With the Possum and the Eagle

Map shows range from Eighth Air Force bomber bases in England.

With the Possum and the Eagle

The Memoir of a Navigator's War over Germany and Japan

Ralph H. Nutter

★
PRESIDIO

Published by Presidio Press, Inc.
505 B San Marin Drive, Suite 160
Novato, CA 94945-1340

Library of Congress Cataloging-in-Publication Data

Nutter, Ralph H.
    With the possum and the eagle : the memoir of a navigator's war over Germany and Japan / by Ralph H. Nutter
        p. cm.
    ISBN 0-89141-754-0
    1. Nutter, Ralph H. 2. World War, 1939–1945—Personal narratives, American. 3. Navigators—United States—Biography.
4. World War, 1939–1945—Aerial operations, American. 5. LeMay, Curtis E. 6. Hansell, Haywood S. 7. Bombing, Aerial—Germany.
8. Bombing, Aerial—Japan. 9. B-17 bomber. 10. B-29 bomber. I. Title.

D811.N88 A3 2002
940.54'4973—dc21

                                            2001044808

Printed in the United States of America

Contents

To my wife Dale

Acknowledgments

This book relates my recollection of events that happened more than fifty-five years ago. I have examined many of the official orders, memoranda, flight data, and log sheets prepared during the years 1942 to 1945. They have been an invaluable assistance in verifying many of the events I have described. In some cases I have been obliged to rely on my memory of the specific events.

The histories of the Eighth and Twentieth Air Forces have been told before. *With the Possum and the Eagle* is about the World War II careers and operational decisions of Maj.Gen. Haywood Hansell Jr. and Gen. Curtis LeMay.

Although I began collecting material many years ago, I started writing this book in 1998 when many of the men involved in this history began passing away. A few remained from our 305th Bomb Group. Colonel William Sault, our group operations officer, provided me with original pictures of our group. My cousin Keith Nutter gave me insight into B-24 Liberator operations. Brigadier General Henry Huglin, group commander on Tinian, gave me photos of B-29 operations in the Marianas Islands in the Pacific.

Two special friends persuaded me to write the book. Gladwin Hill, a featured writer for the *New York Times*, and Maj. Gen. Joseph Preston, formerly commander of the Vandenberg Missile Base. Both flew on our first United States bombing mission over Germany in January 1943; Gladwin Hill as a reporter for the Associated Press, and then Maj. Joe Preston as pilot. I was navigator for Preston at Muroc, California, Chelveston, England, and the Marianas in the Pacific.

Sam Keker gave me encouragement and obtained pictures of LeMay and Hansell. My family physician, Roger Dunham, a successful author, encouraged me. I wish to thank E. J. McCarthy and Bob Kane of Presidio Press. It was a pleasure to work with them. In all my efforts, my wife Dale gave me continual support and assistance. Many thanks to all.

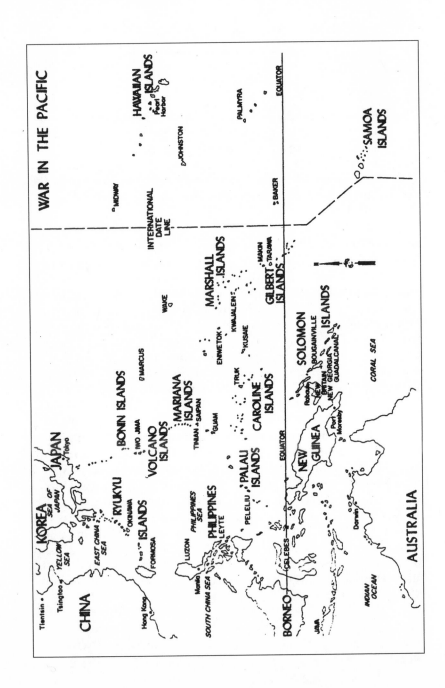

Preface

"The blood-dimmed tide is loosed everywhere the ceremony of innocence is drowned."

—William Butler Yeats, "The Second Coming"

"War is just one living and dying mass of confusion and delusion and stupidity and brilliance and ineptitude and hysteria and heroism anyway."

—Gen. Curtis E. LeMay

I was a navigator on B-17 Flying Fortresses and B-29 Superfortresses for Generals Heywood Hansell and Curtis LeMay in the air war against Germany and Japan from 1942 to 1945. The title of this book is derived from the nicknames of those two general officers. Hansell was called "Possum" by friend and foe alike. LeMay, one of the best known but least understood of the World War II Army Air Forces commanders, was called "Eagle" because of his straightforward attacks on the enemy, military targets, and issues without any evasive action. Hansell never deviated from his opposition to indiscriminate area bombing of civilian urban areas. LeMay attempted to follow U.S. policy and limit heavy bombing to precise military targets in daylight. He abandoned the policy in March 1945 when it appeared to have failed over Japan.

In 1942, LeMay, then a young colonel, was the commander of our 305th Bomb Group, one of four bomb groups serving under Hansell, then our wing commander, in England.

When Hansell and LeMay arrived in England that year, they both believed that strategic bombers could win the war without the necessity of a land invasion and without fighter support to German targets. They were incorrect on both counts. We were confronted by massive attacks from German fighters. More often than not, visual sighting of the targets was impossible because of dense cloud cover. When our crews could not see the target, they attempted "blind" or "overcast bombing" with the aid of the primitive radar then available.

Civilian areas inevitably were hit, which resulted in what was called "collateral damage." Not more than one bomb out of ten came within a thousand feet of the target aiming point.

Our aircrews that bombed Germany in 1943 did so at a terrible cost and with meager results. German military production increased in 1943 and 1944. As our combat losses increased to almost 20 percent, our crews were obliged to confront an even larger number of defending German fighters. By October 1943 the situation became brutally clear: five more missions like those flown early that month would wipe out the entire Eighth Air Force. While the German Luftwaffe faced serious attrition, we were faced with total annihilation if we continued to conduct deep flights into Germany without fighter support.

As I worked for each leader under the most stressful conditions, I observed the demands and problems of combat leadership. In most situations, Hansell was a reserved southern gentleman, warm and friendly. A planner and self-styled intellectual, he believed it was possible to engage in "civilized" bombing by limiting attacks to precise military targets. Those who did not know LeMay considered him to be a "blood-and-guts," hard-shelled, authoritarian commander. His combat units placed the most bombs on military targets with the least loss of combat crews.

In the fall of 1944, Hansell was given command of the B-29s on Saipan in the Mariana Islands. I was his bomber command navigator. LeMay was given the impossible assignment of bombing Japan from western China.

The command problems facing both generals in the Pacific were vastly different from those over Germany. The B-29 was a new, untried aircraft with serious mechanical defects. Engine problems were compounded by fifteen-hour flights over water, increasing the risk that crews would be lost if their aircraft suffered even minor damage or mechanical problems.

The first B-29 raids on Japan conducted by Hansell's XXI Bomber Command from Saipan in late 1944 were wildly inaccurate. Meanwhile, supporting LeMay's 58th Bomb Wing, flying from remote Chinese bases at the end of a tenuous supply line extending from India over the rugged Himalayas, proved to be an unwarranted waste of resources. It was a difficult time for both generals because the president and other senior U.S. leaders were putting immense pressure on them to achieve immediate results against Japan.

Hansell was determined to prove that high-altitude daylight precision bombing was the optimum way to achieve victory with a minimum of civilian casualties. But the bombing under his leadership was ineffective; less than half of the crews hit designated targets. Weather, cloud cover, and the tremendous jet stream winds at altitudes above thirty thousand feet made accurate bombing practically impossible. As an alternative, the air staff in Washington urged Hansell to firebomb Japanese cities. Hansell, believing that firebombing would inflict unwarranted Japanese civilian casualties, rejected the idea.

In January 1945, Gen. Henry H. "Hap" Arnold, commander of the U.S. Army Air Forces, replaced Hansell with LeMay. He viewed LeMay as a "doer," whereas he saw Hansell as a planner and not an effective combat commander.

I was again reunited with LeMay. After reviewing Hansell's operations, LeMay attempted to continue high-altitude precision daylight missions against industrial targets. After six weeks, there was no improvement in bombing results and aircrew casualties continued at the same rate. LeMay, believing he had no other choice, ordered the incendiary bombing of Tokyo at night at altitudes of five thousand to seven thousand feet. The result was the most destructive assault on an enemy city in history. The civilian casualties exceeded those of the A-bomb attacks on Hiroshima and Nagasaki.

LeMay did not completely abandon precision daylight bombing, however. When the weather was favorable, he ordered raids on industrial targets but at lower altitudes. In addition, he mined all major Japanese harbors, thus denying the enemy access to seaborne military supplies, raw materials, and foodstuffs. His tactics reduced crew losses from 6 percent to 1 percent, a loss rate lower than that of the air training command in the United States. As the B-29s continued to torch Japanese cities in the spring of 1945, LeMay told the U.S. Joint Chiefs Staff that his bombers could end the war by October 1945. The chiefs summarily rejected that idea and plans for the invasion of Japan continued.

Hansell blamed LeMay's shift to area bombing to pressure from higher authority. He remained convinced that high-altitude daylight precision bombing of military targets would have succeeded if higher authority and the American people had not been so impatient to end the war. He argued that precision bombing had fatally weakened Germany and could have done the same to Japan. In his view, precision bombing was the only moral and ethical way to bomb urban areas. It was not necessary to destroy entire cities to eliminate a few factories. Even if the Japanese leaders acted like beasts, he reasoned, we should not act in the same manner.

LeMay, on the other hand, was convinced that firebombing was necessary to defeat the Japanese. He also felt that atomic bombs were unnecessary—after all, "the verdict was already in." He changed his mind about the use of nuclear weapons after the war, however.

Most Americans have forgotten LeMay's accomplishments in the air war against Germany and Japan: they now remember him for his leadership in the Cold War against the Soviet Union. Perhaps the story of how U.S. policy shifted from precision daylight bombing to area bombing in World War II may assist our leaders and citizens in evaluating our country's future defense policy.

Part 1: The Air War Against Germany

1: A Second Lieutenant Meets Colonel LeMay

It was seven o'clock on Sunday evening, 7 December 1941. I was studying in the dormitory of Perkins Hall at Harvard Law School. I heard the sound of tramping feet in the hall and the voice of my classmate Sander Johnson, yelling in a military cadence, "hut, two, three, four; hut, two, three, four." I opened the door of my room and yelled back, "Sander, I'm trying to study!"

He kept on marching with several classmates behind him, then looked back at me and said, "Throw away your books Ralph. The Japanese have bombed Pearl Harbor. We'll all be in the army!"

My roommate turned on the radio. There were hysterical reports that the Japanese were going to bomb San Francisco. I decided that Sander Johnson was right. I pushed my books off the desk into the wastebasket.

I had tried to join the navy air arm in November but was rejected because of my eyesight and a sinus condition. Perhaps physical standards would be relaxed now that we were at war.

The next morning I went to the air corps recruiting station in Boston. At 8 A.M. there was already a line of men extending around the block waiting to enlist. I stood in line until eleven when I was finally given a physical exam. After telling me that I had failed the eye examination, the flight surgeon said, "You can always join the infantry as a private." I was horrified. As a teenager I had seen the movie *All Quiet on the Western Front* and read the book *Over the Top*, an account of the horrors of trench warfare. I wanted to avoid the infantry.

"You really want to join the air corps don't you?" the flight surgeon said. "Have you ever flown in an airplane?"

I told him I had never flown or been in an airplane, but I had always wanted to fly.

He looked at me for a moment and said, "I'm going to lunch. I'll leave the door unlocked and return at one o'clock."

I accepted his "suggestion." As soon as he was gone I memorized the eye chart and calibrated the depth perception apparatus. I passed my retest and took the oath that afternoon. I returned to law school to say good-bye to my friends and classmates.

I was shocked and surprised by comments made by two of them. "What's your hurry?" asked one. "It'll be months or perhaps a year before we're drafted."

"Yeah," chimed in the other. "You're a sucker to enlist. We'll get in another year of law school and be way ahead of you as lawyers after the war."

I made no reply. I couldn't believe that they didn't understand the crisis our country was in.

New air corps recruits were given train tickets for Montgomery, Alabama. We were to be aviation cadets there at Maxwell Field.

A tough army sergeant met us at the Montgomery railroad station and marched us to a truck for the ride to Maxwell Field. We arrived at 9 P.M. and were told there were no available sleeping quarters on the base. The sergeant then took us to an empty factory. He gave each of us a blanket and said he would return at 6 A.M. We slept on the floor with no mattress or pillow. This was not the romantic air force I had read about.

Things were no better the next day. We spent the entire day playing touch football at the athletic field. At 5:30 P.M. we lined up in our first army chow line. After dinner, a captain told us that we would sleep on the football field for the next two nights. He returned and gave each of us a blanket again. We rolled up in the blankets to keep warm.

On Wednesday morning the captain told us there were no facilities or planes available for training aviation cadets and that we could return home on a sixty-day leave.

"This is ridiculous," I told him. "I quit law school because I thought I was needed. What am I supposed to do for the next two months?"

"No one expected this war," he replied. "We have no instructors or equipment available for pilot training. If you don't wish to accept the sixty days leave, you can start training as a navigator at Mather Field in Sacramento. We have a DC-3 leaving for Sacramento tomorrow morning."

My first flight was in that DC-3 cargo plane. There were no seats, and I sat alone in the windowless cargo cabin with assorted military equipment. It was a most unusual way to start a military career.

I graduated from navigator school in July 1942 and received orders assigning me to the 305th Bomb Group at an airfield in the Mojave Desert at Muroc, California. My fellow graduates and I were picked up by an army truck for transport to the base, which was located about thirty miles from Los Angeles.

We drove up a steep grade and looked down onto a desert wasteland. The temperature was over a hundred degrees. The landscape appeared to be a vast moonscape without greenery or vegetation—a godforsaken place if ever there was one. It looked like an appropriate place to train for combat. The sand blew against the windshield. I feared we were entering a sandstorm. The only examples of vegetation were cactus and Joshua trees.

As we approached the entrance to the base, we saw huge dry lakes, great flat expanses shimmering in the hot sun. There were only two buildings, and three B-17s (four-engine bombers called "Flying Fortresses") were parked alongside a single runway. We could see wooden silhouettes of battleships at the end of the runway. The driver let us off in front of what he called the mess hall. He recommended that we try to get something to eat before checking in.

I opened the door and saw officers eating lunch. All of the tables were crowded except for one in the corner, where I promptly sat down. The entire room suddenly fell silent. After taking my seat, I noticed that a full colonel, two majors, and a captain were at the table. As we drove up from Los Angeles the driver told us that a tough colonel named Curtis E. LeMay was commanding officer of the 305th Group. I had violated military protocol by sitting at the command table reserved for senior officers. All eyes were on me. No one at the table spoke. I knew I had done something wrong so I tried to eat as quickly and as unobtrusively as possible and leave.

I caught a glimpse of Colonel LeMay out of the corner of my eye before leaving. He was about five-foot-ten, full-faced, and stocky, with a broad chest, black hair, and piercing olive-colored eyes. He gave the immediate impression of enormous self-confidence, but without arrogance. It was a look of stern, unflappable strength and indominability, which in the next three years never changed.

He didn't look like a glamorous pilot. There was no vanity in his appearance. He didn't eat or smile while I sat at the table. I learned later that his silence and serious demeanor were not because of my presence—he was not a conversationalist by nature. It was not unusual for him to be silent, having little or no time for small talk or social amenities. He always seemed to be calm. Speech was for a purpose. He thought a man could learn more by listening than talking. He used just enough words to demonstrate his meaning and intentions.

I had experienced tough, no-nonsense professors at law school. Their approach to learning was trial by fire, so I was not surprised by LeMay, and I was pleased to have him as our leader in combat. I soon learned that his stern, disciplined demeanor was a combat asset. He always faced danger and responsibility calmly. He was not grim or gloomy that first time I saw him at Muroc mess hall—or ever in the future, no matter what the circumstances. His tough approach was the antithesis of the romantic fliers I had seen in Hollywood motion pictures. I soon learned that bombing was not a dashing adventure, but a grim, dangerous, and demanding task that required meticulous teamwork and discipline. LeMay never displayed any emotion. Physical and nervous energy were not to be squandered; they were to be conserved for essential matters.

After lunch I went to my assigned tent and met my crew: the officers I was to fly with for the next five months, a friendly and relaxed group who made me immediately at ease. O'Neill, the pilot, was a down-to-earth practical Irishman. Collins, the copilot, was the son of a northern Vermont dairy farmer. He had a great sense of humor and was almost always smiling. Galloway, a huge former All-American football player from Texas, was our bombardier. His repeated references to his football exploits at Texas A&M did not seem to fit in with the quiet confidence of O'Neill and Collins.

It was about 1:30 P.M. when I arrived at our tent, and the temperature must have been 110 degrees. O'Neill explained that our bomb group had only three B-17s. We were not going to get in much flying time with only three aircraft to be divided among the group's four squadrons. He said that our most important job at Muroc was to set our priorities, the first of which was to try to stay cool at all times. He picked up a large fire extinguisher and started squirting water on the tent ceiling.

"Unless we're flying or on other duty," he told me, "each member of the tent is assigned to squirt the ceiling with water every fourth day. The door flap must always be kept closed because the wind will blow sand into the tent. Otherwise you'll think we're in the French Foreign Legion. It's also a good idea to keep the tent flap tied down securely to keep the rattlesnakes out."

"What is there to do around here when we're not on duty?" I asked.

Collins laughed. "Aside from going to Pancho's place, nothing—except shooting rattlesnakes."

"What is Pancho's place?" I asked O'Neill.

"It's called the Inn," he replied. "Pancho's Inn. Pancho is a real pistol. She only likes fighter pilots, not bomber pilots. She calls bomber pilots and aircrew members 'truck drivers.' If she sees your navigator's wings, she'll probably call you a useless son-of-a-bitch, a goddamned gofer, or a bookkeeper. If you're persistent, I could probably get her to let you buy us a drink."

O'Neill offered to take me to Pancho's that night, since I probably wouldn't have an assignment on my first day. To put it mildly, O'Neill did not exaggerate about Pancho or her inn. Both were weather beaten. Her face was wrinkled and leathery, probably from incessant cigarette smoking and flying in an open cockpit. The screen door needed several patches. Behind the bar I saw several pictures of carefree pilots sitting in the cockpits of ancient open-air biplanes and prewar fighters. We found a seat at the bar, and O'Neill finally got Pancho to serve us drinks. She eyed my navigator's wings as if I had leprosy.

"What the hell do you need a goddamned navigator for?" she asked me. "I've been flying for twenty years. I never got lost. Are you some kind of goddamned accountant?"

I smiled sheepishly. The screen door banged. I'd been saved by a new customer. From then on, Pancho ignored me and directed her attention and scathing remarks at the new man. He was a P-39 fighter pilot.

"Why are you flying that death trap?" she asked him. "I saw one lose its tail yesterday and go straight down. The pilot couldn't even bail out!"

The next morning I learned a bit more about the 305th Group. It had four squadrons: the 364th, 365th, 366th, and 422d. I was assigned to the 366th; our commander was a major from Minnesota, Joe Preston. Preston was one of only three pilots in the entire group who had experience flying four-engine bombers. At the time of Pearl Harbor, Preston was stationed at Clark Field in the Philippines. He lost his B-17 on the ground, from Japanese strafing, on 10 December 1941. Like LeMay, Joe Preston was the strong, silent type, a man of few words.

At our first squadron meeting Preston told us we shouldn't complain about Muroc. The flat desert and dry lakes were perfect for training our inexperienced pilots and crews. It was an ideal place for emergency landings. We had only one problem: we didn't have enough planes to fly. Preston said he would do his best to get us flying time. Until we had more aircraft we would have to be satisfied with ground training, such as it was. We were supposed to get new B-17s, but he had no idea when. I asked if I could get a sextant to practice celestial navigation.

As we walked back to the tent after our squadron meeting, I asked O'Neill to tell me about Colonel LeMay.

"Well, I don't know much more than you," he said. "At least you had lunch with him. That's more than any of the rest of us. I've been here a week and I'm still trying to get him to check me out on a B-17. I've heard some of the guys say LeMay's nickname is 'Iron Pants,' but from what I hear, he's really an 'Iron Ass.' He's as tough and rough as he looks. They tell me he's only thirty-six. He looks older. No one has even seen him smile. He's always serious. You're lucky; unlike most pilots, he thinks navigators are necessary. He likes navigators. They say he's the best navigator in the air corps. He'll give you lots of attention."

LeMay wasn't a West Pointer. He had a degree in engineering from Ohio State. Although originally a fighter pilot, he thought like an engineer and had been flying bombers for about five years. He flew the U.S. mail during the depression and was in charge of a Civilian Conservation Corps camp. Shortly before the war he was the lead navigator for a series of practice bomb runs on ships at sea and on two long-distance flights to South America. He was as tough and competent as he looked, a man of few words.

He talked in quiet phrases with a pipe or cigar in his mouth, rather than complete sentences. He didn't repeat himself, never showed emotion, and wasn't interested in social amenities. Some people called him "Smiley" or "Old Poker Face."

"When he gives you an assignment," said Major Preston, "get it right the first time. When he asks a question, get to the point. He doesn't want to hear any bullshit. I hear you went to law school. He doesn't like lawyers, he thinks they're talkers, not doers. He believes talk is cheap, and that you learn more by listening than talking, so he doesn't judge people by words or promises. He judges them by what they do. Performance is the beginning and the end for him. He's fair, but tough as nails."

I asked Preston why LeMay always looked so stern and serious. He told me the flight surgeon said it was because he had Bell's palsy— a form of paralysis of the facial muscles on the right side of his face; he couldn't move those muscles and tried to compensate for it by keeping a cigar or pipe in his mouth. He believed in discipline and teamwork—as a matter of survival, good enough for all of us. Preston said the colonel was loyal to his people, so we were lucky to have him as our commander.

After talking to Preston and O'Neill, I was reassured about LeMay. I still didn't feel like a soldier. I had a lot to learn about discipline and teamwork. It was apparent that, with the exception of four senior officers and LeMay, we were all no more than raw recruits: civilians in uniform, inexperienced and undertrained. We needed a leader like LeMay if we were going to survive fighting the Nazis.

I soon learned that Muroc was probably the world's safest place for new bomber pilots. Most of our pilots had never even flown in a two-engine bomber, let alone a four-engine aircraft. Only LeMay, Preston, and Major De Russy had flown B-17s. The next day, O'Neill told me that LeMay was going to check him out as first pilot. We walked the flight line. Our first flight together as the crew of a B-17 was an experience none of us would forget. I didn't know it at the time, but it was the first of many flights I was to have with LeMay. Just before takeoff, I saw him drive up in a command car dressed in a flight suit.

"I'm going to be copilot," he told Collins. "You can ride between the seats."

This was also my first meeting with the other members of our crew. In addition to me, O'Neill, Collins, and Galloway, our bombardier, we had six enlisted men: a flight engineer, radio operator, ball-turret gunner, left and right waist gunners, and a tail gunner. Sitting at the navigator's table in the nose of the plane for takeoff and landing practice, I had nothing to do but listen to the interphone while LeMay checked out O'Neill as pilot. LeMay said little. Preston was right; he spoke only when necessary. O'Neill's practice takeoffs and landings were smooth, with few bumps. On the fourth landing LeMay ordered O'Neill to pull up to the hardstand.

As he climbed out of the cockpit, I heard him say to O'Neill, "You'll do."

Then he turned to Collins and said, "I'll check you out tomorrow morning at seven."

By this time our crewmembers were on a first-name basis. Collins's first name was Warren, but we all called him "Sonny." He was a fellow New Englander, and we became best friends. I was with him in London on leave the night before he was shot down in April 1943.

The 305th Bomb Group remained at Muroc until the middle of August 1942. We waited in vain for our new B-17Fs. The cloudless skies over the Mojave Desert would have been perfect for flying and bombing practice except for the fact that we never had more than three aircraft for our entire group. We spent a lot of time in our tents. I thought we would die of either heat prostration or boredom.

It was so hot in July and August that if we took our positions in the aircraft after ten in the morning we couldn't touch metal equipment without gloves. There was also the danger of vapor lock if we took off in the middle of the day. While we were training in the Muroc desert, General Patton was training his troops in the desert near Barstow in preparation for the invasion of North Africa. Patton and LeMay both used tough methods to train their troops for combat.

There were a lot of rumors and scuttlebutt as to where we might be assigned for combat—the Pacific or England. We made no long-distance flights. Our bombing practice was limited to a few practice runs on chalk circles drawn in the desert sand. The sky was almost always clear in the desert, visibility almost perfect.

Those practice bomb runs in the desert with our new Norden bombsight gave us a false sense of optimism about bombing accuracy. We believed the press releases that boasted we could place our bombs in a pickle barrel from high altitude. No one explained to us the contrast between making an unimpeded, peaceful bomb run in the cloudless desert skies and bombing a Japanese island covered with dense jungle, a zigzagging ship at sea, or a heavily fortified, cloud-covered, camouflaged German city defended by hordes of fighter planes and a blanket of flak. We were given no maps of either Europe or the Pacific. I took advantage of the cloudless starry desert nights to practice with my sextant, shooting stars and learning to identify constellations at a glance.

We did engage in a little gunnery practice and enemy fighter identification. We spent one day at a primitive gunnery school in Las Vegas. I made a fleeting acquaintance with .30- and .50-caliber machine guns. My only prior experience with guns had been shooting at rats in a garbage dump with a .22. At Muroc, I tried shooting rattlesnakes outside of our tent with a .45-caliber pistol. They were our only moving targets. This experience didn't teach us how to track an enemy aircraft approaching us head-on at a closing rate of several hundred miles an hour.

Our B-17s had two .30-caliber machine guns in the nose for use by the navigator and the bombardier. Later, we found out that these guns were no better than peashooters against German fighters. We made low-level strafing attacks on a mock wooden battleship in the Muroc desert. I was surprised that anyone would consider using a four-engine bomber for strafing. We never attempted dry-run bombing attacks on urban targets in the Los Angeles area. Since we never had more than four aircraft, formation flying and celestial training in the air were impossible.

After our first week at Muroc, LeMay announced his leave and recreation policy, saying, "I don't expect I can make you into combat crews if the brass don't give you planes to fly. We're going to have to make up for this loss of practical training time with on-the-job training when they assign us to a combat area. I'm going to have a liberal leave policy now. I'll give each crew every other weekend off in Los Angeles. Enjoy it. Don't think this is my combat policy. If you want to raise hell, get it out of your system now. Once we get overseas you'll be confined to base until I decide you can hold your own in combat. It may take a long time."

I knew that it was just a matter of time before I would observe or experience a serious accident involving one of our aircraft. It finally happened in the first week of August, and it was a scene I have never forgotten. Fortunately, it didn't involve one of our planes.

I was checking weather reports at the flight tower with Pat O'Neill when we heard the roar of an aircraft overhead. I looked up and saw a P-39 Airacobra from the fighter squadron based at Muroc headed toward the tower in what seemed an uncontrolled dive.

We could hear the pilot shouting over the tower intercom: "I've lost my tail unit. I'm trying to bail out. I don't think I'm going to make it."

We rushed out of the tower just as his aircraft hit the edge of the runway and exploded in a tremendous ball of fire.

O'Neill shook his head and said, "It looks like gravity must have prevented him from ejecting. Aren't you glad you aren't a fighter pilot?" I didn't reply. I had just seen my first casualty of the war.

We were all pleased when LeMay announced that we were leaving Muroc in late August to be assigned to an air base at Tucson, Arizona, to wait for a full complement of new B-17s. We packed up and climbed aboard an ancient train for the long, steaming-hot trip to Tucson. Of course those sooty old passenger cars weren't Pullmans. We speculated that they had been used to transport troops to Florida in the Spanish-American War in 1898.

As the train lumbered through the desert, we talked endlessly about our eventual combat destination. The news was not good for the Allies in August 1942, but we were unconcerned. We were young and confident and believed that if given a chance we would win the war with our bombing. A few camp followers climbed aboard the train, but nobody objected. Some stayed until we got to Tucson. We passed the time on the train playing poker, telling impossible war stories, and trying to sleep in the uncomfortable straight-backed seats. The heat in the trains was almost unbearable. We couldn't sleep more than a few hours at a time. I read one mystery after another and learned the boredom that goes with army life.

After two weeks of more boring downtime in Tucson without aircraft, we were told that the new planes would be delivered to us in Syracuse, New York. The trip to Syracuse was a repeat of the ride to Tucson, only worse. After getting over the Rocky Mountains, we experienced scorching heat accompanied by unrelenting humidity. Again, there were no sleeping facilities during the five-day trip across the country. There was no dining car; we were fed sandwiches that appeared to have been made for troops in World War I.

In spite of these conditions, we had a particularly moving experience in the Chicago stockyard. At midnight, as our train pulled slowly out of the stockyard headed east, on the next track, headed west, was another overcrowded troop train. All of the windows were open on both trains. Strangely, there was no gallows humor passed between the troops. No one spoke. We put out our hands and slapped the palms of the troops going in the opposite direction, a gesture that would later be called a "high five." Like us, they were probably traveling to an unknown combat destination. We were wishing each other luck, and needing it more than we realized.

We pulled into Syracuse in the first week of October 1942, wearing our summer uniforms. It was cold, but I didn't mind. I was delighted about being there: I had been a student at Syracuse University from 1938 to 1940.

After our arrival, new Boeing B-17Fs were finally delivered to the crews. Our crew was given aircraft number 41-24592, in which we flew across the Atlantic and into our first encounters with the Nazis. We named it *Royal Flush* and had a picture of a skunk painted on the nose flushing on Adolf Hitler.

We were told our group would soon be going overseas, but still no one knew where. What we did know was that Colonel LeMay was concerned that we weren't ready for combat. There were conflicting rumors as to whether we would go to Europe or the Pacific. Preston told me that LeMay's preference was England because he believed we should defeat the Nazis first. We didn't have appropriate clothing for either England or the Pacific. LeMay sent our supply officer to order clothing for Europe. When orders came assigning us to the Pacific, LeMay resisted, telling General Arnold's staff that we were already outfitted for Europe. He was usually one step ahead of headquarters when it came to protecting his men.

In early October, when it appeared that we would be leaving for combat in a week or ten days, I asked O'Neill if I could fly to Boston from Syracuse on a commercial airliner and visit my folks.

"Why not?" he said.

With O'Neill's approval, I didn't bother to check with LeMay or with Major Preston, our squadron commander. Apparently the colonel checked the roster and found I was missing and unaccounted for that Saturday. When I returned on Sunday night I got a huge surprise. I stepped outside the door of the American Airlines DC-3 and was astonished to see LeMay sitting there in a car alone. He motioned for me to get in. Neither of us spoke during the ride to the base; his face was inscrutable as usual. I sat there in the dark, speculating on what he might do to me for being absent without formal leave. As the car approached my quarters on base, I decided it was time to determine, if possible, the extent of my infraction and the colonel's plans for me.

I cleared my throat and said most respectfully, "I will get out here, sir."

He stopped the car. I opened the door, got out, saluted, and turned toward the barracks. He said nothing. He never mentioned the incident to me again. He didn't have to. His meaning was clear. I had committed a serious offense by not obtaining proper clearance for my visit home. His personal trip to pick me up underscored his opinion of my infraction.

Whatever the colonel may have thought of me, apparently our crew was not in the doghouse with him. The day after my return to Syracuse, Major Preston ordered our crew to report to LeMay for a special assignment. We waited in the operations room. I wondered if it concerned my recent unauthorized trip. LeMay entered smoking his pipe.

Speaking in a low voice, he told us, "I have been ordered to select a special crew for an unusual and possibly dangerous assignment. I have checked out O'Neill and Collins. They are adequate."

He looked at me with a slight smile and said, "Apparently Nutter has a lot of moxie. You are to take off today for Eglin Field, Florida. They are experimenting with some type of glide bombing where they put a bomb with wings under a B-17. I don't know if it really is a glide bomb, if it's practical, or exactly what is involved. I picked your crew because I think you can handle it if anyone can. When you finish at Eglin you are to report to the base at Harrisburg, Pennsylvania, for further modification of your aircraft for combat. If there are no questions, get packing. Good luck."

As we were leaving, O'Neill asked me if LeMay had mentioned this assignment when he picked me up at the airport. I told O'Neill of our nonconversation.

"Maybe this is your punishment," he said. "I don't think we need this."

After we arrived at Eglin Field we were sent to look at a bomb with wings attached underneath the bomb bay of a B-17.

"That's going to be one hell of a drag when we take off," said O'Neill. "What if it doesn't release properly and the damn thing gets caught in the underpinning? How can we land with that goddamned bomb ready to explode? I'm not about to try landing with that thing underneath us. You guys better check your parachutes and be ready to bail out!"

The takeoff was hairy. For the first time I wondered whether we would make it. O'Neill kept the wheels on the ground until the last second, and then pulled back on the controls. We barely cleared some ambulances parked at the end of the runway. It didn't take much imagination to figure out why they were there.

I gave O'Neill a course for our target, a raft in the center of the Gulf of Mexico. Galloway, our bombardier, lined up the raft in his bombsight and released the toggle switch. Suddenly, the plane lurched upward; we were free of our unwanted cargo. We all breathed a sigh of relief as we watched for an explosion. A geyser of water went straight up.

O'Neill called me on the interphone: "Okay, Ralph. Let's get the hell out of here. Give me a course for Harrisburg."

I was more than happy to oblige. I never heard of anything like that glide bomb again until I learned a similar device exploded and killed young Joe Kennedy during a test flight over the English Channel.

2: Across the North Atlantic

When we returned to Syracuse from Harrisburg, we were informed that we should get ready for our flight to England. We were not going to lie under palm trees and exchange visits with the Japanese in the Pacific. We were to make social calls on Nazi Germany from the air. The first stop was to be Gander Lake, Newfoundland.

The night before we left, our group had a boisterous and raucous party at the Hotel Syracuse. We sang the air force song, "Off We Go into the Wild Blue Yonder," and threw our drinks and glasses into the fireplace. My guest at the party was a blind date from Syracuse University. I didn't know what to say to her as I escorted her back to her dormitory. As I said good-bye at the door, we both kept asking, "When will we see each other again?" Two and a half years later we were married after I returned from England.

The next morning, as we walked toward our aircraft for our take-off from Syracuse, Sonny Collins turned to me and said, "This is it, Ralph. This is where we separate the sheep from the goats."

I didn't reply. Ever since I had gone to the recruiting station I had tried to anticipate how I would react in combat. Now, in a matter of days or weeks, someone would be shooting at me. I hoped I would return. At the moment, I had an immediate, more pressing challenge. With less than a hundred hours of flying time, I had to rely on the accuracy of my navigation to guide us across the North Atlantic in an arctic storm to Prestwick, Scotland.

My concerns about combat against the Nazis were premature. We almost didn't make it across the ocean. Our troubles began before we reached Gander Lake. After less than an hour out of Syracuse, our number three engine began to run rough. Sonny Collins suggested his hometown of Burlington, Vermont, as an opportune emergency landing field. We radioed ahead and landed on a fog-shrouded runway lined with local townspeople. No four-engine bomber had ever landed in Vermont. The B-17, the famous "Flying Fortress," was a symbol of the war and a glamorous new weapon.

O'Neill approached the short runway as low as possible. We came to an abrupt stop at a New England stone wall and he then taxied the aircraft to an area in front of the control tower. As we walked to the tower, a Vermont University coed asked me what I was carrying. It was a small case containing my shaving kit, but I told her it was our secret Norden bombsight. She was impressed. They put us up in a University of Vermont dormitory. The next morning, O'Neill and a local mechanic made temporary repairs on our problem engine. O'Neill assured us that, if necessary, we could make it on three engines and obtain replacement parts at a Bangor, Maine, air force depot.

After another day at Bangor, and further repairs, we headed for Gander Lake, the jump-off point for our flight across the big pond. Next to Muroc, Gander was the most isolated place I had ever experienced. An impenetrable evergreen forest surrounded all of the airport except for the end of the runway facing the water. We were warned not to venture into the forest because if we got lost, we probably would never be seen again. The weather at Gander was as forbidding as the landscape. There was always a chilling damp fog and low cloud cover. They told us an arctic storm was coming from the north. We waited for the weather to clear.

After waiting another day, LeMay called a group meeting. He told us he couldn't wait any longer for the weather to break. We were overdue in England. His weather briefing was pessimistic.

"Metro tells me there is rough weather ahead for us in the North Atlantic," he said. "I've flown this route to Prestwick many times ferrying B-24s. At this time of year, icing can be a very real problem. Be sure your deicers are working, and if possible check for icing in the carburetors. The weather will make it rough for you navigators. You may not be able to check your course with celestial navigation. At this time of year there is always the possibility of a blizzard coming down from the Arctic. If possible, you must check your course every few minutes. If you don't correct sharply to the left, you will drift too far south. Then you will never hit England, let alone our destination in Scotland.

"Without a correction to the left, if you don't run out of fuel by Land's End, at the south tip of England, the Nazi fighters will be waiting for you off the French coast. You can't rely on radio aids or directional finders. The Nazis have set up a false beam with a frequency identical with the RAF [Royal Air Force] radio beam in England. Don't be fooled. You are on your own. I realize that most of you have never flown over water or navigated for long distances. You navigators must trust the accuracy of your computation.

"In the States you relied on your pilots and radio aids. Now the pilots and crews are relying on you. Don't let them down. I'll give you the first course out of Gander. We aren't sure it'll be accurate. Check the course and wind on your drift meter as soon as you level off if you can't see the stars. Good luck!"

We somberly filed out of the operations room. As our crew of four officers rode in a jeep to our plane, I looked up at the sky for stars. Without stars, there was no way I could take a celestial fix. With strong winds coming from the north, dead reckoning would, at best, be an educated guess. I was careful to conceal my concern from the crew.

I climbed in the plane and sat quietly for a moment at the navigator's table. The takeoff for England and armed combat against the Nazis would be the beginning of a new and uncertain future for all of us. I had just turned twenty-two. I remembered that only fifteen years before Lindbergh's nonstop flight across the North Atlantic had been a noteworthy achievement.

The flight in a projected blizzard was to be the first major event in a new chapter of my life as a flying officer. It was the beginning of three years of events and circumstances beyond my comprehension. This was more responsibility than I had ever contemplated. My crewmates were relying on me to navigate and direct a route, without radio aids, in almost impossible weather with a limited supply of fuel. A misdirected course or error in navigation could lead to ditching in the cold ocean and death for all of us. My contemplation was interrupted by the increasing roar and rhythm of our four engines. O'Neill gave the *Royal Flush* full power, released the brakes, and we were on our way.

The plane roared down the runway in darkness, toward the black unfriendly skies ahead. Just before the wheels of our speeding plane left the runway, our emergency life raft flew out of the top emergency hatch.

"Let's turn back and get a new life raft!" our top-turret gunner yelled on the interphone.

"What the hell," O'Neill replied matter-of-factly, "In this weather and storm, a life raft wouldn't do us any good anyway."

We started climbing to our planned altitude of nine thousand feet. It was a half an hour before we leveled off. I looked for an opening in the cloud cover and finally spotted a break in the clouds and took a celestial fix on Polaris, the North Star, and another star for latitude. I couldn't believe it when my first celestial fix showed that we were fifteen miles off course. I remembered LeMay's parting words. We had to have confidence in the accuracy of our navigation. I reported my findings to O'Neill.

"I don't believe it," he replied. "Take another fix."

I was able to get more celestial shots and plot a fix on three stars. The lines of position on my map indicated that we were seventeen miles off course to the south. I again reported my findings to O'Neill.

"I hope you know what you're doing," he said. "It's your ass as well as ours. I'll change course as you requested."

I kept taking more star sightings and asked O'Neill to make further corrections to the north. I was finally using the lessons they taught us in school. Suddenly the sky became covered with clouds. Blinding snow covered the Plexiglas nose and my astrodome. There could be no more celestial navigation until the storm abated and there was a break in the clouds. This was only the beginning of our problems.

In a matter of minutes, we heard the number three engine sputter and die. O'Neill feathered the engine to stop the air drag on the windmilling propeller. When an engine stops and a propeller spins without the benefit of lubrication, the propeller shaft becomes overheated. Eventually the propeller falls off and there's the danger of it striking some part of the aircraft and causing serious damage. We were able to maintain altitude with only three engines. No one spoke. The interphone was quiet. After flying another hour, the number two engine quit. Now we all knew we were in serious trouble. Fortunately we had two engines left, one on each side of the plane.

O'Neill's voice came over the interphone: "Pilot to crew. We have to eliminate all extra weight. Throw all baggage, personal items, tools, guns, and ammunition overboard. Everything that isn't tied down goes. No exceptions."

"If there are any loose bodies back there, don't tell O'Neill," Galloway whispered.

We started to lose altitude. I was concerned about our drift to the south caused by the storm. I suggested to O'Neill that if we could level off above the waves, with the assistance of the landing lights I might be able to compute our wind drift and velocity from the white caps of the waves with my drift meter. Then I could make course corrections by dead reckoning. O'Neill turned on the landing lights and dropped down to a few hundred feet above the water. I was able to spot the white caps on the waves and compute our wind drift to the south.

I continued to ask O'Neill to make further course corrections to the left. Every member of the crew was silent. After what seemed like an eternity, and more corrections to the north, I started looking for the approach of dawn in the east, toward Ireland. The two remaining engines ran smoothly. I hoped that if the cloud cover cleared in the early morning light, I might be able to make celestial sightings on the sun or even a late moon. Finally, just before dawn, I was able to take three celestial shots of stars through holes in the cloud cover.

"We're on course," I announced on the interphone. "Northern Ireland should be dead ahead in a matter of minutes."

I left my navigator's table, climbed up to the pilot's compartment, and stood behind O'Neill and Collins, between the seats. Suddenly we broke out of the cloud cover and saw a green coastline directly ahead in the bright sunlight. It had to be Ireland, the Emerald Isle. It was the most beautiful sight of my young life.

"We're going to make it!" I yelled.

O'Neill laughed. "Of course. There was no doubt about it, but I guess you didn't think so."

I didn't reply. We cut across the coast of Northern Ireland and I looked down on the city of Belfast to the south. At last we were in Europe. I gave O'Neill a direct course for Prestwick.

Our lumbering flight halfway across the Atlantic on two engines had delayed our arrival, and we landed an hour later than the other crews from the 305th. As we taxied to a revetment, I noticed a large crowd lining the runway. Colonel LeMay drove up to our plane in a jeep. I recognized some members of the 305th, but I also saw what appeared to be local Scottish townspeople lined up to greet us. O'Neill killed our two remaining engines. As we wearily climbed down from the plane, the Scots cheered us.

"What took you so long?" a Scotsman shouted. "We've been waiting for you Yanks for nearly two years!"

It was an emotional scene. Some of the women had tears in their eyes. I didn't know what to say. I was exhausted. I was afraid to show my emotions.

"We stopped for some beer in Dublin," I replied.

"What happened to your engines?" LeMay asked O'Neill. "How long did you fly on two?"

After O'Neill described our flight, LeMay complimented him and told us to get some sleep. There were no military quarters for us, so the townspeople took us into their homes. It was the warmest greeting of my life. As I sat eating my first porridge, I noticed the house wasn't heated. Our hosts told us they couldn't turn on the heat while we were in the rooms. What they really meant was, there was no coal or fuel to heat their homes at any time. Contrary to what I had been told, I found the Scots to be the warmest people I had ever met. I had been trained in college to be an Anglophile. I felt I had made the right choice.

The next day, after making temporary engine repairs, we flew to our new home in East Anglia, between Cambridge and Northampton: Grafton Underwood. The entire base was a field of sticky mud. We soon changed the name to "Grafton Undermud." Mud, fog, and a damp chill were to be with us for the remainder of my tour in England.

3: Training for Combat

In October 1942, the Eighth Air Force had seven bomber bases in the Northampton-Cambridge area of East Anglia in England. After we landed at Grafton Underwood, I walked to our new barracks, a half-cylinder-shaped metal Quonset hut. The only heat was from a coal stove in the center of a room housing twenty-two first and second lieutenants. Only a few would survive combat over Germany. A year later, only two of our original group from Muroc remained. As I unpacked my gear, I thought about the immediate future. I knew we were undertrained and lacked the expertise to confront experienced Luftwaffe fighter pilots in battle. Colonel LeMay didn't give us any time to worry, however.

The next morning he called a group meeting and told us: "You are all confined to base until further notice. Our first combat missions will be against the German submarine bases on the French coast. It'll be on-the-job training. Every member of each crew is to study aircraft identification. We will have no fighter protection in target areas. Our fighters don't have the range to escort us to the targets. When you see a fighter turning into our formation, there will be no second chance. Shoot at it. You've got to learn to identify and distinguish German fighters from RAF and American fighters.

"Navigators and bombardiers are to study maps of the French coastline, the pictures of the sub bases, and the surrounding areas. The weather here is terrible. It may be our worst enemy. You must learn to recognize landmarks and targets immediately. You won't have a second chance. We've got to learn to fly in fog, to navigate, and to bomb in bad weather and through holes in the cloud cover. It's going to be difficult to hit a target at high altitude, in cloud cover, over a crowded urban area. The English have barrage balloons tethered all over England as a defense against low-flying Nazi fighters and bombers. When you come back to base in bad weather you must know exactly where you are or you'll lose a wing on the cables."

We started in-flight formation and gunnery training for the first time. LeMay flew in a gunner position in the lead plane. The formation flying and gunnery practice was nearly disastrous for Mac Mc-Donald, one of our senior pilots. Mac towed a long cloth sleeve behind a twin-engine A-20 bomber. The gunners tracked Mac's plane and attempted to hit the sleeve with machine-gun fire. One of our gunners missed the target sleeve and hit McDonald in the shoulder. He made a remarkable landing with only one hand on the controls. He used his teeth to cut back the throttles.

LeMay was furious at the gunner. After we landed, he ordered all crews to the skeet range. "I knew that the gunnery stunk, but I didn't know it was that bad!" he said angrily. "You guys are so lousy that I'll outshoot every one of you."

He kept his word; he wasn't through. Although we were exhausted after a long day, he then led the group in formation flying. It was the first tight formation we had ever flown. LeMay rode in the top turret of the lead aircraft and issued instructions over the radio to each plane to get in as close as possible to the wing tips beside it.

"We've got to circle our wagons," he said gruffly. "We won't have any long-range fighter protection. Our only chance of survival is to maintain a tight formation. A tight, close formation will concentrate two hundred guns anytime the Nazis attempt to fly through our formation."

We soon learned that the close, flat formation other groups had been using left us vulnerable to fighter attacks. LeMay devised a new staggered box formation with a lead, low, and high squadron. This revised formation had a dual purpose: it maximized the number of bombs on the target and gave us more concentrated firepower than a level formation.

We also had to learn to cope with the cloud cover that concealed the targets as well as the freezing cold. Temperatures of 40 degrees below zero were a continual problem, so we wore sheepskin-lined leather jackets and boots. Oxygen at high altitudes helped keep us warm, but the oxygen masks would often freeze to our faces. To make matters worse, I had to take off my mittens and gloves while using my navigation instruments and plotting courses on maps.

We had three training missions before a mission was scheduled against a target in Germany. The German fighters were to be our instructors. Our first flight over enemy territory might be our final examination, with no make-up possible.

No one had ever discussed whether we could bomb German targets without fighter escort. We had been told that we could hold our own against enemy fighters, that our B-17 aircraft was a self-sufficient fortress and didn't need fighter support.

"We'll shoot our way in and back from a target," LeMay told us.

After our first mission I knew that he was acutely aware that our leaders had miscalculated the ability of the German fighters to stop us. Lack of fighter escort was only the beginning of our troubles. Our outnumbered forces were to be sacrificed for the invasion of North Africa.

In the second week of November, LeMay ordered our aircrews to assemble for a special meeting in the briefing room. He introduced us to Brig. Gens. Heywood S. Hansell Jr. and Fred Anderson of the Eighth Air Force Bomber Command. We wondered what two generals were doing visiting us. It had to be a special occasion. Preston told me that Hansell was in charge of planning for the Eighth Air Force. His nickname was "Possum." It was not a derogatory term; Hansell signed his personal letters as "Possum."

They gave us a sudden and devastating dose of reality. Anderson spoke first. He told us that three of the Eighth Air Force's seven heavy bomber groups would be transferred to support the North African invasion, which had begun on the eighth. The transfer of those groups to North Africa was a matter of highest security. He warned us that if we were shot down over German-held territory and taken prisoner, we were to give the Germans only our name, rank, and serial number. We were not to tell them that almost half of our forces had been sent to North Africa.

Hansell asked if we had any questions. I looked at LeMay. His face was inscrutable, as usual. I waited for some comment from our group leaders. No one spoke. We were in shock.

I glanced around the room one more time and raised my hand. Hansell nodded in my direction and I stood up and said, "If three of our groups are sent to North Africa it means we'll have only four left to compete against the Nazis. We won't be able to send more than seventy-five planes on a mission. Can we protect ourselves or do any real damage with such a small force against hundreds of German fighters?"

He didn't reply. "We have no fighter support beyond the enemy coast," I continued. "Will we have enough firepower to defend against Nazi fighters with such a small force?" I could see that Hansell was reluctant to answer my question.

"This transfer of groups to North Africa was not our decision," he finally replied. "We have no choice. We must continue bombing the targets Pinetree assigns. Washington will not permit our planes to sit idly on the ground until we get replacements. The British are asking what we are here for, and why we're using up all these resources if we aren't going to hit the Germans."

"It looks as if we are expendable," I replied. The room was silent. "What about our flying with the RAF at night until we get fighter support?"

Hansell stood fully erect and said, "The RAF engages in area bombing. It is contrary to air force policy. Our planes are not equipped for night bombing. Our crews are not trained for it. It would take several weeks training before we could start bombing at night. We're all disappointed by this decision. I know missions with a smaller force will be rough. We have no choice. It's Washington's decision. It's out of our hands."

LeMay looked at me and barked, "Okay, that's enough. This is reality. We have to fight with the crews and planes that we have."

Hansell dismissed the meeting. I wondered whether we were about to face hopeless odds. How long would it be before we would receive replacements for the loss of three groups? There was a general grumbling as we filed out of the room. I noticed that neither Hansell nor Anderson had made any promise as to when our losses would be replaced. I asked Preston if he had any idea when the lost groups would return.

He told me he had no way of knowing. "But Hansell is in charge of planning and selecting our targets," he added. "He has to know that without replacements his plans for a strategic bombing victory over Germany will be delayed for months or even years."

As we filed out of the meeting, Doug Venable, one of my closest friends, remarked, "They call this North African invasion Operation Torch. It looks more like we're the ones who will be torched. When they tell us to keep 'em flying, they mean flying and dying. Our odds for survival just took a nosedive. Ours is not to reason why, ours is but to fly and die. Mother, you can get ready to put my star in your window. It won't be long now." He was correct.

4: Group Navigator for Curtis LeMay

The decision to send nearly half of our forces to North Africa meant that the bombing of strategic targets in Germany would have to be put on hold. We were ordered to make the German submarine pens our first bombing priority. The submarines were a serious threat to Allied troops on the way to North Africa, as well as the supplies of food and war materials to the British Isles.

On 17 November 1942, our 305th Bomb Group was selected for a diversionary mission to the German submarine base at Brest on the Brittany peninsula in northern France. LeMay told us that we were not scheduled to drop any bombs. Rather, it was planned that our group would be a decoy. We were to be bait for the Nazi fighters. The mission planners hoped that we would divert the German fighters' attention away from the main effort of the three groups bombing Lorient, another submarine base south of Brest.

General Hansell attended the mission briefing and made a short statement. I could see that he was unhappy. Bombing German submarine bases was a far cry from bombing strategic military targets in Germany, as he had planned.

We took off for Brest in the early morning. Our plane was at the lowest point in the formation and the last plane in the 366th Squadron. This position at the rear of the group formation was called "Tail-end Charlie" or "Purple Heart Corner." We were alone and the aircraft most vulnerable to enemy fighters. Except for our tail and ball-turret gunners, our formation had no other guns in range to help us against fighters attacking from below and to the rear.

We were each given an escape kit to be used in the event we bailed out or crash-landed in German or occupied territory. I had a French passport with a picture of me dressed as a French farm worker. I was told that I was not to attempt to speak French. My New England accent would be a dead giveaway. Instead, I was to use sign language and act as though I were a mute. The instructions printed on the outside of the escape kit read: "Do not open—Emergency-use only." The kit consisted of a celluloid pamphlet containing soap, a needle, thread, a jackknife, water purification tablets, powdered coffee, matches, razor, compass, and a map of northern France. We were told not to carry our .45-caliber pistols over France. I wasn't looking forward to using a parachute. However, I surmised that if it became necessary I would not hesitate to do so.

As we prepared to take off for our first flight over enemy territory, I had mixed feelings of exultation and apprehension. I had been in the Air Corps and at war for eleven months. What would be my response, and the response of our crews, the first time we encountered experienced German fighter pilots? Galloway sat ahead of me in the bombardier's seat. As we prepared to take off, I looked over his shoulder down the runway at the plane taking off ahead of us. O'Neill gave our four engines full power. Their roar as we sped down the runway seemed a fitting and proper way for us to start a confrontation that would change our lives forever.

Since we were flying a diversion we carried no bombs. We were quickly airborne. We followed Major Preston, our squadron commander. He led us through heavy cloud cover to the assembly point, where we rendezvoused with the 305th's other squadrons. Because we were "Tail-end Charlie," it was not necessary for me to navigate. All we had to do was follow the leader. I felt I could rely on the lead navigator in LeMay's plane.

We headed across the English Channel toward Brest. We saw no German fighters as we approached the French coast. The diversion had not fooled them. After a feint toward the Brest submarine base, Colonel LeMay turned back and led our group across the Channel toward Plymouth. The English coast was a welcome sight as I watched RAF Spitfire fighters coming out to escort our formation back to Grafton Underwood.

As we approached the coastline, I saw that all England was socked in with 100 percent cloud cover. I computed the force and drift of the wind with my drift meter and used dead reckoning to plot a course to our base from Plymouth. In the meantime, we continued to follow the group as the last plane in the formation. When we arrived over the Cambridge area in East Anglia, the group started circling. LeMay was looking for a hole in the clouds so we could land. As he circled the area, we followed.

While listening to the command frequency on the radio, I heard LeMay tell the group, "My navigator can't seem to locate our position or lead us to our base. We can't keep circling at this altitude. We're running low on fuel. There are barrage balloons down there that could cut off our wings. Is there any navigator who has not just been following the leader, but knows where we are?"

"Yes, sir," I replied. "This is five-four-nine-two. We're about ten miles from base."

"Okay," said LeMay. "Take the lead. We'll follow you in. You had better be sure of your position and the location of the barrage balloons. We're counting on you."

The group commander's plane dropped back and permitted us to pull into the lead position. I moved into the bombardier's seat to look for a hole in the clouds. I spotted a small opening through which I could identify the trees and rural landscape surrounding our base. I saw no barrage balloons. I spoke to the group on interphone: "There's a hole in the clouds. I've spotted the base."

"Lead us in," replied LeMay. "We'll follow you."

We dove down through the hole in the clouds with the entire group following us, and every plane made a safe landing.

As soon as we rolled to a stop I slowly dropped down through the hatch in the aircraft's nose. I was surprised to see the colonel walking toward us.

Without any words of introduction he told me, "You are now group navigator for the three-oh-fifth. You'll be in charge of navigation and lead us on every mission you fly from now on."

O'Neill and Collins looked at me. They were as astonished as I was.

After a moment's hesitation, I managed to reply, "Sir, I—I'm only a second lieutenant. I can't give orders to first lieutenants and captains."

"Tell me if they don't obey you," LeMay growled as his command car rolled to a stop in front of us.

"Come here," he said, motioning to me. "Get in my car with me. We'll go to operations and critique today's mission. You'll find that I appreciate navigators. I'm a navigator by nature."

This was my second ride with him. I vividly remembered the first occasion as I climbed into the backseat. I hesitated to look back at

O'Neill and Collins. I knew that my assignment as group navigator would mean I would not be flying with my old crew anymore. I would have new duties as a member of the group operations staff. As we rode toward headquarters, LeMay told me that our most pressing problem was our failure to come even close to achieving bombing accuracy.

"We pay the price in lost planes every time we go on a mission," he said. "But we're not getting a return on our investment in bombing results. Some changes have to be made."

He ordered me to analyze the reconnaissance photos of our training missions. I studied the pictures of our practice bombing. The photos made it clear that, even in those cases where the bombs of our lead aircraft hit the targets, many of the other aircraft in our group scattered their bombs all over the landscape. If we did this over France we would either plow up farmland or kill innocent civilians. LeMay told me that the training command back in the States had always assumed that navigators and bombardiers were relatively equal in terms of their ability when they headed overseas. They expected that each aircrew could hit targets individually with a reasonable degree of accuracy. In practice, however, there was a great difference in the bombing accuracy and performance among the individual crews. Their response to the stress of flying in combat in European weather varied tremendously.

LeMay called a meeting of our squadron commanders and group operations leaders.

He explained the problem in his usual direct way, saying: "Those training-command types don't know the difference between flying a peaceful bomb run in cloudless desert skies and a bomb run at twenty-five thousand feet, in cloud cover, over a camouflaged target, in a crowded urban area, with flak bursting all around. Only our best crews have been hitting targets consistently. Some crews just can't concentrate in combat. An 'A' crew in the states may be a 'D' crew over enemy territory. Our strike photos indicate that more than sixty-five percent of our bombs are unaccounted for and no more than three percent of our bombs are landing within a thousand feet of the target.

"The bomb run is sometimes half over before the bombardiers have picked up the target. The results obtained by our average crews are not good enough. Only our best crews will lead the missions. The crews behind will toggle their bombs when they see the bombs dropping from the lead plane. That way the bombs will make a pattern to cover the front, back, and both sides of the target."

Preston, Charles Malec (our group bombardier), and I left the meeting convinced that although the colonel was correct, selection of the lead crews would be difficult. There would be resentment from pilots, navigators, and bombardiers who were not selected to become mission leaders. Those who became leaders would become eligible for promotion.

LeMay instructed us to set up a lead crew school. I was in charge of training the navigators, and Preston became the principal. The school became the hallmark of LeMay's training program in England and later for our B-29 crews in the campaign against Japan. We developed an automatic flight control procedure for the bomb run that allowed the bombardier to control the aircraft in the final minutes before bomb release. In March 1943 I received a commendation from Hansell and LeMay for developing this procedure. Our group bombing accuracy began to improve dramatically.

The Germans were quick to learn the importance of the lead plane to the success of the mission. They discovered that if they could shoot down or disable the lead plane the entire mission might be a partial or total failure. Increased head-on attacks focused on the lead plane took the pressure off the rest of the formation and "Tail-end Charlie" was no longer in the most vulnerable position. Although it was an honor to be selected as a lead navigator or bombardier, with the honor went the increased danger of being the fighters' primary target.

Shortly after Generals Hansell and Anderson suggested that we were expendable, Colonel LeMay gave us a new challenge. Standing before us in the briefing room during the last week of December 1942, he surveyed the room, his eyes glaring at us under his bushy eyebrows, removed his pipe, and said: "I've been studying the photos of our bombing results. They stink. Every time we take off and fly into enemy territory we're bound to have some losses. We pay a price every time we go out. There's no point in making a bombing run if we're not going to hit the target. I assume most of you understand plane geometry. The accuracy of our bombing depends on the accuracy of a geometric triangle. The angle must be exact for the bombs to hit a target. Even if the bombardier inserts the correct math in the bombsight, including course, speed, and wind drift, accurate bombing is impossible if our planes are twisting and turning on the bomb run. The bombs must leave from a stable platform.

"I know some of you will say evasive action is a defense against fighters and flak. That may be partially true, but we have to fly straight and level on the bomb run from the initial point (IP) until the bomb-release point. We either get the bombs on the target or concede the air war to the Germans now. You can't hit a target with a ten-second bomb run while we are taking evasive action. Those civilians below us are probably on our side. When our bombs don't hit military targets we may be killing civilians who are our friends and supporters. I can't blame them for being upset when our bombs land on their homes, schools, churches, and hospitals. The smart boys back in Washington call that collateral damage. I'll be leading this first straight-and-level, no-evasive-action mission with Preston, Nutter, and Malec. If some of you are wondering whether or not you'll make it back, quit thinking about it. Losses go with the territory. Any questions?"

Someone from one of the crews said, "If we abandon evasive action and fly straight and level, we'll be sitting ducks for both the flak and fighters. The fighters and flak guns can line up on your lead plane, get a bead on you, and then pick us off one at a time."

"I'm not saying you're wrong," LeMay replied, his voice taking on a fatherly tone. "But I've been studying artillery and antiaircraft manuals and I think we can take their flak. When we get to the target area, we will have paid the admission price. We're going to reap the benefits of that price by getting our bombs on target. A mission that doesn't hit the target is a wasted effort. If they line up on our lead plane, we'll have no choice but to sit there and take it. So will the rest of you. There will be no exceptions. There are no foxholes in the sky. If any of you don't have the stomach for this, maybe you'll be happier in the infantry. See the adjutant if you want a transfer."

"When are we going to get fighter support all the way to the target and back?" someone else inquired.

"I can't answer that," said LeMay. "We'll just have to get used to bombing with the limited fighter support we have."

On 23 November we tried out LeMay's new tactic on Saint-Nazaire. At our dawn briefing the group commander stood and pointed at the map. "Saint-Nazaire is the most important German submarine base," he announced. "It's south of Brest, where we made our diversion. The sub pens are covered with twelve feet of concrete. We know that our five-hundred-pound bombs will probably bounce off the top and can't penetrate the sub pens, but if we can get the bombs to land in the water at the entrance to the sub pens, then the force of the explosion may wreck the subs inside.

"I hear some of you are still grousing about my no-evasive-action policy. I wouldn't try this unless I believed it was going to work and improve our bombing accuracy. Both Malec and Nutter agree that this is the only way we're going to get our bombs on target. Keep a tight formation. It makes for a closer bomb pattern and protects us all.

"Each bombardier is to toggle his bombs when he sees the bombs from our lead plane. We will fly our usual one hundred fifty-five miles per hour indicated air speed as we approach the target at twenty-two thousand feet. As we turn off the target, we'll cut back to an air speed of one hundred fifty so the rear squadrons can keep up with us. This turn off the target is a critical time for those of you behind us. If you're a straggler, it will probably be all over for you. The German fighters are like a pride of lions waiting for a lone zebra. Don't be the zebra! If you don't keep up with our formation, we can't slow down and risk the whole group to wait for some unfortunate straggler. We fly in formation together as a group, or we all go down separately."

The 1st Bomb Wing sent fifty-eight aircraft to Saint-Nazaire. We led the wing with twenty, but six crews did not make it to the target. When a plane did not bomb the target, we called it an abortion. There were inevitably mechanical problems. This time, however, I wondered if some of the abortions from our group were for good cause, or if the crews were trying to avoid complying with LeMay's geometry lesson.

As we approached the IP, I wondered if the price would be too high. We were going to make it easier for both the German fighters and the antiaircraft gunners to pick us off.

It was zero hour. LeMay spoke to the group on the command frequency, ordering the planes behind us to tighten up the formation. The Saint-Nazaire bomb run lasted seven minutes. It seemed much longer. I expected the worst, but it never happened. Although the temperature was thirty-five degrees below zero, the weather was ideal for bombing. There was not much cloud cover, and I had no difficulty picking out the sub pens in the harbor below. We approached the IP on the French coast on time and in accordance with our flight plan. I waited for a barrage of flak and a concentrated fighter attack. I didn't have to wait long. The flak hit our aircraft, first in the right wing, then in the left wing. It appeared that the Germans' antiaircraft gunners had us locked in their sights. We had to keep going and prepare for the worst. There was nothing we could do to protect ourselves; we couldn't shoot at the antiaircraft gunners. The force of the two strikes of shrapnel on our wings rocked our plane and upset the level bomb platform we were trying so hard to achieve. The second hit knocked us off course and we started to lose altitude. LeMay told Malec that he was taking the plane off automatic pilot and that he would fly the bomb run manually. He managed to get us back to our planned altitude and on a straight-and-level course.

Finally, Malec yelled, "Bombs away!" As we unloaded our six thousand pounds of bombs, the plane lurched upward. I saw the bombs hit the water next to the entrance to the sub pens. This was better than a direct hit on the twelve-foot slab of concrete on top. We turned toward the ocean and then north toward England. No German fighters followed us. We lost two planes to fighters, none to flak. Our group had twice the number of bombs on the target than the other three groups. LeMay's no-evasive-action procedure was a success. At the mission critique, Malec told me that black clouds had interfered with his bombing accuracy.

"Chuck," I said, "those weren't black clouds, that was flak."

Although our bombing was accurate, the strike photos showed that attacks on the submarine pens were no more than a nuisance to the German war effort. Twelve feet of concrete prevented any major damage to the subs and maintenance equipment inside. Our leaders would not accept reality, though. Bomber Command ordered us to continue to hit the German sub bases.

Although the bombing was a wasted effort, we were learning a lot about German fighter tactics. During those first missions over enemy territory, our bombers and the German fighters were like two boxers sparring in an effort to evaluate the strengths and weaknesses of an unknown opponent. We were impressed with the technical ability, bravery, and ferocity of the German pilots. On the route to the target, our greatest need for protection was after the Spitfires turned back for England. I was always sorry when I saw them waggle their wings and turn back. Occasionally the German fighters followed us across the English Channel to our home base. The RAF Spitfires were more than an equal match against them over England.

The future didn't look promising for us unless we could obtain long-range fighter support. I asked Preston about our chances of getting fighter escort to the target and back.

"Don't count on it," Joe replied. "I think the brass in Washington have hung us out to dry while they try that North African caper. I don't even know if the U.S. has any long-range fighters. I've been told that the British are working on a long-range fighter that's being built in the U.S. They call it the 'Mustang,' but I don't know whether the U.S. is planning to produce or use it. I have a feeling we'll be on our own for a long time. At least we have LeMay. He never gives up. If we survive this, we'll have him to thank."

I felt that if ever there was a man in the right place, at the right time, it was Colonel LeMay. I finally understood what he had been trying to do with our group ever since July back at Muroc. His tough discipline and what originally seemed like iron-ass demands began to make sense to me.

Later, I told Doug Venable about Preston's pessimism regarding our chances of getting fighter support to and from the targets, that Joe believed that LeMay's leadership was our only chance to survive.

Doug laughed and said: "That's our boy. He doesn't know the meaning of 'can't do.' It's always 'can do' with him."

"Doug," I said, "you just gave our group a name."

I mentioned the name to Preston and he told LeMay. They immediately liked it. We had an insignia made with the slogan on it and "Can do" became our group motto. It sounded corny and old-fashioned, but as long as LeMay was our leader, most of us believed we could hold our own against the Germans. Failure was not in his vocabulary. We believed in him and each other, and as time went on he believed in us. The 305th had become a unit. We had a confidence and loyalty in LeMay that was absolutely necessary to our success and survival.

In late December we moved to a larger base at Chelveston, halfway between Cambridge and Northampton. It was larger than Grafton Underwood and had longer runways; there was also more mud. The coal in the Quonset huts was hardly sufficient to keep us warm in the bone-chilling English dampness.

5: The Possum Becomes Our Commanding General

In the first week of January 1943, we were informed that Brig. Gen. Heywood "Possum" Hansell, would succeed Brig. Gen. Lawrence S. Kuter as commanding general of the 1st Bomb Wing, which included our 305th Bomb Group. I remembered Hansell's announcement in November that we were losing three of our groups to North Africa. I asked Joe Preston what he knew about Hansell and he told me that Hansell was expected to be a star in the air force. He had been an observer of the RAF operation in England prior to the war and was in General Arnold's inner circle. He had been the chief planner for Maj. Gen. Carl Spaatz, the Eighth Air Force commander, in the summer of 1942. Arnold had picked him to command our wing for the first bombing assaults on the Nazi homeland.

Joe predicted that LeMay would try to persuade Hansell to order the other three groups to use his new staggered formations. They might be our only chance to survive.

I rode with LeMay, Preston, and Malec to our first wing operations meeting. Hansell's headquarters was in the former estate of an English lord in Brampton, a village west of Cambridge. We assembled in what had probably been the formal dining room. The commanding officers and headquarters operations people, including group navigators and bombardiers, from all four groups were present.

Hansell entered the room carrying a swagger stick, the British symbol of military command. He was slim and of average height with brown, sandy hair and small eyes. Although he had sharp features, his face was warm and friendly. He smiled nervously at the four group commanders staring at him. I wondered whether he was comfortable as the commander of a combat unit about to confront the toughest and most challenging air force assignment of the war. It was apparent that he wanted our respect and approval. I learned later that this was his first combat command. I compared him with LeMay. After working for LeMay for almost six months, I had the utmost confidence in his leadership. It seemed apparent to me that he was born to command a combat unit.

Hansell, on the other hand, knew the formalities of military command but gave no appearance of charisma or inner strength. I wondered whether the qualities that made him a successful staff and planning officer for General Arnold were sufficient for a combat command. Hansell's face became animated when he discussed the strategic importance of a particular military target. He clearly enjoyed the intellectual exercise of analyzing the enemy's economics and production needs and the bomb tonnage required to destroy a vital military target. He deferred to group commanders when combat tactics and procedures were discussed.

Hansell was three years older than LeMay, and the contrast in their backgrounds was striking. Hansell came from a military family, his father having been an army surgeon. He grew up on southern military bases. He personified the grace of the Old South. As a small boy he had been fascinated by the study of military history, and Robert E. Lee was his boyhood idol. Like Lee, he tried to wage what he conceived to be a civilized war by bombing only military targets avoiding civilian casualties. He graduated from Georgia Tech in 1924.

He had an impressive history in the Air Corps. He taught at the prestigious Air Tactical School (ATS) at Maxwell Field, Alabama, and LeMay had been one of his students. He was deeply committed to Brig. Gen. Billy Mitchell's prewar theory that victory could be achieved through airpower by bombing vital military targets. He believed that heavily armed bombers could out-fly enemy fighters, bomb targets without fighter protection, and return to base with reasonably acceptable losses.

Hansell had learned to be secure and at ease in the corridors of influence and power. He had been the chairman of a unit to make plans for the expansion of the Air Corps in 1941 and 1942. He was a proud military theorist, but he had never been accepted as one of the boys in an operational unit.

At the ATS he taught LeMay and other students that high-altitude precision bombing could achieve total victory without the casualties of a land invasion.

LeMay had spent his career in the lower echelons of the Air Corps. Never having served at air force headquarters, he knew none of the top leaders. His path to group command and the rank of full colonel had been founded on merit alone. Although he was conspicuously lacking in Hansell's social graces, his flying and tactical abilities could not be overlooked in time of war.

The disparity in the two men's demeanor was striking. LeMay's face was stern and inscrutable. He seemed a man apart. He made no attempt to impress the other group commanders. He spoke softly and sometimes mumbled. He asked tough questions and, when pressed, gave tough, direct answers.

In contrast to LeMay, Hansell appeared anxious to reach a consensus of the group leaders. I wondered whether consensus building was the type of leadership required of a combat commander.

After we had attended a few of Hansell's meetings, most of us had negative thoughts about him as our commanding general. He did not appear to be strong and confident. When a group commander would ask him when we could expect fighter support, he never gave a direct answer. He was uncomfortable with the question, and rather than answer it, he would change the subject. When the meetings involved the discussion of tactical problems like formations, bombing procedures, gunnery, and the performance of the combat crews, he usually was silent. He did not seem interested in the nuts and bolts of combat operations and tactics. He was willing to let the group commanders work out tactical problems in their own ways. It was apparent that these wing meetings with the group commanders were an ordeal for him. Later, when I worked for him on Saipan, he told me they were soul-searching experiences.

LeMay did not participate in the social amenities or give and take with the other group commanders. He was silent when Hansell discussed the importance of particular German targets, but became the dominant member of the meeting when we discussed tactical problems.

In the winter and spring of 1943, none of the group leaders suggested to Hansell that high-altitude precision daylight bombing without fighter escort was impractical or that we should fly with the RAF at night. LeMay continued to seek new ways to improve our bombing procedures and training methods. Many of the other group leaders considered his tactical innovations bold, even radical.

LeMay did not appear to be bothered by their criticism. He

pointed out that the formation and bombing techniques we had been taught back in the States were a carryover from peacetime training methods. They were founded on untested theories that would not be successful in combat against the Germans. Unless we made changes, he contended, not only would our bombing efforts be unsuccessful, our groups would face annihilation.

In spite of their differences in personality, I noticed no tension between Hansell and LeMay. Although LeMay presented his views in a strong and forceful fashion, he was never disrespectful of Hansell. Hansell, always a gentleman, gave LeMay wide latitude to express his views. Indeed, I believe Hansell welcomed his suggestions. After our first missions and wing staff meeting, I wondered what circumstances might have produced LeMay's indefatigable courage, realism, and ability to respond to the most adverse conditions. What motivated him? Was it his family background or some event in his childhood?

LeMay's executive officer was Lt. Col. Don Fargo, his closest associate in the 305th. On many nights while we were waiting for weather clearance for our missions, Don told me LeMay's family history. LeMay was born in 1906. Unlike most of our group, he was not a child during the Great Depression. His formative years were in the years before World War I. He grew up in joyless semipoverty. He was the oldest of seven children born over a period of twenty-two years. His first childhood home, although not in a slum, was in a poorer section of Columbus, Ohio.

Throughout his childhood, his father had difficulty staying employed. He lost his first job working on the railroad and later worked at odd jobs performing carpentry and painting. He was a dreamer, always looking for new horizons and opportunities. During LeMay's early years, the family lived in four different locations in Columbus. When it seemed there was no longer any opportunity in Ohio, he announced they would be moving to Montana.

The family's move to Montana in the dead of winter was arduous. The train trip in unheated railroad coaches was especially difficult for the children. They had no money to buy food, so they were obliged to carry it with them on the train. Typically, his father promptly lost his first job in Montana. The family had to move once again—this time in an open wagon during a raging blizzard, to the Nez Perce area of Montana, twenty-five miles from the nearest neighbor. There, young Curtis learned to love the beauty of outdoor activities, self-reliance, hunting and fishing, and a sense of adventure that was to be with him for the rest of his life. At the age of eight he had to catch fish to put food on the table.

Next came a family move to Emeryville, California, where his father found work in a cannery. Again, this did not last long, and soon the family was on the road again—to Pennsylvania, northeast of Pittsburgh. Curtis worked at odd jobs, including a paper route, until the end of World War I. Food was often scarce, and he frequently ran away. When the young truant was located, his father punished him, but without success. He continued to run away and was forever changing schools. He grew up without the tranquility of a permanent home, having no time to establish childhood friends. Throughout those years of hardship and a nomadic existence, he relied on his mother's strong sense of serenity and responsibility for stability. She accepted life as it was without complaint; whatever hardship might come, she would find a way to survive.

LeMay was like two other World War II heroes and leaders who were close to their mothers—Gen. Douglas MacArthur and General Patton. But, unlike them, he had no military background. His father was of rural French-Canadian heritage, and his mother was descended from English settlers in Virginia. Like his mother, LeMay's sense of duty, courage, and responsibility were his most dominant traits. Reality was a tough disciplinarian. He learned to face reality as it was, not as he wished things were. In contrast to his father, whom he considered a dreamer, LeMay prided himself on being practical. He learned to distrust intellectuals at an early age and frowned on them as theoretical dreamers.

The family returned to Ohio in 1919, and Curtis helped support his younger brothers and sisters, bought his own clothes, and paid all of his personal expenses. In high school he had no time for the normal social life of young people his age. His life was work, work, and more work. In the fall of 1924 he enrolled at Ohio State University, where he studied civil engineering. His college life was more of the same: all work and no play. He worked the graveyard shift in a foundry from 5 P.M. to 2 A.M. six days a week and failed an early morning class because he constantly fell asleep. In 1928, having failed to obtain a degree, he enlisted in the army and promptly fulfilled his boyhood dream when he was transferred to the fledgling Air Corps. The following year he was able to make up the course he had failed and graduate from Ohio State.

Hansell always opened his staff meetings by asking each of the group commanders to give a brief summary of his group combat experiences and immediate problems.

Hansell was uncomfortable with questions concerning fighter support. He knew that the P-47 fighters then in production could fly no farther than the RAF fighters, and he tried to reassure the group commanders by informing them that the Wright Field materiel command was working on a design for auxiliary fuel tanks for the P-47s. He gave us no date when they would be available. LeMay was not satisfied.

"Without fighter support, we'll be unable to protect our crews," LeMay said bluntly. "Fighter attacks on the bomb run affect our accuracy. It's difficult for our navigators and bombardiers to locate camouflaged targets in cloud cover when tracers, shells, and shrapnel are knocking our planes around on the bombing run. So far, we've been lucky if we get one percent of our bombs on the target. How would those pickle-barrel theorists in the States do if they had to bomb under the conditions our crews are facing? It's a hell of a lot different dropping bombs on German territory than a chalked circle in the open desert of the Southwest."

LeMay wasn't through. "Who was the sad sack who put those thirty-caliber peashooters in the nose?" he asked. "They're a joke. They don't have the range or power to do us any good. We need at least two sets of twin fifties in the nose. I noticed that on our last mission the Nazis were changing their tactics. They were attacking us head-on. They're also using a new long-range cannon with much greater range than our guns. They can sit out there and pick us off one at a time."

Hansell was concerned and uneasy about the tenor and tone of LeMay's remarks. Our group commander's comments were nothing like the genteel dialogue Hansell had experienced at headquarters' staff meetings. He knew that the group commanders were aware he had been the guiding force in preparing the air force's war plans in 1941 and 1942—plans that had no provision for the development or production of long-range escort fighters for bombers.

Hansell had been told that LeMay hardly ever spoke more than a few words. Now his strong views were dominating the wing meetings.

LeMay still wasn't finished. He shifted from discussing weapons to the gunners themselves: "They stink. The exaggerated claims headquarters is making about the number of German fighters we are shooting down are bullshit. Maybe it makes good PR in the States, but they're not fooling the Germans. I'm starting a concentrated in-flight training program for our gunners."

He hesitated for a moment, then went on: "I would also like to talk about the accuracy of our bombing—or perhaps I should say *in*-accuracy. If we hit military targets one percent of the time we're lucky. We're plowing up a lot of farm fields and killing a lot of innocent civilians. What's the use of flying over a target if we're not going to hit it? Evasive action on the bomb run is ridiculous. By the time we reach the target we've already paid a price in men and planes. Our group doesn't have any greater losses than the other group by flying straight and level without evasive action."

The room was quiet. I could see that the other group commanders were displeased with LeMay's remarks. Hansell, visibly upset, turned to LeMay and said, "Curt, before I issue any orders directing no evasive action on the bomb run, I think you had better fly some more missions. I'll fly with you in the lead plane on the next mission. Then we'll discuss it."

LeMay paused. His stern expression remained unchanged. "Do you want me to diagram my new staggered formation?" he asked.

Hansell nodded and LeMay went to the blackboard and drew the formation we had been practicing for the past week. Hansell, seeming to be impressed, said, "It looks like a better concentration of firepower. We'll try it out on the next mission and see how it works."

When no one responded, Hansell mentioned a few housekeeping matters and then dismissed us.

I thought about the meeting. Hansell did not seem displeased with LeMay's strong views about combat tactics and bombing procedures or the fact that LeMay was criticizing him personally. His new tactics and training programs would improve bombing accuracy and our defensive capability. His candor could actually be refreshing if he would just use a little more tact.

LeMay was silent on the drive back to Chelveston. He made no comment about the meeting. On the way back to our barracks I asked Preston why we were flying daylight missions when both the British and Germans had given up on daylight bombing because of their disastrous losses. Joe said he could not answer my question.

Our first mission with Hansell was delayed by the weather. It was not unusual for a mission to be canceled at the last minute because of weather problems. More often than not, we had to take off in thick, pea-soup English fog. Heavy cloud cover usually accompanied the fog over our base. After takeoff, our groups flew to a designated assembly point on England's east coast, each aircraft flying blind through the clouds. It was often the most dangerous part of the mission. Visibility in the clouds was often no more than fifty feet. If we saw a plane while we were climbing through the fog or clouds, it was usually too late to avoid a catastrophic collision.

The weather prevented us from flying more than four or five missions a month. On days we were not able to fly because of the weather, LeMay scheduled practice bomb runs and formation flying, as long as there was daylight. Gunners who were not flying practiced at the gunnery and skeet ranges. Navigators and bombardiers studied target maps, photos, landmarks, possible bombing runs, and potential routes to enemy cities. In planning the route to the target, I always tried to avoid areas where there were heavy concentrations of antiaircraft guns and to pick out targets of opportunity in case the primary target was covered with clouds.

The weather finally cleared and, true to his word, General Hansell appeared at our group in the second week of January. He announced that he would ride with our crew on a mission to Lille in northern France as LeMay's copilot. Sixty B-17s were dispatched on the mission, with our 305th Group leading the wing. Although

Hansell, a brigadier general and our wing commander, was in command of the mission, he did not speak on the interphone or assert any direction or control. I wondered what he thought about the cramped condition of the cockpit quarters and the chaos of a combat mission. This was a sharp contrast to the well-ordered comfort of his headquarters.

There was seven-tenths cloud cover as we approached the target, a German armaments plant in Lille's heavily built-up industrial area. After we turned at the initial point of the bomb run, LeMay gave the bombardier control of our plane on automatic pilot. I leaned over Malec's shoulder and strained to pick up some landmark that I could identify and give him a precise aiming point. We were two minutes into the bomb run before I could point out the target. While I was looking for it, five FW190 fighters came at us head-on, twisting and rolling, with their machine guns and cannon blazing. I swung my .30-caliber machine guns around and fired what I knew were ineffective bursts at the approaching enemy fighters. I could hear cannon shells and pieces of shrapnel hit our aircraft.

I looked back and saw two planes from the 306th group collide. I counted twenty parachutes. No one spoke. I could feel the jolts from the antiaircraft fire and more shell fragments hit our plane. LeMay took the plane off automatic pilot, straightened out our course, and we made a successful bomb run.

We turned off the target and headed for the English Channel. As we approached the white cliffs of Dover, we let down to an altitude of ten thousand feet. The flight engineer, who doubled as top-turret gunner, appeared at my navigator's table and handed me a Spam sandwich.

"Compliments of General Hansell," he said with a grin.

It was the first and last time I was given lunch by a general. As we climbed out of the plane on our return to the base, I turned to Hansell and said, "Thank you for the sandwich, sir."

He smiled. "Those head-on fighter attacks on the bomb run were not pleasant; you deserved it," he replied. "I don't know how you were able to pick out the target in that cloud cover. You did a great job. I must say, this mission was not a happy experience."

I looked at LeMay. He did not speak or react to Hansell's statement. His face was impassive. As usual, he was frugal with praise or compliments.

While we were waiting for a jeep to transport us to debriefing at operations, Hansell commented about the intensity of the fighter attacks during the bomb run. LeMay replied that it was impossible for our top and ball turret guns to defend against such attacks, and the .30-caliber machine guns in the nose were no better than a child's BB gun. I asked Hansell if it would be possible to install a .50-caliber turret under the nose and two sets of twin .50s for use by the navigator and bombardier. He said he would look into the matter.

He then turned to LeMay and said, "You did a great job of holding our course straight and level on the bomb run. I'm surprised that we managed to get through all that flak."

"I know the flak was rough, but I don't deviate on the bomb run," LeMay replied. "We got our bombs on target."

"Perhaps the crews could have armor protection with some type of flak vests," I interjected. I paused a moment and then asked if it was possible to put armor plating or metal protection under our seats. "Shouldn't we try to protect American manhood?" I concluded facetiously. I could see that LeMay was not amused by my suggestion about putting armor under the seats.

Hansell looked at me and said, "I'll discuss putting in more nose guns and body protection with Eaker's armament people at Pinetree." He then said he would order the other groups to use our no-evasive-action policy on the bomb run and that he hoped to ride with our crew again.

I learned later that Hansell received a medal for his leadership of the mission.

After the mission, LeMay sent a letter to the training command describing our group's experiences. He offered tentative conclusions concerning our performance in combat and added a postscript describing the Lille mission. The letter is in Appendix A.

LeMay was economical in his display of emotion, compliments, and sentiment, but he gave me support and recognition where and

when it counted. In December 1942 he promoted me to first lieutenant, and three months later I became a captain. He demonstrated
his concern about my welfare in other ways. As group navigator I was
responsible for checking Teletype messages from VIII Bomber Command to determine if a mission was scheduled. After Bomber Command designated the target, I checked with our weather officers for
an estimate of cloud cover and wind velocities and direction on our
target routes. The wind velocity would affect our ground speed and
our arrival time at various points along the route. An error of as little as one minute could be critical. I had to compute the exact time
of arrival at each checkpoint.

The first critical time was the group assembly point, from which
we would depart to join other groups and wings. I also gave notice
to Allied fighters of our flight schedule and time of rendezvous at
the English coast. Because the fighters didn't have sufficient fuel to
accompany us to the target, they would fly back to England after escorting us to the enemy coast. On our return they would attempt to
meet us at a designated time and place. When our group was scheduled to lead a mission, I would also designate the exact time for the
beginning of the bomb run and the arrival time over the target.

Each evening about 11:30, LeMay would come to the operations
room to check the flight plan. Invariably, he would ask me if I were
going on the mission.

If I replied in the affirmative, he would then say, "Go to bed. I will
do your work."

On one occasion, I had listed myself as navigator for a mission another group was scheduled to lead.

After examining the flight plan he asked his usual question, "Are
you flying on this one?"

When I replied that I wasn't flying with Joe Preston, but as lead
navigator with another squadron, he picked up the telephone and
called the squadron commander who was to be the lead pilot on the
mission.

"Let your own navigator lead this mission," LeMay said gruffly. "I
need Nutter here."

He dropped the phone back in its cradle, turned, and left the
room without a word of explanation. Later that day I had a strange

feeling when the plane on which I had planned to fly did not return. I never mentioned it to LeMay. I don't think he would have given me an explanation.

On another occasion, at the debriefing meeting after we returned from a mission, LeMay turned to me and said, "Nutter, you don't look too good. Are you sick?" When I told him I had the flu, he told me I shouldn't have gone on the mission because if I'd had to bail out and became a prisoner I would not have survived.

On more than one occasion he told me that the commanding officer was not supposed to have any friends. He couldn't afford the luxury of making combat decisions because of personal feelings. "I'm not supposed to be liked," he said. "I don't have the luxury of liking or disliking people."

In May 1943, when my close friend Doug Venable was killed, LeMay's only comment to me was, "Command is a lonely job. I'll write a letter to his family."

He wanted to be sure that all of his decisions were made for the group as a whole. There could not be a hint of favoritism in his assignments. Members of the group should not be sacrificed to protect some inept or unfortunate individual. A sentimental, romantic gesture for comrades in trouble would be counterproductive if it endangered other members of a crew or the group. He taught me that some loss of life had to be expected in every battle. Loss and death went with the territory; if victory were to be achieved, some lives had to be sacrificed for the greater good.

The first time I heard LeMay express the brutal truth that there is no room for sentimentality in fighting a war, the statement seemed harsh. I have never forgotten the circumstances.

We were returning from a mission over Germany. LeMay was the pilot and Joe Preston the copilot. As we turned off the target, I looked up at our high squadron and saw that one of its planes was in serious trouble. Smoke was pouring out of two engines. As it started to lose altitude, three German fighters moved in for the kill. The plane went into a steep dive and I counted eight parachutes. As the men in parachutes dropped down together, I saw a German FW190 fighter circling them. Then, to my horror, three more German fighters proceeded to strafe the defenseless men. One of the planes in our squadron broke formation and attempted to defend our parachuting comrades. The results were inevitable. Other German fighters pounced upon the Good Samaritan plane and, isolated and without the protection of the formation, it also became a victim, going down with the loss of ten more men. None of our crew mentioned the incident on our interphone. After we landed, I rode with LeMay, Preston, and Malec to the briefing room. None of us spoke. LeMay was more grim than usual. I knew that the critique of the mission would be difficult. I expected LeMay to have some harsh comments about the break in formation leading to the loss of the second crew.

After we assembled, there was absolute quiet. He seemed reluctant to speak. Finally he took his pipe out of his mouth and his words came out in a voice that was louder than usual. Looking directly at the assembled crews, he said: "There's no room for sentimentality in fighting a war. I know most of you saw what happened today. There's no excuse for breaking formation under any circumstances, unless you receive a direct order from the mission commander. Sentimentality and discipline don't mix in combat. We aren't fighting a Hollywood war here. Leave the glory, the false heroics, and sentimentality to the actors and sob sisters. The loss of one plane was unfortunate. The loss of the second crew was the result of a direct breach of group discipline.

"If one of our planes is disabled on a mission, if it is possible, we will slow our formation down to one hundred fifty indicated air speed to give the crippled plane a chance to keep up with the formation. But that is the best we can do. No one will break formation if they can't keep up."

LeMay's impatience with the inept and unfortunate became legendary. Later on, he expressed similar thoughts in circumstances that were not quite so dramatic.

When we were not flying, LeMay had a staff meeting every Wednesday and Friday at 8 A.M. One Wednesday morning he asked the group adjutant, a captain, to report on the status of certain equipment and supplies in the quartermaster department. He instructed him to place the report on his desk by the following Friday. At our next meeting, the adjutant started the meeting by apologizing to LeMay for not submitting the report as ordered and said he would have it on LeMay's desk in time for the next meeting.

"That won't be necessary," LeMay replied.

"Don't you want the report?" the captain asked.

"Yes," replied LeMay, "but you have a new assignment. You are now the group mess officer. I said it before, and I'll say it again. We don't have time for the inept or unfortunate in this war."

On another occasion, during a staff meeting, an unusually long-winded intelligence officer had difficulty coming to a conclusion. LeMay asked him to come to the point. He continued in his rambling manner until, with no end in sight, LeMay again interrupted him.

"Sir," said the captain, "I'm not finished."

"The hell you aren't!" snapped LeMay. "Sit down!"

LeMay taught us that discipline saved lives in combat. Sentimentality was the antithesis of discipline. There was no room for individual heroics in a combat operation that depended on teamwork.

LeMay never spoke to me personally about how he felt about our losses. He kept those thoughts to himself. I knew that he spent many hours late in the night writing personal letters of condolence to the families of our crewmembers lost in combat.

The increasing number of empty beds in our barracks and empty seats in the mess hall were a constant reminder of our daily losses. We were losing 8 percent of our force on every mission. It was a case of here today, gone tomorrow. We never talked about our missing comrades. We had an unwritten rule that no one should show emotion or concede that we probably wouldn't complete the required tour of twenty-five missions. We knew we would have to be incredibly lucky to complete even twenty missions. It was just a matter of time before our luck ran out. When a crewman was killed but the plane returned, most of us decided that funerals were not for survivors. I never attended a funeral, either in England or in the Pacific. We memorialized them by painting the names of those we lost on the barracks walls, with their hometown and the name and date of their last mission.

6: Casablanca—The Air Force Rejects Area Bombing

In December 1942, at a meeting of the U.S. Joint Chiefs of Staff, General Arnold said that if he could get more bombers for the Eighth Air Force, Germany could be defeated without an invasion.

Admiral Ernest J. King, the chief of naval operations, replied that the Eighth had nothing to show for its efforts given that it hadn't dropped so much as one bomb on Germany.

Arnold, trying to contain his temper, reminded King that half of the Eighth's groups had been sent to North Africa. King replied that Arnold would get a chance to explain the Eighth's failures to the president, British prime minister Winston Churchill, and the joint chiefs at a strategy conference in Casablanca in January.

The bombing directives formulated at Casablanca in January 1943 had a momentous effect on the future bombing policy of the Allied air forces for the remainder of the war. The policy was so vague and ambiguous that, as the war progressed, the proponents of both precision and area bombing used the policy to justify any type of bombing mission against enemy urban areas.

As Admiral King predicted, U.S. Army and Navy leaders came to Casablanca determined to abolish high-altitude precision daylight bombing. The Eighth Air Force had been in combat for six months and no bombs had been dropped on the German homeland. British leaders considered our daylight missions in France and the Low Countries to be no more than a nuisance, an unwarranted waste of resources. The joint chiefs and Churchill hoped to convince Pres. Franklin D. Roosevelt that his abhorrence of area bombing because of the danger to innocent civilians was unrealistic in the context of a total war against a brutal enemy. Apparently they succeeded, because not long after their arrival at Casablanca, Gen. George C. Marshall, the army chief of staff, told Arnold that the president agreed with Churchill and the joint chiefs that the Eighth Air Force should give up daylight bombing and join the RAF in night area bombing.

Arnold was disturbed and shocked. This would mean the end of the long-standing effort by air force leaders to achieve victory with airpower and would prevent the air force from becoming independent from the army and navy. He was convinced the North African invasion had been an unwarranted concession to Churchill's Mediterranean strategy. It was a mistaken diversion of attacks on the source of Hitler's military power in the German homeland.

Feeling alone and isolated, Arnold sent a cable to England ordering Maj. Gen. Ira Eaker to fly to Casablanca. Eaker was the air force's best diplomat. Like Arnold and other senior air force officers, he believed that Eighth Air Force bombers could fly to German targets without fighter escort and return with acceptable losses. Eaker had been trained as a lawyer and had been effective in his dealings with the RAF. Arnold knew that some RAF leaders agreed that area bombing had not been effective in destroying military targets. It was no more than terror bombing, and there was no evidence that they had been effective in persuading the German people to withdraw their support of Hitler and the war.

Arnold and Eaker believed that only daylight precision bombing would force Hitler to commit his fighters to battle. Unless the German fighter force was destroyed and the Allies attained air superiority, no invasion could possibly succeed. Arnold felt that he could not stand up to the force of Churchill's rhetoric and personality. He was too emotionally involved to confront Churchill, and he had serious health problems. Eaker could make the case for high-altitude daylight precision bombing in a way that would appeal to Churchill's sense of the dramatic.

On 20 January 1943, Eaker met with Churchill alone. The prime minister began by pointedly telling Eaker that the Eighth Air Force had not dropped a single bomb on Germany, although it had been based in England for almost six months. Eaker agreed, but informed Churchill that the Eighth would commence bombing the German homeland as soon as he returned to England. He handed Churchill a lengthy memorandum titled "The Case for Day Bombing." Churchill glanced at it and told Eaker he would discuss it with the RAF later. He then asked Eaker to explain his main points.

Eaker said that if the Eighth Air Force continued to bomb in daylight and the RAF at night, together they would bomb around the clock, giving the Germans no rest. He said it was necessary to destroy the Luftwaffe and gain air superiority. He explained that the RAF's gunners were no match for the German night fighters, whereas Eighth Air Force gunnery and bombing had steadily improved. Moreover, he said, it would take too long to modify the B-17s and train the crews for night operations. Neither Churchill nor Eaker mentioned the need for fighter support for the American bombers. Churchill subsequently told his aides that there was no point in trying to persuade the Americans that daylight bombing could not succeed without fighter escort. The Americans would not accept advice from the RAF; they would not modify their daylight bombing tactics until they learned about the need for fighter support from their own experiences.

Arnold, Eaker, and Hansell believed that the American B-17s and B-24s were superior to British bomber designs. They were convinced they could fight their way in and back from German targets in daylight, with reasonable losses, and without fighter escort. In the adverse climate at Casablanca, Arnold and Eaker dared not suggest that they had engaged in faulty planning or that the air force needed a long-range fighter. The crews would have to continue bombing without long-range fighter support.

Arnold's and Eaker's promise at Casablanca that the Eighth Air Force would start bombing German cities within a week meant that the air war was to enter a new phase for our combat crews.

Our missions to occupied France and the Low Countries in 1942 had fighter cover to within a few miles of the target areas. Our losses were low: only thirty-two aircraft, a loss rate of less than 3 percent. A new aircrew member could possibly finish twenty-five missions at that rate. However, the odds for surviving a combat tour were about to change. We would soon learn that Churchill's judgment about our leaders' blind adherence to their prewar bombing theories was correct.

7: Our First Mission over Germany

On 26 January 1943, Hansell called a meeting of group leaders to plan our first bombing mission over Germany. He opened the meeting by telling us that at the Casablanca conference General Arnold had ordered General Eaker to launch immediate missions against the German homeland. He told us that we must make a maximum effort and, if possible, put as many as ninety planes over the target.

LeMay asked Hansell if we were ready to fly into Germany without fighter support.

Hansell said we had no choice. Arnold insisted on an immediate mission. LeMay made no comment. The other group commanders looked grim. Hansell terminated the meeting without further discussion.

We returned to Chelveston to plan the mission. I worked out our group flight plan with LeMay and Preston and didn't get to bed until 11:30 P.M. Wake-up call was at 3 A.M., and after a breakfast of powdered eggs and Spam at 4 A.M., our crews assembled in the briefing room.

I pulled back a large curtain covering a map of Germany. I had placed a red string on the map indicating the route from our base at Chelveston in East Anglia, across the North Sea and the German Frisian Islands, to the Bremen-Vegesack area adjacent to the Weser River, where the Germans had their largest submarine construction yard and aircraft plant. The room was silent. The crews had been anticipating a mission over Germany for a long time.

LeMay stepped forward and pointed to the map, saying, "Germany is the target for today. This is what we're here for. Our targets are the aircraft and submarine plants in Vegesack near Bremen. If there's cloud cover and you can't see the target at Vegesack, then Major Preston, who will be leading the mission, will turn to a point along the coast and bomb our secondary target, Wilhelmshaven. Wilhelmshaven is the German naval headquarters and the largest naval and submarine base on the German coast. Look for pocket battleships in the harbor. We have reports that the *Scharnhorst* is based there. Keep a tight formation. The fighters are looking for stragglers who break formation.

"You'll be on your own as you approach the German coast. You'll have no fighter support beyond the Frisian Islands. That means you're going to have to shoot your way in and back from the target. Navigators and bombardiers will remain for a special briefing. If there are no questions, the meeting is dismissed."

I conducted the briefing for the navigators and bombardiers. We reviewed the bomb runs and photographs of the target areas in both Bremen and Wilhelmshaven. No one spoke as the crews filed out of the briefing room. I rode out to our plane in a jeep with Preston and Malec. I looked at the dark, overcast sky. I knew that this mission was crucial for Eaker and Hansell. Arnold and Eaker had promised we would bomb Germany in January. It was the end of the month. We had to go, in spite of the uncertain weather, with no break in the cloud cover above our base, so we would probably have to take off on instruments in foggy drizzle. I wondered if we could break through the overcast and assemble the group above the clouds without a collision.

This first mission over Germany began a new phase in our combat operations. Our previous missions over German-occupied territory in France, Belgium, and Holland had been warm-ups for the real thing. Our losses had never been more than 5 percent. This was the major league of aerial combat. Up to this point I had been too busy learning how to be a group navigator to think seriously about the hazards of flying over the German homeland. I had been in the Air Corps since 8 December 1941, the day after Pearl Harbor. Now, a little more than a year later, I would be in combat in the toughest league of them all. In the three and a half months since we had been in Europe I had seen the grim faces of German fighter pilots as they thundered through our formations. I knew they would consider an attack on their homeland as payback time.

This first mission to a German target was to be our ultimate test. The time for brave talk was over. I had no qualms or reservations about causing what our intelligence officers called "collateral damage" to nonmilitary targets and civilian areas. I looked upon Nazi

Germany as a special case. When we bombed German-occupied countries I was concerned about our bombs missing the targets and killing or maiming friendly French, Belgian, and Dutch citizens. I had no such reservations about bombing Germany. As far as I was concerned, the Germans were either Nazis or Nazi supporters or sympathizers. We could expect no quarter from the Germans. These thoughts went through my mind as I sat at my navigator's position, waiting for the flare from the control tower that would signal the pilots to start their engines. As the mission leader we were to be the first plane to take off.

As the propeller turned over on engine number one, I saw LeMay salute us and drive away. Joe ran each engine up to full throttle before taxiing to the end of the runway. I felt excited. I had expected to be nervous and apprehensive, but any fears I may have had were drowned out by the roar of the engines of the planes behind us, waiting for us to take off. As we paused at the end of the runway, I could hear the screeching of brakes as the planes behind us maneuvered into position. We sat waiting for the takeoff signal from the control tower. As the red flare rose in the sky, Preston released the breaks and we roared down the runway and started our climb through the low cloud cover. The remainder of the group took off behind us at one-minute intervals.

We flew blindly in a slow spiral up through the clouds and kept a close watch for other aircraft. We broke into sunlight at twenty thousand feet and circled the assembly point, waiting for the other squadrons and groups to form behind us in formation. We kept our wheels down so the rest of our planes could identify us. Soon the groups and squadrons were strung out behind us and Preston ordered them to tighten the formation. He retracted our wheels and I gave him the heading for Vegesack.

I made entries in my navigator's log sheet every ten minutes. As we crossed the English coast and headed across the North Sea, Joe told us to keep our eyes peeled for German fighters. We leveled off at twenty-five thousand feet and I could see ships in the water between the Frisian Islands and the German coast.

I told the crew we were over Germany. The Frisian Islands were covered with snow—a beautiful, peaceful scene. In the east there was a handsome blue sky in the sunlight. Germany looked like a winter wonderland, not the home of a mortal enemy. Military targets would be hard to pick out in a countryside blanketed with snow. Suddenly, I saw what appeared to be black specks approaching us. The natives were not about to give us a friendly greeting.

Our top-turret gunner yelled over the interphone, "Two o'clock high, here they come!"

I looked up and saw two radial-engine FW190s rolling and diving at us head-on, shooting tracers at our aircraft. This was not the beautiful "wild blue yonder" of the Air Corps song we had sung in cadet school.

As the lead navigator, I didn't have time to worry about the attacking fighters. I looked at the heavy cloud cover beyond the German coastline and wondered how I would be able to pick out the targets at Vegesack under such conditions. A German fighter passed by my window and I could see the pilot's grim face. The noise of our machine guns was beyond belief. It sounded like a hundred jackhammers.

"It looks like the primary targets at Vegesack are socked in," I yelled to Preston over the interphone. "There's no way we can make a visual sighting."

"Roger," Joe replied. "Give me a course to our secondary target at Wilhelmshaven."

I spotted a peninsula on the coast that I recognized as being about thirty miles from Wilhelmshaven and gave Preston a new heading. As we started the bomb run, I looked down and tried to locate the battleship *Scharnhorst* in the harbor. The Germans had attempted to camouflage the area with smoke pots and netting.

I reminded Malec, our bombardier, that Wilhelmshaven was the headquarters of the German navy, their largest submarine base, and that possibly the *Scharnhorst* was here. Malec, hunched over his bombsight, didn't reply. Finally, he told me he had a large ship in his crosshairs.

Joe put the plane on automatic pilot and we tried to fly a straight and level bomb run with no evasive action. The German fighters continued to dive at our plane head-on. They seemed to be enjoying themselves, darting around us in what seemed like a dance of death.

They wheeled, swung, and soared around us, diving directly at us with guns blazing. I saw tracers coming toward our aircraft and black clouds of smoke from antiaircraft guns exploded all around us—so close that we felt like we could get out and walk on them. I understood what crewmembers meant when they said they were becoming "flak happy."

We had been told that if we saw those black clouds of flak, the danger of a hit was over. They were wrong. Shell fragments peppered our plane and we lurched up and down from the force of the explosions. It was impossible for Malec to make a straight and level bomb run on automatic pilot. Preston took over the controls and tried to hold us steady manually. At the last minute of the bomb run, we leveled off.

Malec pressed the release toggle on his bombsight, and yelled, "Bombs away!"

I turned my drift meter toward the bomb bay and watched the bombs as they fell toward the target. They seemed to go across the harbor like an unrolling carpet. I saw three strings of bombs hit docks adjacent to what appeared to be a large naval ship, and another string landed outside the target areas.

I jumped up and down and yelled excitedly into the interphone, "We hit it!" Unfortunately, I knocked my oxygen mask off. I put it back on as we turned off the target toward the North Sea.

Joe cut us to an indicated air speed of 150 miles per hour so that the rest of the planes in the formation could keep up. I gave him a course for England, and we headed back across the North Sea. After following us for ten minutes, the fighters broke off their attacks. I leaned back in my seat. We had been under attack for no more than one hour, but it had seemed an eternity. *So far, so good,* I thought.

Our first mission over the enemy's homeland had not been as tough as we expected. We lost two planes to fighters and one to flak. I had used up a can of ammunition. We had surprised the Nazis. Perhaps they had thought we would not be so foolish as to bomb their homeland without fighter support.

At the mission debriefing, LeMay told us he would reserve further comment about the success of the mission until he examined the strike photos. Hansell said he was disappointed that although ninety-one planes had taken off, only fifty-three aircraft had bombed the secondary target area.

General Arnold's headquarters and the press wrote up the mission in the States as if it were a great success. Gladwin Hill, of the Associated Press, rode as an observer in our aircraft. He sent back glowing reports of the first American bombing effort against the German homeland. He embarrassed me by reporting to the *Boston Herald* that I was the first Harvard man to lead a raid on Germany. Fortunately for me, nobody in our group read his misleading story.

The next day, Hansell called a meeting of the wing's operational leaders. He told us that Eaker was not unhappy with the results; he thought the mission proved that daylight strategic bombing of military targets could be successful. LeMay disagreed. He said that 40 percent of our force never got to Wilhelmshaven and that he didn't think our bombing accuracy was any better than our efforts against the sub pens in France. We were kidding ourselves if only 1 percent of our bombs hit the target. He was right. We had to return to Wilhelmshaven on two more occasions.

I looked at Hansell. I could see that he and the other group commanders were not pleased with LeMay's critical remarks. They felt that the mission was a success if we returned with a loss of no more than three planes.

We soon learned that LeMay's prediction about our future missions over Germany was correct. We had brought the war directly to the German homeland in daylight. Hitler and Hermann Göring had told the German people that no Allied planes would or could bomb Germany in daylight. Hitler considered the roar of our bombers overhead in daylight an insult to him and the German people. He promised them that the daylight missions would be stopped; he would make us pay a price we could not afford.

In the next few weeks, Hitler transferred hundreds of fighters from the Russian and Mediterranean fronts to defend the German homeland. Eaker had accomplished one of the objectives he had promised Churchill at Casablanca: We had forced the German fighters into a battle for air supremacy.

On the next mission, 4 February, we sent ninety-one bombers to Hamm in Germany. It was the Germans' turn to surprise us. We were confronted with blankets of flak and cannon fire from their fighters, which allowed them to shoot at us from beyond the range of our machine guns. We lost five bombers and several crewmen aboard the planes that returned were wounded. The Germans had a new weapon: a twin-engine fighter, the Me210. The battle for air superiority was to continue until the late spring of 1944.

Arnold was not to be deterred by the German response. He ordered Eaker to schedule more frequent missions over Germany. Two group commanders asked Hansell if he thought our small forces were having any real effect. He replied that our missions were the substitute for an Allied second front until there was an invasion. Bombing was the only way the Allies could bring the war to the German people. Air force leaders had promised the American people dramatic results and victory through airpower. We would keep that promise.

The American people were not told the truth about the mediocre results of our missions, or the extent of our losses. After each mission, Arnold's headquarters put out press releases suggesting that our bomb tonnage on a target area was equivalent to bombs on a precise military target. The average American citizen did not know or understand the difference between area and precision bombing. They were satisfied to know that American planes were dropping bombs on the enemy, and they believed the widely inflated reports that we had destroyed hordes of German fighters.

Washington was engaging in a numbers game similar to the one that was later used in the Vietnam War. Instead of a bogus body count, Army Air Forces headquarters released grossly exaggerated reports of Nazi fighter losses and the tonnage of our bombs that hit German targets. The reports, intended to reassure the American people that we were winning the air war, did not fool the Germans. They had accurate figures on both target damage and aircraft losses—theirs and ours. They knew that as summer approached they could bring the Eighth Air Force close to annihilation if we didn't get fighter support.

In February 1943 we were averaging no more than seventy-five bombers per mission. In addition to the planes we lost, 40 percent of the returning aircraft had serious battle damage. No one had to tell us that unless we received replacements for our lost crews and long-range fighter support we were facing a bloody summer. German fighters outnumbered our bombers by more than ten to one. Without fighter support to and from German targets, we were fighting a losing battle for air supremacy. LeMay told Hansell privately that the Nazis were cutting us down to size. We couldn't continue to lose 5 to 8 percent of our force on each mission without replacements.

Hansell had to know that whenever we bombed "targets of opportunity" or through clouds, we were probably engaging in area bombing. There was almost always a substantial chance that the clouds would prevent or interfere with the accuracy of visual bombing. Moreover, the demand for a greater frequency of missions increased. Although we were always scheduled to hit precise military targets, in reality we were compelled by circumstances to engage in daylight area bombing on most of our missions.

In defending their homeland, German pilots had a substantial advantage over our invading bombers. A disabled Nazi plane could land and the pilot return to battle and fight again the same day. On the other hand, even if our crews parachuted successfully, they became prisoners of war and were lost to us for the duration. We knew that conditions would get worse before they would get better. I led two other missions to Wilhelmshaven. We lost seven aircraft on 26 February and three more on 3 March.

In February our loss rate approached 10 percent. I was always pleased when LeMay was command pilot. When he led a mission, we believed that he would somehow make it a success. His determination and confidence were infectious. On one occasion, we lost an engine after we turned off the target. LeMay knew that we could not maintain formation, so as we started to lose altitude he ordered a squadron commander to take over leadership of the group. I was concerned that we might not make it back without the protection of the group. I saw another group flying ahead of us at our lower altitude and called him on the interphone and suggested that we join their formation. His answer was short and direct: "Hell no! They don't know where they're going."

Although we were a lone aircraft and a tempting target for German fighters, we managed to reach the German coast and continue across the North Sea at an altitude of fifteen thousand feet. We started to relax. I smelled smoke coming from the pilot's compartment. LeMay had taken off his oxygen mask and lit a cigar. He had the flight engineer bring me a cigar in the navigator's compartment. The radio operator reported to LeMay that the waist gunners were dismantling their guns and cleaning them for our next mission. He ordered them to restore the guns for combat and said they would look silly if we were attacked by German fighters and didn't have any guns to fight back. As we limped toward Chelveston on three engines and prepared to make our final approach for landing, we were shocked to hear the sound of machine guns behind us.

"There are two FWs strafing us at six o'clock," the tail gunner yelled.

I wondered if we would be shot in the back. I had never expected we would be shot down above our own air base. LeMay didn't reply. I knew he would get us down on the ground if it were humanly possible. We landed safely. It seemed a miracle that none of us was wounded. Our plane looked like a sieve. We had used up one of our nine lives.

8: Prelude to a Bloody Summer

Contrary to his glowing public relations statements to the American people, General Arnold was privately dissatisfied with our bombing results in the winter and spring of 1943. He criticized General Eaker's senior command personnel and told him that he was overly protective of his combat crews. The Eighth Air Force was not flying enough missions; Eaker had not made adequate use of our available bombers or the short-range P-47 Thunderbolt fighters.

The assistant secretary of war for air, Robert Lovett, defended Eaker. He informed Arnold that we were fighting against the toughest odds in the world. Even when our bombers returned from missions without personnel casualties, many of our planes were often so badly damaged that they could not return to combat for several weeks.

Each month during the spring of 1943, our losses increased. We lost seventy-five crews and less than a third of them were replaced. Our increasing losses had to have become apparent to the Germans. More fighters rose to meet us on each mission. They had to know the size of our attacking force was important to our success. As our forces became smaller, we not only dropped fewer bombs, but we had less firepower to defend ourselves. The Germans were winning the battle for air supremacy.

At our wing operations meetings, Hansell told the group commanders that the solution for our losses was in Washington. LeMay did not join the other group commanders in their criticism of the lack of support from air force headquarters. He was not about to concede that we were defeated. He continued to insist that survival was in our hands.

By the first week of April 1943, we were in a deep crisis. Arnold had assured the president and the joint chiefs that the Eighth Air Force would bomb Germany's inland military targets with large bomber forces, and he also told Eaker that he would replace our losses. Both promises were unfulfilled. In public, Arnold continued to praise our efforts by stating that no bomber attack had been turned back by enemy action. His statement was accurate, but it had been at a terrible price. The chance of a combat crew completing a twenty-five-mission tour was all but impossible. Eaker continued to risk Arnold's wrath by demanding long-range fighter support. His requests were ignored.

On 4 April 1943 we were scheduled to attack the German Renault armament and tank factory in Paris. We were told it accounted for 10 percent of the Nazis' tank production. It was a day I have never forgotten.

My old crew was still flying as "Tail-end Charlie" in my former squadron. The day before the mission, Collins and I had been on leave together in London. At a few minutes before midnight, a messenger from the base knocked on our door at the Park Lane Hotel. He told us the weather had cleared and we were scheduled for a mission. Collins asked if I would speak to LeMay about moving them to a safer position in the formation. After the mission planning meeting, I mentioned Collins's request to LeMay. He stared at me but made no reply. It was apparent he considered my request an inappropriate sentimental gesture.

As I walked to the flight line with O'Neill and Collins, Collins asked, "What about it, Ralph? Did you talk to LeMay?"

I told him of my abrupt conversation with the group commander and sheepishly added that I had done the best I could. Neither of them replied. They turned without a word and walked toward their plane.

I was lead navigator for the mission. Our group mustered eighteen aircraft, and we bombed at twenty-three thousand feet. As we turned off the target over Paris, I looked for my old crew at the back of our squadron. I could see that the German fighters were concentrating on the aircraft there. I was anxious and troubled. I should have taken a stronger stance with LeMay.

As I looked back, my worst fears were confirmed. My old crew was in serious trouble. Smoke was pouring out of their number-three engine. They started to lose speed and altitude, dropping below and behind our formation. Soon they were all alone. I held my breath, knowing what was coming. Three fighters started strafing them. Flames engulfed their number-two engine. I saw men coming out of the plane's hatches and counted ten parachutes. I felt relieved to know they had all made it out. I was in deep shock. This was the reality that LeMay had been telling us to accept. Our group received a presidential unit citation for the mission, but it was no consolation to me. It was a long time before I learned that the entire crew survived as prisoners of war.

The mission was a moderate success, although we received an unexpected message from the French. Some bombs missed the target and hit a racetrack adjacent to the Renault plant. The French underground informed us that although they welcomed our bombing of the German targets in Paris, they would appreciate it if we would leave their racetrack alone.

Joe Preston knew that O'Neill and Collins were my close friends. As we climbed out of our plane, I was sure that Preston was talking about their loss when he said, "Ralph, I don't know whether you and I will be much good, even if we do survive this."

Until the war ended, Joe and I were truly comrades in arms. I later flew with him in B-29s in the Pacific. After the war he became a major general and commander of Vandenberg Air Force Base, California.

The loss of O'Neill's crew not only hit me hard, but it also was the cause of an unpleasant experience for my parents. Although I had been transferred to LeMay's headquarters as group navigator in the fall of 1942, the Eighth Air Force still had me listed as a member of O'Neill's crew. When word of their loss was reported, the Eighth Air Force sent out a form letter advising my family that I was missing in action. It took me about two weeks to rectify the error. I sent my folks a V-mail message that, as with Mark Twain, my demise was a matter of much exaggeration.

By mid-April the weather had improved, so on the sixteenth we were ordered to bomb the U-boat yards and Focke-Wulf aircraft factory in Bremen. We called Bremen "Flak City." Preston, Malec, and I were selected to lead the mission. As we were about to climb aboard our aircraft, I saw Maj. Gen. Fred Anderson and LeMay approaching. I recalled Anderson's announcement in November that we were going to lose three groups to support the North African invasion. LeMay told us that Anderson would ride with us to Bremen as an observer.

Preston told him that if he were ready to go, he should get a parachute chest pack and a Mae West life preserver. While the general was getting his equipment, Joe told me that Anderson was a West Pointer and about to take over Eighth Air Force Bomber Command. He was considered to be both brilliant and tough. Preston said that if Anderson had not been an aviation classmate of LeMay's, we would probably be feeding the sharks in the Pacific. I thought that LeMay must have a lot of confidence in our crew if he suggested that our new commander should ride with us to Bremen. At our morning briefing, the intelligence officer had warned us that the Germans had beefed up Bremen's defenses after our previous mission there.

After Anderson obtained his gear, he returned and sat in the pilots' compartment between Preston and Clint Breeding, the copilot. However, he took no active part in leading or directing the mission. Preston assumed command in his quiet, determined way. One hundred six aircraft took off for Bremen, but I was not conscious of Anderson's presence during the seven-hour mission.

Our flight across the North Sea to the Frisian Islands had become routine. I didn't expect any fighter opposition until our escorts turned back toward England, at which point German fighters appeared like clockwork. It was the heaviest attack we had encountered. I looked up and saw a group of what seemed like twenty-five German fighters approaching us head-on. Before our gunners fired a shot, cannon shots began exploding in our formation. I leaned down to pick up my Weems navigation plotter on the floor. As my head went below the navigation table, shell fragments shattered the window above it. I looked up and saw a hole in the window at my usual head level. It was a good thing I'd dropped my plotter.

Joe Preston yelled into the interphone, asking if I was okay.

"Yes," I replied, "but it's a little breezy down here now."

This was the beginning of the roughest day of my young life. Bremen was living up to its reputation as "Flak City." Its intensity and the fighters were the worst we had seen. For the first time, FW190s and Me109s attacked us in waves. They cut back and forth through our formation. Until that day, I had never attached my parachute to my chest harness because of its bulk. That and my heavy sheepskin jacket and Mae West life preserver restricted my movement in our cramped forward compartment. I had to navigate, assist the bombardier with locating the target, and man the machine guns.

It was clear enough for me to look over the bombardier's shoulder and shoot at the oncoming German fighters at the same time. There was a tremendous explosion. Pieces of shrapnel had burst around my parachute on the floor. I didn't hesitate but grabbed the chute and hastily put it on. I had no way of knowing whether it had been pierced. I hoped it would be safer on me than on the floor. I also grabbed my steel helmet. As we turned onto the bomb run, flak continued to explode around us. Preston fought to keep our course straight and level as the full force of several explosions shook our plane.

Another burst hit in front of me, behind the bombardier.

I asked if he was alright and yelled, "Will you be able to make the bomb run? Do you want me to take over?"

He shook his head. He continued to adjust his bombsight as if nothing had happened.

The mission was a partial success. Although our bombs hit the target, we did not have a force large enough to inflict substantial damage. Although 106 aircraft took off for the mission, many of them did not reach the target area. We lost sixteen aircraft; the 14 percent loss was our heaviest of the war to date. Another forty-six of our planes were heavily damaged. Many crewmembers were killed or seriously wounded. After Joe and I inspected the damage to our wings and fuselage, I told Joe our luck was still with us.

I was about to leave for the debriefing when Hansell and LeMay drove up to our aircraft to greet General Anderson. Anderson asked them to wait until he had his picture taken with our crew. After the crew picture was taken, Preston and I rode back with the brass for a critique of the mission. On the way, Anderson asked Hansell if he had received the report of our loss of sixteen aircraft. Hansell didn't reply.

"Now I know what you have been talking about," Anderson said. "The Germans came at us in waves. They swarmed all over us like a herd of bees. We need fighter support all the way to the target and back. I didn't see any P-47s."

Hansell hesitated. I could see that he didn't want to discuss our losses and the lack of fighters in my presence.

Finally he said, "Hap is under tremendous pressure. The joint chiefs are giving him hell about our air force budget. The army and navy are claiming that Arnold has spent too much money on fighters and the millions spent on our new B-29 bomber. His staff is concerned that if he doesn't take things easier, he is going to have another heart attack."

I could see that my presence was making the conversation difficult for Hansell. I left the meeting to talk to my navigators and check on the extent of injuries to my bombardier. While talking with them I learned that while we were on the bombing run one of our gunners in another squadron had his arm blown off at the shoulder. He was bleeding so badly that the crew knew that he had no chance of surviving the three-and-a-half-hour flight back to Chelveston. They wrapped him in a parachute to keep him warm, pulled the ripcord on the second chute, and pushed him out the rear door in hopes that the Germans on the ground could save him.

On a later mission, my friend Jess Duval, a bombardier, was wounded. I visited him in the base hospital. He was his usual cheerful self, but he told me that he'd had enough excitement.

"Ralph," he said, "when I get home to Oklahoma, I'm going to buy a Model A Ford, lock it in low gear, and not drive faster than fifteen miles per hour."

Jess didn't keep his word about changing his lifestyle. While I was at Salina, Kansas, in the spring of 1944, I flew to Ardmore, Oklahoma, and visited him at the base hospital there. Both of his legs were in casts.

"What happened to you?" I asked.

He smiled. "Well Ralph, I didn't get a Model A. I got a Buick and cracked it up going eighty! What are you doing in Salina?"

I told him I was training to be a radar navigator bombardier in the B-29 program. As we said good-bye, he struggled to his feet and hugged me, "Ralph, don't push your luck in the B-29s. I think you've already used up your share."

On one occasion when we were returning from Germany, I looked ahead to the Zuider Zee in Holland. It was always a welcome sight. I scanned the sky for friendly fighters. We had been told at the mission briefing that the P-47s now had auxiliary fuel tanks and that they might join us at the Dutch border. We had an inflexible rule that when we were over enemy territory and a fighter turned its nose toward our formation we would not hesitate to shoot at it.

Because our P-47s and the German FW190s both had radial engines it was impossible to identify whether they were friend or foe when they approached us head-on. I looked up and saw an aircraft with a radial engine turn toward our formation. The bombardier immediately started shooting at him. As the fighter passed in front of us, he yelled, "I got him Ralph!"

He had indeed: he'd shot off the fighter's tail. As it plunged toward the ground I saw the American star on the fuselage. It was a P-47. I didn't see a parachute.

"You got him alright, you son of a bitch!" I shouted. "That was a P-47!"

After we returned to base, we learned that the "kill" he'd made was a full colonel, the commanding officer of the first P-47 group to fly in support of our bombers. LeMay told the bombardier he would be flying as a tail gunner from then on—that way our fighters would be safer. He was the only captain I know of who finished his tour as a gunner.

The fighter pilots were not ready to forgive us for the loss of their commanding officer. A few days later I was on leave in London. I was standing at the bar at the Park Lane Hotel when a P-47 fighter pilot asked me if I was in the 305th Bomb Group. "If you are," he added, "you'd better get the hell out of this bar. If my buddies here learn that you were one of the truck drivers that shot down our CO, you'll be lucky to escape with your life!" I took his advice.

The Zuider Zee was the scene of another harrowing experience for our crew. I was lead navigator, flying with another squadron from our group at twenty-five thousand feet. As we approached the Zuider Zee, an explosion shook our aircraft. Both the pilot and copilot were hurled from their seats and the plane went into a steep spin, out of control. The copilot yelled for me to come up to the cockpit because the pilot was wounded. I crawled to the pilot's compartment; equipment was tossed all over. The copilot and I struggled to pull the plane out of the dive, concerned that the g forces would break off the wings. We pulled slowly back on the controls and were able to straighten out at a thousand feet, just above German boat traffic headed for the Frisian Islands.

The ships below started shooting at us as we leveled off and we returned the fire with all of our .50-caliber machine guns. We were probably the only bomber that strafed German shipping at low level. I was still upset about our wounded pilot and our close call in a dive to eternity. I cheered when I saw the crews on the German ships jumping overboard.

Doug Venable was my closest friend in the 305th. We started out together as aviation cadets in navigation school at Mather Field, California, and arrived together for our first assignment as navigators at Muroc. Doug was a most unusual aviation cadet and navigator. A native of Texas, he was a well-read poet and student of foreign languages—a mixture of poet and philosopher. He was more than six feet tall, blond, and blue eyed.

While other cadets were struggling with trigonometry tables and the mathematics required for celestial navigation, Doug sat at his desk writing poetry. He had a great sense of humor, a quick smile and jovial remark for almost every situation, and was popular with both officers and enlisted men. When we went to London on leave he did not hesitate to engage reserved English passengers in cultural discussions of the merits of the poetry of Byron and Shelley. His happy-go-lucky exterior concealed an extremely sensitive nature.

In early May 1943, I noticed that Doug had become withdrawn. He spent his free time alone in the barracks. For several weeks he had been doing a great deal of serious thinking about the civilian casualties caused by our bombing. On several occasions he asked me what I believed the German pilots thought of us. I told him I didn't think about it and he shouldn't think about it either. He also asked me how I felt about killing innocent German civilians. I told him that I tried not to think about it, as that was the only way we could survive. I didn't like it, but killing was part of our job. It went with the territory. I suggested that he was overtired and should take some time off at our rest and recreation facility. He denied that he was overtired, or that he had any problems.

I talked to his pilot, Bill Whitson. Bill told me Doug had been talking to him about the effect of our bombing missions on the Germans civilians, and even the Luftwaffe pilots. He was asking questions about the ethics and morality of our bombing. We both wondered whether this would affect his ability to function in combat. Combat flying was not the time for philosophic musing about the enemy. We were faced with a situation of kill or be killed. Reaction in combat had to be automatic, almost a matter of instant reflex.

Bill and I decided to take up the matter with LeMay. He acknowledged that some of our crewmembers were mentally and physically exhausted from the stress of long and tiring combat missions. He agreed that Doug should go to the "flak farm" for some rest and relaxation.

Doug stayed there for only five days. When he returned he told me that he had rested enough and that he belonged back with his crew. I asked him about his experience at the R&R center; he ignored my question.

"Ralph," he said, "I've been doing some writing. Would you like to read my latest poem?"

I nodded and he handed it to me (the complete poem is in Appendix B). It was titled "A German Focke-Wulf Pilot Speaks to an American Prisoner of War," and its theme spoke for itself. While we were fighting for survival on our missions, Doug was thinking about the Nazis and their reaction to our guns and bombs.

Four days later, 13 May, we were scheduled to return to the huge German naval yard at Wilhelmshaven. Doug came to me again and said he wanted to rejoin his crew for the mission. I suggested that he should wait at least a few more days, as LeMay had ordered.

Then he said, "Ralph, aren't you my best friend? Will you speak to LeMay for me so I can fly on the next mission?"

I agreed and recommended to LeMay and Bill Whitson that Doug should be returned to combat status.

The experience of Venable's crew on this mission gained national publicity. Their plane was named *Old Bill*. A well-known artist had painted a cartoon of an overweight Cockney soldier known as "Old Bill"—a lovable character with a huge, old-fashioned mustache—on the nose of the Whitson plane. They were flying behind us with the 422d Squadron as we approached the German coast and fighters attacked *Old Bill* head-on near the German island of Heligoland. A cannon shell shattered the aircraft's Plexiglas nose and the blast hit Doug in the chest, killing him instantly. Whitson and several other members of the crew were seriously wounded. I looked back and saw *Old Bill* drop out of formation.

We continued on and made a successful attack on Kiel. After we landed, I rushed up to the control tower to await the return of Whitson and the rest of our group. As *Old Bill* approached the runway someone on board fired a red flare, meaning that they were in trouble and had wounded on board. The German fighters had shot out their brakes and disabled their flaps, making it impossible for the seriously wounded pilot to control the landing speed. I watched as they shot down the runway with practically no let-up of speed. Bill managed to bring the plane to a halt with a ground loop at the end of the runway. We held our breath as crash trucks, field ambulances, and fire engines raced toward the smoking aircraft.

I rushed down the control tower steps and drove LeMay to the scene. I ran to the shattered nose and saw Doug's mangled body lying on the floor of the shattered navigator's compartment. I was overwhelmed by the thought that Doug might not have lost his life if I had not made a sentimental gesture for a friend. He should not have been on that mission. By giving in to his plea, I had cost him his life.

LeMay came up behind me and put his hand on my shoulder as he looked at the plane. They were removing Doug's body and the wounded.

"Come on, Nutter," he said. "There's nothing we can do here; we'd better critique this mission."

I turned away and followed him. It was too late to help Doug.

The medics took Whitson and the other wounded crewmen to the hospital.

A few days after we lost Venable we had two more situations involving crewmembers who suffered what is now called combat fatigue or post-traumatic stress disorder. In World War I, combat veterans who suffered mental and emotional difficulties from their war experiences were said to be "shell shocked."

I had a good friend, a copilot, who came from a long line of distinguished army officers. His father was an infantry general in Alaska. His troubles started after our third mission over Germany. His pilot reported that as soon as they crossed the Dutch coast, my friend would tell him he was going blind. He couldn't read the instruments or even see out of the aircraft. As soon as they crossed the North Sea on the way home to England, he would regain his sight. LeMay grounded him. Some of our personnel accused him of being "yellow." I was one of the few officers who would speak to him. I played Ping-Pong with him at the officers' club while he was waiting for a transfer back to the States.

A bombardier had similar stress problems in combat. As soon as we started on the bomb run he would tell me he couldn't see objects in his bombsight or operate the controls properly. On one occasion I slapped his face and forced him to complete the bomb run. A few days later, after he made anti-Semitic remarks and attacked a Jewish bombardier, I reported the situation to LeMay, who had him transferred out of our group.

In the winter of 1943 I was officer of the day at group headquarters. Two army psychiatrists appeared at my desk and requested an appointment with LeMay. When I told him they were there he said, "I'm not interested. I don't have time to talk to a couple of headshrinkers."

I explained that they had given a battery of psychological tests to some of our officers in aviation cadet school and that they were conducting a survey to determine if the tests might predict how they would respond to the stress of combat.

He told me to bring them in, adding, "I know the difference between no-gooders and our people who are really stressed out and need time at the flak hospital."

After listening impatiently to them for a few minutes, LeMay said: "I don't think you men can help us. This group gets the most bombs on the target with the least losses. We try to avoid talking about combat fatigue or morale here. We teach our crews how to face reality. We're not fools. Anyone who doesn't fear flying over Germany is either a fool or a liar. Fear goes with the territory.

"I don't claim to know much about psychology. I understand you psychiatrists believe that people can respond to stress by talking about it on a couch. If a man can't do his job for any reason, we ground him and either send him home or to the infantry. If a man cannot live with fear and still do his job and protect his crewmates, I don't want him and, more importantly, his crewmates don't want him.

"It's my job to give my men the confidence that I will do everything possible to make them ready for anything these Nazis throw at us. These aircrews are the most unselfish group of men you can find anywhere. They are members of a team. I want them to think of only one thing over Germany: how to get the bombs on target and kill as many Nazis as possible. If you want to learn about combat conditions, I'll arrange for you to fly on a mission." The psychiatrists turned and left without any further comment.

Winston Churchill called the joint effort of the United States and Great Britain the "Grand Alliance." Throughout the war it worked remarkably well. Generals Montgomery, Eisenhower, Bradley, and Patton had different personalities and leadership styles. In spite of their differences, they were able to coordinate their land tactics and campaigns. This was not true of the air campaigns of the RAF and the Eighth Air Force.

Generals Spaatz, Eaker, and Hansell arrived in England in 1942 determined to engage in independent daylight bombing restricted to precise military targets. They disapproved of Air Marshal Arthur Harris's area bombing policy. Hansell considered it both uncivilized and inefficient. He resented Harris's criticism of his plan to wipe out key German bottleneck industries, which Harris called an impractical panacea.

As chairman of the Eighth Air Force planning committee, Hansell worked well with his RAF counterparts in selecting key military targets. Most of the RAF planning officers were graduates of Oxford and Cambridge and members of the British upper class. As a gracious southerner, Hansell was at ease with the British. He enjoyed English social life.

Unlike Hansell, LeMay's prewar acquaintance with the English was limited to his delivery of B-24 bombers, which he ferried across the North Atlantic. He became acquainted with RAF pilots and navigators, and he was impressed with their bravery and technical competence. He marveled at their ability to bomb Germany at night with primitive bombers under the most hazardous conditions. He was ready and anxious to learn from the RAF's experience.

When I became LeMay's group navigator in November 1942, he arranged for me to fly two night missions to learn how, and in what manner, they used radar as an aid in navigation and bombing. He persuaded the British to assign one of their most experienced radar navigators as my instructor and adviser, and the officer they chose, Flight Lieutenant Conlon, became a close friend. He taught me the rudiments of British navigational aids such as Gee and Loran. Later, when the RAF developed a self-contained radar system called H2S, Conlon taught me how to use it.

The most important lesson we learned from the RAF was the use of pathfinders to lead bombing missions. It didn't take them long to learn that only a few of their crews were hitting targets within miles of the designated aiming point. In an effort to improve accuracy they selected their best navigators and bombardiers to become leaders or pathfinders on the missions. LeMay adopted this concept of using lead crews for our daylight bombing missions.

The English generally had no criticism of high-ranking American officers. They were entertained and most graciously received in English homes. Lower-ranking American officers and the enlisted men were another matter. Our military personnel became acquainted with the English rank and file in London and the villages surrounding our air bases.

When we weren't scheduled to fly on a mission we would ride bicycles in the blackout to pubs in the villages of Rushden and Higham Ferrers near our base. We enjoyed drinking English ale, playing darts, and socializing with the local residents. On one occasion, I

rode to Rushden with Clark Gable. He had volunteered to make a
gunnery film as a member of the air force motion picture unit in Culver City, California. He was as friendly and likable in person as he
was in the movies. Unlike some such heroes, his courage was not
make-believe. He told LeMay that he couldn't make an appropriate
training film for gunners unless he flew as one on a combat mission.

LeMay told him that we didn't have the time to train him as a top-
or ball-turret operator. If he wanted to go on a mission, he would
have to fly as a waist gunner. Waist gunners stood at open windows
in the middle of the aircraft manning pedestal-mounted .50-caliber
machine guns. At altitudes higher than twenty-five thousand feet the
temperature was usually forty degrees below zero.

"That's what I'm here for," Gable replied. "I want to learn the
problems of gunners in combat conditions."

When we arrived at a pub, it was not a relaxing occasion for Gable.
Girls crowded around him at the bar. His friendly and infectious
smile was a magnet for everyone. After about an hour, he told me it
was time to return to the base. He said he needed to find a quieter
place if he was going to get some rest.

English pubs were an ideal spot to meet and barter with the local
farmers. Our breakfasts at the base usually included a travesty called
powdered eggs. Occasionally they served us the standard GI meat:
Spam. Many of us ignored this offering. Sometimes we were issued
genuine American candy bars and gum, which we took to pubs and
swapped for fresh eggs. Some of our personnel traded their candy
bars for other favors that they were treated to in the surrounding
haystacks.

My first experience with the differences between the English and
American cultures was at an RAF bomber base in southern England.
We were returning from a mission against a Nazi submarine base in
France in late 1942 and all England was socked in by heavy fog. The
RAF warned us that we should not attempt to land at our base at
Grafton Underwood. Many of our aircraft had been damaged by flak,
and I was delighted when LeMay told me to give him a course to an
RAF bomber base on the coast.

After landing we were assigned rooms in the RAF barracks and
then invited to afternoon tea and cake at the officers' club. Our officers sat on one side of the room across from the RAF officers. There

was an awkward silence as we sat staring at each other. An attendant brought in tea and traditional English biscuits and cake. He placed them on a table in the center of the room.

It had been ten hours since our early morning breakfast of powdered eggs. Without any invitation from our hosts, we left our seats and crowded around the table. The tea and cakes quickly disappeared. While this was going on, our hosts remained seated and watched with amusement at our lack of courtesy and consideration. I looked at LeMay. I could see that he was embarrassed by our behavior. He ordered us to leave and return to the barracks, where he gave us a lesson in social sensitivity.

He told us that he could understand that we were hungry after the mission, but English tea and cakes was not the place to satisfy our appetites. He was embarrassed by our rude conduct. The English were our closest allies and had been fighting the Nazis almost alone since 1939. Afternoon tea was more than refreshments to them. Their traditions had kept them going for three years. It didn't mean they weren't tough. We should make allowances for their customs and traditions. He then told us that it had been reported to him that some of us had been getting into fights with Englishmen. He was not asking us to turn the other cheek, but he made it clear we were to avoid trouble with the English if at all possible. Then he said, "If you do have a fight, then win it. I'm going back to the RAF commander and apologize for all of you. You had better not put me in this position again."

The RAF had another custom that was an even greater surprise to me. I was fortunate to be assigned to a private room. At about seven o'clock in the morning I was awakened by a knock at the door. A member of the Woman's Army Air Force (WAAF) opened the door and entered carrying a towel and a pan of hot water. It was a pleasant way to wake up. She was young and pretty.

She told me she had heard that we'd had a tough encounter with the Nazis and asked if would I like her to give me a hot bath.

I was in my underwear. I was still a young, bashful, naive New Englander. Not knowing what she had in mind, I blushed and said, "No thank you."

When I told Collins of this encounter he could not believe I had not returned her kind offer of English hospitality. He told me that

I had already violated LeMay's instruction about reciprocal courtesy with the English.

A few weeks later, I was invited to have tea and cakes with O'Neill and Collins at the home of the famous Church family of Northampton, a few miles from our base. I learned to appreciate the importance of English tea and the tradition that goes with it. Just as we were sitting down for afternoon tea, we heard the roar of a strafing fighter plane. We assumed it had been strafing our air base. Our hostess smiled and continued to pour the tea. "I'm sure that you boys are not going to let the Germans interrupt our tea," she said.

When King George VI and Queen Elizabeth visited our base, LeMay ordered us to redecorate the officers' club and remove some of the more salacious paintings and aircraft names on the noses of our aircraft.

On my first visit to London in the early fall of 1942, Warren "Sonny" Collins and I arrived by train at the railroad station north of the city. A German air raid was in progress. We heard bombs falling and the roar of the sirens, but no one seemed to be upset or rushing to air raid shelters. We passed a tearoom and saw waiters in formal dress still serving tea. We asked an attendant where we could find a good hotel. He looked us over and said, "I'm sure they will have rooms for you at the Savoy." I didn't know it then, but the Savoy was one of the most luxurious hotels in London, the favorite watering hole of royalty and Arab princes.

After taking a taxi to the hotel, Collins and I walked into the magnificent lobby. It was almost empty except for several uniformed attendants. We asked for a room and the clerk inquired if we would like the royal suite. I asked him about the room rate, not knowing that people who stayed at the Savoy didn't need to ask how much it would cost. He said we could have a suite for twenty-five pounds.

"This is our first trip to London," I told Collins. "Let's take it."

I had never before spent a night in such a fancy hotel. The bellboy carried our bags to a suite of three rooms. I was looking out the window at the Thames River when Collins yelled, "Come here, Ralph. What's this contraption next to the toilet?"

I had read about bidets in romantic novels, but had never seen one. I told him it wasn't exactly a commode; it was for bathing a crotch.

Sonny replied that he would write his brother about the bidet: They had no gadgets like that in Vermont.

Later we were served a dinner that must once have been a succession of elaborate courses. Three waiters in formal attire served a sparse meal on the best chinaware, changing the plates for each course. It made no difference that there was no food available on the plates for the course. After the waiter had completed this ritual for two courses, I asked him if they had dessert. After assuring me that the Savoy *always* had dessert he brought us a few tablespoons of cream of wheat placed in the center of a white plate. We were astonished. I asked the waiter if we could have some milk and sugar and he replied that the hotel had exhausted its ration of those items.

When the weather was unfavorable and we were not scheduled to fly a mission, we occasionally had Saturday night parties at the officers' club. I saw LeMay there only once; he did not attend social events. He was usually working in his office.

During one party, things were more relaxed than usual. Beer and liquor were flowing freely. Most of the officers had removed their coats and ties. About eleven o'clock, LeMay and Hansell unexpectedly appeared at the club entrance. They were both in full uniform. They stared at us and the room became quiet.

An English guest did not seem to be aware that she was in the presence of the commanding officer and a brigadier general. She walked up to LeMay and said, "Come and join us. Let me help you take off your coats and ties."

Hansell smiled awkwardly and backed away. LeMay didn't move. As she started to reach for his hat and tie, he gave her his classic stern and piercing stare. She pulled back and retreated quickly to the other side of the room. LeMay and Hansell turned and left with no comment.

Every two weeks if no mission was scheduled, LeMay gave us a forty-eight-hour pass to London. Most of our group's officers stayed at the Park Lane Hotel opposite Green Park and Buckingham Palace. After my old crew was shot down and Doug Venable was killed, I enjoyed going to London with our group bombardier, Hank Wodyalla, a free-spirited Pole from Chicago.

Once, while taking the train from Wellingborough, the station nearest to our base, Hank said: "Ralph, wait until you get a load of my new girlfriend. She's the most beautiful redhead you ever saw. She's a thousand times better than those Picadilly commandos in London. She's going to meet us at the station. Boy, does she have class. She's the daughter of an English Lord. She tells me that her husband also has a title. He's a major in the Eighth Army with Montgomery in North Africa. She told me that she hasn't seen him in two years. She seems so lonely. I'm trying to comfort her."

He laughed, then continued: "We do have a problem though. She says that somehow her husband seems to think that she's having an affair with an American. It couldn't be me, though. She thinks he's having her followed when she leaves the manor."

"I hope her husband doesn't have any buddies from the Eighth Army following you," I replied. "Those desert rats are tough. They're teaching Rommel and his German troops lessons in desert warfare. If we hear any hobnailed boots behind us in this blackout, we'd better run like hell."

She greeted us warmly as we got off the train. Hank was correct about his redheaded girlfriend: Her beautiful hair was a striking background for her flawless English complexion.

I was right, too—about the hobnailed boots. We left the station in the blackout and I heard the sound of heavy boots coming up behind us. Hank grabbed his girlfriend by the arm and we ran all the way to the Park Lane. When we got there she persuaded the bartender to serve us some rare scotch. Suddenly we heard the roar of German bombers overhead. A bomb hit the hotel and Hank and his girlfriend implored me to run outside. I told them I was not about to permit the Germans to deprive me of the first scotch I'd had in six months.

A few days after my night mission to Munich, our group was scheduled to lead a mission to Gdynia, a Polish city on the Baltic coast occupied by the Germans. Hank told me that he was scheduled to be the lead bombardier on the mission. His parents were Polish and he had a personal score to settle with Hitler and the Nazis.

The day before the mission I couldn't find Hank. I finally located him in the armaments room. He said he had a surprise for the SS and German intelligence. Hank was leaning over a blue practice bomb. Practice bombs were filled with sand and weighed a hundred pounds. I told him that it smelled like a latrine in there, not a chemical and armaments room. He turned and offered to let me see what he was putting in the bomb casing. It was *not* explosives. The bomb was a personal statement to Hitler and his SS men. On the outside of the bomb he had written with chalk: "To Adolf. All the worst! This is what the Polish people think of you. I hope you and your henchmen enjoy this greeting. Love and kisses, Hank W."

"Wait until those Nazi bastards send their SS men to examine this baby," he said. "They'll think it's an unexploded secret weapon, but when they open it up they'll find only shit and garbage."

We sent 109 bombers to Gdynia. The crews were in the air for more than ten hours. The round trip of fifteen hundred miles equaled the length of our trip to Munich on 4 October. We lost six aircraft. True to his promise, as soon as he dropped his high-explosive bombs on the target, Hank rushed back to the open bomb-bay doors and threw out his special greeting to Hitler.

After I became the division navigator I arranged to meet Hank for leave in London. We were walking in Piccadilly Circus in January 1944 on the way to our hotel when we met George Patton Jr. By that time Patton was the most famous—and in the minds of some, most notorious—ground general in the U.S. Army. After the American defeat at the Kasserine Pass in North Africa, he had reorganized the demoralized troops there and led them to victory. Then he violated Eisenhower's instructions and beat General Montgomery into the port of Palermo in Sicily. It was a great victory that was spoiled by the press.

I knew that LeMay admired him. He had the same direct approach to combat as Patton, but none of his public relations skills. The day before I left for London, LeMay suggested to me that Eisenhower had overreacted to the press' criticism of Patton.

I was astonished to see Patton approaching us in Piccadilly Circus. He had on his usual dress uniform. Hank and I were wearing the traditional air force A-2 leather jacket and officer's hat with the wide rim removed, giving it a crushed appearance. Patton glared at us and ordered us to stop and stand at attention.

"You men are out of uniform!" he roared.

I hesitated, then decided to try a little legal doctrine. I wondered if it would work with Patton.

"Sir," I replied, "we're in the air force. You don't have any jurisdiction over us." Without waiting for his response, I turned to Hank and said, "Come on captain. We have an important appointment to keep."

We walked away as fast as possible. I braced myself for his reaction but heard nothing. We kept walking.

I never related the details of the incident to LeMay but I did mention that we had talked to Patton in London. I said that if he ever had the opportunity, I would appreciate an autographed picture. A few weeks later I got one in the mail.

Americans and the English have a different attitude about Christmas. I will never forget Christmas day, 1943. I was the division navigator for the 1st Bomb Division at Brampton. Brigadier General Robert Williams had succeeded Hansell as commanding general. Williams, who had led the division on the first Schweinfurt mission, lost an eye in a German air raid. He always wore a patch over it, but it didn't seem to affect his ability as a pilot. The people at Brampton told me that Williams could land a bomber better with one eye than most pilots could with two.

I was scheduled to go to London on Christmas day to make a radio broadcast for the people back home. Williams suggested that I fly down with him as his copilot. We took off on a typically cloudy and foggy day. As we approached the city, Williams called the airport tower for landing instructions. His repeated calls for clearance to land were ignored. Finally, Williams said, "To hell with them, Nutter. I'm going to land. There doesn't seem to be much activity at the field."

We had no problem landing and went to report to the airport tower. There was only one RAF officer present, and it was apparent that he had already begun celebrating the holiday.

"I might have known that some Goddamn yanks would be flying on Christmas day," he said, slurring his words. "Don't you people know that even the Nazis celebrate Christmas? We have an armistice on Christmas. We don't bomb them and they don't bomb us."

We wished him a happy holiday and took a taxi to the radio studio where I made my radio greeting to the folks at home. I made the mistake of telling the radio audience that the war was going well in England and that I was ready to take on Japan in B-29s. Williams was upset. He said I had committed a serious breach of security by mentioning the B-29s. I told him that I had read about the B-29s in the *Stars and Stripes* and that I was sure the public press reports were available to the Japanese.

Later I attended a Christmas party for RAF and Eighth Air Force officers. My wife refused to believe me when I told her that I danced with Fred Astaire's sister Adele at that party. She said it was impossible; I was the world's worst dancer.

We returned to Brampton the next day. After we landed I decided to visit my RAF friend, Flight Lieutenant Conlon. He asked me if I would like to pilot a Tiger Moth that the RAF used for recreational flying. It was a two-seat biplane made with canvas, lightweight wood, and baling wire. LeMay had permitted me to fly copilot for him on several occasions in a B-17, but I had never been the pilot in a biplane.

Conlon permitted me to make three landings and then said, "Ralph, I think you're ready to solo. Take her up and fly to Oxford and return here."

I jumped at the opportunity. The fighter pilots of World War I were romantic knights who had fought with chivalry. They didn't bomb cities. They wouldn't dream of strafing parachuting enemies, as I had seen happen to my comrades over Germany.

I took off in the Tiger Moth and set a course toward Oxford, less than a hundred miles away, at a speed of about sixty-five knots. The wind from Oxford was toward Cambridge in the northeast and about the same velocity as my airspeed. I flew for an hour and looked down. I was only over the university at Cambridge. I decided it was time to land. The last thing I wanted to do was run out of fuel.

The residents of the rural area surrounding our base gradually became accustomed to some of the boisterous conduct of our personnel at their local pubs. We were a good source of revenue, but I was sure they were not pleased by the noise coming from Saturday night parties at the officers' club. Occasionally they had good reason to object to noise and even gunfire coming from our barracks.

High-stakes poker was our favorite recreation during the long winter nights. We played with five-pound notes.

Lieutenants slept in the open barracks area in Quonset huts. Personnel who were scheduled to fly usually didn't join in the nightly poker games. They tried to get some sleep. Those who were not flying played poker huddled around a coal stove with light from a naked light bulb hanging over them.

When a mission was scheduled, "lights out" was supposed to be at 10 P.M. The poker players often did not honor this rule and requests that they turn out the light and go to bed were usually ignored. As a captain, I had a room adjacent to the open barracks area. Whenever I heard the words "Ready, Aim, Fire!" I knew the next sound would be a .45-caliber pistol shooting out the light over the poker table.

LeMay became concerned about the number of planes that were failing to complete missions. He issued orders that no plane should turn back, except in an emergency, without a direct order from him or the mission leader.

Later, after that directive came out, we were headed for Hannover on a mission to central Germany. The weather was atrocious, and when we reached the Zuider Zee in Holland, LeMay ordered the group to turn back. After completing the maneuver we looked back and saw Harry Benson's plane still headed for Hannover. Just before nightfall, he landed at our base on three engines. His aircraft was riddled with shrapnel holes. He told us he had continued to Hannover alone because he had not heard LeMay's order to abandon the mission. I knew he was upset, so I walked back with him to the officers' club.

After we'd had several drinks, Benson persuaded three of us to play poker with him. He said it would help him relax and forget the day and LeMay's criticism. We returned to the barracks and had just begun to play when Benson suddenly pulled out a revolver and said, "Let's play Russian Roulette."

"You have to be kidding," I said. "Put that gun away!"

"I'm serious, Ralph," he replied. He spun the chamber, held the gun to his head, and pulled the trigger. The hammer clicked. He handed it to me and I pointed it at the ceiling and pulled the trigger. I put a hole in the roof. Another player, a pilot, grabbed the gun from me and pointed it at our squadron mascot, a dog, sleeping on the floor. On one occasion a crew put an oxygen mask on the dog and took him on a mission. We all yelled in unison, "Don't point that gun at the dog! Put it down!" He ignored us, pulled the trigger, and killed the dog. I ran outside. It was my last poker game of the war.

Although I was in England throughout 1943 and parts of 1942 and 1944, I had practically no time to visit the many cultural and historical centers of the British Isles. I visited Oxford University on one occasion. There, I was introduced to a well-known history scholar and professor. He took me around the ancient colleges. After the tour, we had tea and cakes in his chambers. I attempted to discuss academic matters and the history of Oxford with him, but he brushed off my questions. He was much more interested in hearing about our bombing missions over Germany. In truth, I was not much interested in culture at that time either. I spent my future leaves in London in rest and recreation.

My only visit to Scotland was when we landed at Prestwick, in October 1942. I did visit Wales, though in most unusual and unexpected circumstances. We were returning from a mission over Germany in atrocious weather. After we arrived over our base, we were warned by the control tower that all England was covered with clouds and almost all air bases were engulfed in heavy fog. The controller informed us that earlier that morning RAF night bombers had been unable to land. Several aircraft ran out of fuel and the crews were forced to bail out over England. He advised us to head for southwest England in the area of the Bristol Channel.

LeMay warned me that we were running out of fuel. He said if we didn't get down soon our crews would have to bail out, too. I gave him a course for the Bristol Channel and was shocked to see that the entire area was socked in. I finally spotted a hole in the clouds and what I believed to be an RAF air base. I called LeMay on the interphone for instructions. He informed that we had no choice; we were almost out of fuel.

"Get in the bombardier's seat and lead us in," he commanded. The remainder of the wing followed us. Each of our planes landed safely. I was still not sure where we were. I jumped down from the navigator's hatch and a man dressed in mechanics overalls approached me. He was wearing a civilian flight suit. He spoke to me in Welsh, the guttural words sounded like German. I was exhausted. My God, I thought. Have I delivered our entire wing to the Germans?

LeMay came up behind me and said, "Nutter, you got us down all right—but in the wrong country. This is Wales."

I was relieved, to put it mildly. I knew our plane had suffered severe battle damage. We had lost part of our left wing tip and the top of the rear stabilizer. LeMay knew I was upset.

"I wasn't criticizing your navigation," he said. "This was the best we could do."

9: The Politics of High Command

A s the summer of 1943 approached, our situation was getting worse rather than better. We still had no fighter support, and the Germans kept attempting new techniques to break up our formations. Fighters flew above our planes and dropped parachute bombs timed to explode in the middle of our groups. Twin-engine fighters launched rockets from beyond the range of our guns. The Nazis even repaired a crashed B-17 and flew it alongside ours. We lost two aircraft before we realized it was an enemy plane and shot it down.

Eaker was under pressure from General Arnold to step up the pace of our missions deep into Germany. We didn't know that Arnold had been criticizing Eaker's bomber, fighter, and maintenance commanders. Except for LeMay's 305th Group, bombing results were less than satisfactory. Eaker believed that Hansell was an excellent long-range planner but ineffective as a combat commander. He was nervous, high-strung, overly sensitive to criticism, and seemed to have difficulty exercising the leadership required of a combat commander. Eaker thought it was doubtful that Hansell could physically withstand the trials and responsibilities of the approaching bloody summer.

In mid-June, Eaker and Hansell had a two-hour meeting to discuss command of the 1st Bomb Wing. In his kind and diplomatic way, Eaker suggested that Hansell would be more comfortable if he resumed his former position as director of the Eighth Air Force planning staff. Eaker didn't want to tell Hansell that he didn't think he was tough enough to lead his group commanders. He told Hansell that the summer of 1943 was going to be a period of maximum effort for the Eighth Air Force. It was finally going to get four new groups to replace the crews and aircraft diverted to North Africa. The Eighth soon would be able to send 160 aircraft to a German target. LeMay was going to take over the 3d Bomb Wing from Fred Anderson, who was taking over the VIII Bomber Command. Bob Williams, a tough, demanding disciplinarian, would replace Hansell as 1st Bomb Wing commander.

Hansell was upset. He knew that combat command was necessary for any regular officer aspiring to a top leadership role in the post-war air force. He told Eaker that he had suffered through the learning period of the first missions over Germany. Now, with a larger force and replacements available, the 1st Bomb Wing could make meaningful strategic attacks on the German war machine. He wanted to be a part of that campaign. It was unfair to remove him and let Williams and LeMay benefit from his learning experience.

Eaker appealed to Hansell's interest and past experience in planning. The RAF was planning a massive attack on Hamburg in July. He said he would appoint Hansell as chairman of a committee that would select vital German targets for destruction by both the RAF and Eighth Air Force. He reminded Hansell that the joint chiefs had approved missions to wipe out Germany's vital ball-bearing production at Schweinfurt and its oil facilities at Ploesti in Romania. Arnold's operational analysts and Assistant Secretary of War Lovett, had determined that ball bearings and oil were the chief bottlenecks in German war production. Destruction of the facilities at Schweinfurt and Ploesti might shorten the war and even make an invasion unnecessary.

Hansell was interested. He asked Eaker if the RAF would participate in missions to Schweinfurt and Ploesti. Eaker said that he had been unable to convince Air Marshal Harris that the RAF Bomber Command should join the Eighth in around-the clock bombing of those key targets. Harris considered a mission to Schweinfurt to be a dangerous risk for his crews. Furthermore, he didn't believe Schweinfurt was a true bottleneck target. Germany obtained ball bearings from many sources, including Sweden and Switzerland. The targets at Schweinfurt were too small and the distances were too great. The large losses that surely would be suffered did not justify a mission at this time. Eaker told Hansell that they had no choice; Arnold and his staff were determined to bomb Schweinfurt—with or without the RAF.

Arnold needed a successful mission to demonstrate to the joint chiefs that strategic bombing could shorten or win the war. Hansell asked Eaker if the Eighth Air Force could put up enough planes to destroy the targets at Schweinfurt. An attack on Schweinfurt seemed contrary to Arnold's earlier agreement that the Eighth would avoid a deep penetration of Germany until we had more heavy bombers and fighters capable of escorting them to the target. Eaker replied that Arnold had determined that Ploesti and Schweinfurt were exceptions. The targets were worth the risk, even without fighter support.

Then Eaker played his trump card. He told Hansell he was the best planner in the air force. He would be working with the top echelons of Arnold's staff and the RAF. Target selection would be his responsibility. Moreover, he would get the credit if he could persuade the RAF to join us. He would attend high-level conferences with the British and the joint chiefs and work directly with Generals Marshall and Arnold. If he did an effective job on this planning committee, Arnold might give him command of the B-29s in the Pacific.

Hansell decided that he had no choice. He would have to make the best of the situation. He was relieved that LeMay would not replace him as commander of the 1st Wing. LeMay was his junior in both age and rank. He respected him as a tough and resourceful group combat commander, but he was still a colonel. Without fighter support, the Eighth Air Force would face a bloody summer. It remained to be seen if LeMay could handle group commanders in the tough way that he handled his subordinates in the 305th.

LeMay had a lot of rough spots. He could use some lessons in tact and diplomacy. Hansell wondered whether LeMay's tough policies would be effective when he was not leading his crews in person. If he didn't do well as a wing commander his career would be in jeopardy. It was going to be a difficult summer for any wing commander. Hansell left the meeting with Eaker convinced that, on balance, the change in assignments would be best for both him and LeMay. Eaker sent a cable to Arnold recommending that LeMay be promoted to brigadier general as soon as possible.

There was gloom at Chelveston when we heard that LeMay was leaving us. We had lost many close friends and comrades, but we knew that we owed our survival to him. To us, he was the 305th.

The operations staff attempted to arrange a farewell party for him before he left, but he would have nothing to do with it.

"Thanks, but no thanks," he said.

After dinner, a few of us met with him in our operations room. He made a short speech. It was the only time that he seemed to be sentimental.

"I will never forget this group or the missions I flew with you," he said. "You were my first combat command. This is my and your 305th. I don't think any of us will get over it. It will be with us forever. You have a right to be proud. I am. I am leaving with mixed emotions."

He gave us a half-smile, and said, "Yes, I do have feelings and emotions. I won't be going very far. I hope each of you will drop in and see me. I'm sure I will be working with some of you in the future."

On that day, I had no way of anticipating where and when that might be.

General Arnold had a heart attack on 26 February 1943 and did not return to duty until early June. The week after his return, his deputy, Maj. Gen. Barney M. Giles, gave him a series of memos from Assistant Secretary of War Robert Lovett, General Eaker, and Arnold's chief aide, Col. Emmett "Rosie" O'Donnell. Each memo reiterated the same theme: since early 1943, the air war over Germany had escalated to dangerous levels. The Germans had increased their fighter attacks against the unescorted Eighth Air Force bombers. Each memo stated that there was an immediate and pressing need for fighter support for the bombers all the way to the target and back.

Arnold was especially upset by the tone of the memos from Eaker and O'Donnell. Although neither officer was directly critical of Arnold, their memos didn't pull any punches. They both suggested that faulty planning and broken promises had needlessly endangered men. Eaker compared his aircrews to the American troops lost at Bataan and Wake Island. He said they would pay for the mistakes of their superiors.

O'Donnell also minced no words. After returning from a tour of the Eighth Air Force that spring, he told Arnold that reliance on the short-range P-47 Thunderbolt fighter was "faulty planning. Air crews who were sent on missions without fighter support were like sheep sent to be devoured by wolves."

Lovett joined in the chorus. He suggested that Arnold's staff had underestimated the need for fighter support. They didn't appreciate that combat over Germany was vastly more difficult from that in other war theaters. More than 50 percent of the bombers returning from missions over Germany had suffered serious damage. Each memo demanded immediate long-range fighter support, preferably the P-51 Mustang.

Arnold was disturbed about their call for P-51s. Lovett and O'Donnell had to know about the Wright Field Materiel Command's unqualified support of the P-47 and rejection of the P-51. Lovett was now telling him that German fighters were superior to the P-47 in maneuverability, vision, and simplicity of control. Arnold was sensitive about Wright Field's recommendations. Major General Kenneth Wolfe had criticized the Materiel Command's analysis of the B-29 engines. Now it appeared that Lovett was suggesting they had made a mistake in rejecting the P-51 and recommending the P-47.

In his 1986 book *The Strategic Air War Against Germany and Japan,* Hansell wrote:

"The lack of long-range fighters nearly halted the air offensive of 1943; the lack of long-range fighter support was tragic." He later told me that it was luck, not planning, that saved high-altitude daylight precision bombing over Germany. The luck Hansell referred to was the belated introduction of the P-51, which had been designed and developed for the RAF in 1940 at the North American Aviation factory in Inglewood, California.

In his book *Global Mission,* published shortly before he died, Arnold conceded: "It may be said that we could have had the long-range P-51 fighter sooner than we did. It was the air force's own fault. I have debated how much of the story I should tell. For seven years people in aviation in and out of the service have been muttering about it." But Arnold never told the story. He simply stated that the P-51 finally appeared "in the very nick of time. Some of the people who achieved this were the same people who made the initial mistake in 1942." Arnold didn't identify "the people" who made the initial mistake.

The Mustang made its first flight in October 1940. Arnold inspected it at the North American aviation factory in January 1942. He was impressed and told General Spaatz, "We must have the P-51." But he then delayed implementing his decision.

Military commanders, like most people, are reluctant to admit errors of judgment. This is especially true when such mistakes result in the loss of life. There were more military casualties in the Civil War than any other U.S. war, and Gen. Ulysses S. Grant and Robert E. Lee were refreshingly honest about their mistakes. After his defeat at Gettysburg, General Lee, in offering to resign, informed Jefferson Davis: "I am alone to blame. I certainly should have tried some other course." Grant admitted that his 1864 and 1865 campaigns in northern Virginia caused unnecessary losses of life.

The failure of U.S. Air Corps leaders to develop a long-range fighter escort had its genesis prior to World War II. By the mid-1930s they had determined that heavy bombers would be the basic arm of the air force. The development of long-range fighters was not encouraged because U.S. foreign policy was founded on a belief that the United States would not be an aggressor nation. Because planners expected to fight a defensive war from America's own shores, only short-range fighters were necessary for defensive purposes.

Great Britain and Germany also neglected to develop long-range escort fighters for their bombers. Technicians in all three countries believed that it was impossible to develop a fighter able to match the speed, range, and altitude of bombers. They were convinced that fighters could not fly long distances with bombers without sacrificing speed and agility. By the fall of 1941, both the Germans and the British had given up on daylight bombing because they had no long-distance fighters with which to defend their bombers.

Hansell later excused the failure to develop long-range fighters by alleging that the Air Corps had no charismatic leader to advocate fighter support for the bombers, which could compensate for the absence of fighter support with increased defensive armament. By flying in tight formations, bombers would have sufficient concentrated firepower to ward off enemy fighters.

Arnold's staff supported the technical experts at Wright Field, who were openly contemptuous of British aircraft. Shortly after

Pearl Harbor, the Wright Field experts conceded that the American P-39 and P-40 fighters could not compete with their German and Japanese counterparts. They also continued to ridicule the North American P-51 while engaging in an extensive campaign to support the Lockheed P-38 Lightning and Republic P-47 Thunderbolt. The twin-engined P-38 had a longer range than the P-47, but it was no match for Germany's two best fighters, the Focke-Wulf 190 and Messerschmitt 109.

In the face of American parochialism, Churchill was concerned that the U.S. daylight bombing missions over Germany would fail if they did not provide for long-range fighter escort. In mid-October 1942, Churchill wrote President Roosevelt, telling him that the United States had the best long-range fighter in the world, the P-51 Mustang. He told him it was being produced in California for the RAF, but could easily be mass-produced for use by the Eighth Air Force.

In early May 1943, I asked LeMay, "Why don't we have long-range fighter support?"

LeMay stared at me. I could see that he was reluctant to talk about it. He finally told me it was a budget problem: The United States was mass-producing the P-47 and there would be hell to pay in Washington if Arnold tried to cut back on its production.

I decided to discuss the matter with Joe Preston. Joe had been around a long time and knew Arnold personally. He told me that he was concerned that the stress of the Washington political scene and the strain of supervising air force operations all over the world was getting to be too much for Arnold. The army air forces were not independent of the army. Arnold was not a full-fledged member of the joint chiefs. As part of the army, Arnold had to get Marshall's support for all his major decisions. The navy didn't believe that long-range fighters were necessary, or that we should be in Europe. They thought we should be supporting them in the Pacific with tactical operations against the Japanese. Most army ground generals thought the air force should be used as observers and as an adjunct to their artillery. They laughed at the air force for talking about strategic bombing and victory through airpower.

Joe told me some of Arnold's problems. After he obtained budget appropriations from Congress he had to make judgments about the choice of planes and equipment for production. He had to get

Wright Field's recommendations and approval for the new aircraft and engines. Wright Field wouldn't support any aircraft for production unless it was involved in the planning stage. They claimed that because the P-51 had a water-cooled in-line engine it was more vulnerable to battle damage. But the RAF Spitfires and Hurricanes had in-line engines, and they defeated the Luftwaffe in the Battle of Britain. So did the P-38, P-39, and P-40. Only the P-47 had an air-cooled radial engine.

Joe said that Arnold was having a hell of a time with B-29 production problems. It was budgeted for more than $2 billion, and he was reluctant to ask for appropriations for the P-51 or any other long-range fighter. If he did, the navy and the army would remind him that he told them the P-47 could do the job. They were waiting to tell the president and Congress that Arnold was all PR and that he misled the American people about airpower.

Joe's explanation of Arnold's problems was a revelation to me. I had never considered political problems in the context of fighting a war, or the competing pressures between the army and navy. I was appalled at the thought that lives might have been lost because of budget and political problems or personal ambition.

I remembered that, as an aviation cadet, I had been taught that our B-17s were impregnable flying fortresses. No one ever suggested that we would need fighter support. I wondered if someone made a mistake? Who had exaggerated the indestructibility of the B-17 as a "Flying Fortress" in combat? Was the name "Flying Fortress" a PR concept to sell Congress and the American people so they would support a large budget for bombers?

Joe told me about another possibility. Senior Air Corps officers had been working for independence from the army for years. Perhaps the postwar ambitions of some of our leaders had affected combat tactics and strategy. Joe assured me that LeMay would never mislead us; he was loyal to his superiors, but he was also loyal to his men. If there were any way to avoid it, he would never sacrifice a crewmember for an untested theory or a PR concept.

As commanding general of our wing, Hansell tried to balance the groups' requests for fighter support with his plans to bomb key German war production centers deep in the heart of Germany. He was concerned when Eaker told him that Churchill had warned the president that our bombers would face disaster if we ventured deep into Germany without fighter support. LeMay had asked him to find out why Arnold was not obtaining external fuel tanks for the fighters. He was especially displeased with LeMay's acid comment that if we kept up the way we were going without fighter support, the Germans would put us in the garbage can.

Hansell promised LeMay he would speak to General Eaker. Eaker told him that Wright Field had come up with a temporary plan until we obtained long-range fighter support: existing B-17s would be outfitted as convoy aircraft. They would escort the bombers when they went beyond the fighters' range. In place of bombs, they would carry extra machine guns and ammunition. Attacking fighters would have to get past them to attack the planes carrying the bombs.

LeMay was astounded. He asked Hansell if the Wright Field engineers had determined the effect the weight of the additional guns and ammunition would have on the speed of the convoy aircraft. Would they be able to keep up with the faster bombers? Hansell said that he couldn't answer LeMay. We would just have to try them and find out.

The modified B-17s were called YB-40s, and the convoy experiment turned out to be a cruel joke. It was the subject of a great deal of sarcastic comments in officers' clubs and mess halls. LeMay's prediction that the YB-40s could not keep up with our bombers because of the extra weight of the armament was correct. The experiment was quickly abandoned.

As originally developed, the P-51 had an underpowered American Allison engine. The RAF brought one to England and installed a more powerful Rolls-Royce Merlin engine in it. It became the fastest long-range fighter in the world.

The first P-51s arrived in England in mid-December 1943. However, the aircraft was not available to support us in large numbers until February 1944. It ensured the success of high-altitude daylight precision bombing in Germany. It turned the tide of the battle for air superiority over the Luftwaffe and gave the Allies control of the air during the Normandy invasion in June 1944. General Eisenhower told his invading troops, "If you see a fighter, it will be ours." Hermann Göring, the air marshal of the Luftwaffe, put it more directly:

"As soon as I saw the P-51 escorting the bombers over Berlin, I knew the war was lost."

I was to see the P-51 again in the B-29 war in the Pacific. They landed on Guam in April 1945 on their way to Iwo Jima. They escorted the B-29s all the way to Japan from Iwo Jima.

In the context of his other responsibilities, Arnold's steadfast support of the P-47 was understandable. The army and fighter pilots who had not flown the P-51 were satisfied with the Thunderbolt. It was already in mass production in 1943. Wright Field managed to convince U.S. fighter pilots that the P-47 was the Cadillac of all fighters. It had amenities of no other fighter. It operated effectively at high altitude, but had a slow rate of climb. Its two-thousand-horsepower engine could not be matched anywhere in the world. It had eight .50-caliber guns. The army considered it an indispensable adjunct for the support of ground troops.

The appearance of the P-51 over Germany in early 1944 came in the nick of time. The German opportunity to win the war with a superior fighter plane was lost because of Hitler's stubborn effort to seek vengeance against the Allied bombing of Germany. In 1942, Germany developed the world's first jet aircraft, the Me262. It could fly a hundred miles per hour faster than the P-51. However, rather than use it as a fighter to defeat the Allied bombers, Hitler, over the objections of his Luftwaffe commanders, insisted that it be converted into a bomber. When he finally changed his mind in 1944 and attempted to rush production of the Me262 as a fighter, it was too late. By then, the P-51s had shot down so many German fighter pilots that Hitler had only a handful of experienced pilots to fly his jets. Luck had saved Arnold and the Americans.

If Hitler had had his missiles and the Me262 earlier, there might have been a different outcome to the war. There might have been a negotiated peace or President Truman might have been compelled to use the A-bomb on Germany. Hitler's stupidity destroyed the Germans and his opportunity for victory.

The refusal of air force leaders to insist on the production of the P-51 in 1942 almost lost the air war against the Germans. If long-range fighter escorts had been available in the bloody summer of 1943, the lives of many of our crewmembers would have been saved.

10: Bloody Summer

In June 1943, Eaker instructed his staff to plan a summer offensive. He told Hansell to meet with his RAF counterpart on the combined planning committee and plan a coordinated attack on Hamburg. The missions, scheduled for the last week of July, called for the RAF and Eighth Air Force to bomb German industrial cities around the clock for six of the last seven days of the month. The RAF called it "Blitz Week." During the planning meetings, Hansell listened with quiet disapproval as the RAF members of his committee orchestrated a massive firebomb attack on the center of Hamburg. He reluctantly agreed to recommend to Eaker that the Eighth join in a combined effort and carry bomb loads that included 40 percent incendiary bombs. The British would fly the initial mission at night and we would follow in daylight.

Hansell did his best to conceal his feelings about the massive use of incendiaries. This was area bombing at its worst. Hansell thought that Gomorrah, the code name for the attack on Hamburg, was most appropriate. If the Eighth Air Force dropped its bombs on fires started by the RAF, it would be engaged in de facto area bombing. Innocent civilians would surely be killed. Whether air force leaders admitted it or not, this was a change of policy.

The July 1943 incendiary bombing of Hamburg resulted in the firestorms that were unequaled until the bombing of Tokyo nearly two years later. The carnage was greater than the RAF leaders had expected. The firestorms destroyed more than half of the city and killed more than thirty-five thousand civilians. Hundreds of thousands of residents had to be evacuated. The combination of incendiaries and high-explosive bombs made fire fighting almost impossible.

When the fires were finally extinguished, almost 75 percent of the center of the city had been destroyed. High-explosive bombs hit the entrance to subways under the Elbe River, drowning residents who had sought refuge there. Temperatures from the fires reached a thousand degrees Fahrenheit. The citizens of Hamburg were hysterical with fear and rage, and a number of Allied crewmen who thought they were parachuting to safety over the Hamburg area were lynched when they reached the ground. Hitler and Nazi propaganda chief Joseph Goebbels called the leaders of the two Allied air forces brutal barbarians. The missions achieved their objective, however, as military production dropped 50 percent. The RAF's incendiaries caused the bulk of the damage.

In March 1945, when LeMay firebombed Tokyo, the Japanese press accused him of employing the barbarous techniques he had used on Hamburg. In fact, the Eighth Air Force and LeMay had only a small part in the conflagration at Hamburg. Unable to see the military targets designated in the flight plans because of cloud cover and smoke from the fires raging below, our bombardiers aimed for the center of the city at the smoke and fires started by the RAF.

LeMay was impressed by the magnitude of the destruction of military targets in Hamburg. He studied the strike photographs with Hansell. The fires that gutted the city also destroyed submarine and aircraft plants and other production facilities vital to the German war effort. Hansell, appalled by the magnitude of the destruction of the city's residential areas, told LeMay that he did not wish to be involved in any future such missions. LeMay remarked that the RAF's area bombing had located and destroyed military targets by using a new British radar device called H2S. The RAF radar equipment had been able to locate docks, riverbanks, and harbor checkpoints adjacent to military targets, and pathfinder aircraft dropped flares on aiming points for the aircraft that followed. He told Hansell that the radar could assist our navigators in locating target areas. It would be an adjunct to our visual daylight bombing techniques when cloud cover obscured the targets.

Hansell replied that he was not interested in any nonvisual aids to assist with target identification. It was air force policy to sight targets visually. Visual sighting of targets was the only humane and civilized bombing procedure.

LeMay reminded Hansell that our bombers had not been able to locate their targets visually and that if it hadn't been for the fires started by the RAF, the mission would have been a total failure. He said that it was futile to bomb without damaging the enemy. We lost fifteen out of a hundred aircraft—a 15 percent loss rate—and more than two-thirds of our returning planes were damaged. Many of them came back with wounded crewmembers. We paid a heavy price at Hamburg while inflicting little damage on the enemy.

Hansell didn't reply. He was well aware of the casualties, but there was no way that he would participate in planning area bombing missions without a direct order from Washington.

The 26 July Hamburg mission was almost a duplicate of the previous day's. Because of heavy cloud cover, only fifty-four Eighth Air Force planes were able to drop bombs on precision targets in the city. The remaining aircraft bombed "targets of opportunity."

The next day, after looking at the strike photographs, LeMay told Hansell that the second mission was another failure.

Hansell asked him if he was recommending that the Eighth join the RAF in area bombing.

LeMay said that they had to accept reality. If our targets were obscured by cloud cover and we dropped our bombs on targets of opportunity, we were engaged in area bombing. However, if we began using the new RAF radar equipment, we might actually hit some military targets. We were kidding ourselves if we believed we were engaging in pinpoint bombing.

Hansell was disturbed by LeMay's remarks. He wondered if he and LeMay were on a collision course. He knew that Air Marshal Harris, the commander of the RAF Bomber Command, admired LeMay. Harris had told Hansell that LeMay would be the man he would select to lead a dangerous mission. Hansell didn't disagree. He knew that LeMay had the best precision-bombing record in the Eighth Air Force. He would give LeMay the benefit of the doubt. There would be no harm in permitting him to experiment with the RAF's radar. If we were going to use radar, LeMay would be the best man to make it work.

He told LeMay that he would ask Eaker to permit him to work with the RAF to train crews to use the H2S radar when there was cloud cover over the target. I soon became one of the first Americans to use radar on a bombing mission.

• • •

Following the Hamburg missions, we stepped up the pace of our missions to Germany. Hansell had been working on a plan to bomb the German ball-bearing plants at Schweinfurt for several months. When General Anderson suggested that he pick targets in central Germany as a rehearsal for the Schweinfurt mission, Hansell selected the Fiesler aircraft factory at Kassel, less than a hundred miles from Schweinfurt. The factory produced the FW190, the Luftwaffe's most dangerous all-purpose fighter. Hansell and Anderson believed that the German reaction to an attack on Kassel might reveal the placement of their fighters. If we could bomb Kassel and return with acceptable losses, there was no reason that a successful mission to Schweinfurt was not possible without fighter support.

Our group was selected to lead this, the Eighth's deepest mission into Germany to date. Hansell attended the briefing. He was anxious that we not postpone the mission. It might be our last chance to check on fighter reaction before the raid on Schweinfurt. A total of 182 aircraft were scheduled to take off. The weather forecast called for possible heavy cloud cover in the target area. Our route to the target took us over the edge of the heavily defended Ruhr industrial region. As usual, we could expect no fighter support beyond the Dutch coast. I wasn't happy about the designated route. The flak over the Ruhr Valley was the heaviest in Germany. The projected bad weather would be no defense against the radar-guided flak.

Intelligence officers briefed me on the location of the heaviest concentrations of antiaircraft guns in the Ruhr Valley. When they finished, I studied a map of the area and noticed a huge dam on the Möhne River. The reservoir it created would be an ideal checkpoint for avoiding the heaviest flak concentrations.

The antiaircraft gunners started pumping up flak as soon as we crossed the Dutch coast. About halfway across the Ruhr Valley, Col. Del Wilson, the mission commander, called me on the interphone and asked for our precise location. After assuring him that we were on course, I reluctantly added that I had not been able to locate the Möhne dam or the body of water behind it.

"I don't see the dam and water that you're talking about," said Wilson. "We must be either lost or off course."

To reassure him, I asked him to pass down his map so I could compare it to mine. They were identical; I couldn't believe it. I checked the map again. All the checkpoints surrounding the dam area were in the appropriate position. Something was wrong. I had to make a quick decision. Should we proceed on our planned course? I felt I had no choice. I informed the colonel that we should continue. I found out later that our intelligence officers neglected to inform me that an RAF Mosquito squadron had gone in at low level in May and destroyed the dam by skipping bombs over the water into it. Now there was only a huge mud flat where there had once been a large reservoir.

As we approached the initial point of the bomb run, I started looking for the target area at Kassel. The weather was miserable. We were flying above heavy cloud cover. I looked back and saw the vapor trails of the planes behind us. They and the clouds were interlaced with black puffs of smoke. The vapor trails made it easy for the fighters and antiaircraft gunners to track us. We were showered by tracers and shell fragments from a horde of fighters swarming over our formation. Junkers Ju88s sat outside machine-gun range shooting rockets at us while FW190s and Me109s cut back and forth through our formation. I saw a plane from our lower squadron burst into flames, go into a steep dive, and then explode.

As I leaned over the bombardier's shoulder in an attempt to help him locate the IP, Joe Preston called me on the interphone and said that Colonel Wilson was having trouble with his oxygen and seemed disoriented. He said he thought the colonel's oxygen line might be damaged, and he asked me to come up to the cockpit with a walk-around bottle of oxygen and help determine the extent of his problem.

It was usually not possible to know when you weren't getting enough oxygen, which resulted in a condition called hypoxia. I experienced a malfunction in my oxygen line on a previous mission and became unconscious in less than two minutes, so I knew that Wilson was in danger. Without oxygen he could be dead in six minutes. I thought about my responsibilities as the lead navigator and the success of the mission. I was trying to man the nose guns and help the bombardier locate the target. I told Preston that we were approaching the IP and that I should wait until the bombardier located the target before I came up to help the colonel.

Our plane was bouncing up and down from the flak exploding all around us, and it seemed like we were being attacked by more than a hundred fighters. The fighters cut back and forth through our formation at will. Some of them peeled off and dove at us with their guns blazing. Tracers were coming directly at us, and I could feel shell fragments from the flak and cannon bursts coming through our cabin.

As we passed over the IP, Preston called me again and said that several of the groups behind us were turning back because of the heavy cloud cover, the flak, and the fighter attacks.

"We won't have more than two groups behind us," Joe said. "What are the chances of us getting through these attacks and hitting the target in this weather? Maybe we should turn back with the others and you should just come up and help Colonel Wilson."

I looked ahead and spotted a hole in the clouds. "Let's bomb the target first," I replied.

"It's your decision," said Joe.

Within a minute the bombardier had lined his sight up on the target. "Bombs away!" he yelled.

Looking back, I could see flak bursts and a cloud of black smoke over the aircraft factory. I didn't have time to assess the damage. I grabbed an extra oxygen bottle and scrambled up to Colonel Wilson, who was barely conscious. A shell fragment had penetrated his oxygen line. I attached a walk-around bottle to the hose coming from his mask and turned the oxygen up all the way. He gave me a weak grin. I don't think he was aware that he had almost lost consciousness. I said nothing and rushed back to my navigator's position. I knew it was going to be a rough trip home without the protection of the planes that had turned back.

As we turned away from the target, the German fighters renewed their attacks with a vengeance. Suddenly the machine gun I was firing jammed. I pulled off my gloves and touched the hot metal of the weapon's chamber. As I worked to locate the problem, I could feel the freezing cold and hot metal on my bare hands. It was forty degrees below zero. I was burning and freezing my hands simultaneously. I had no choice. I finished cleaning the chamber, fed in a fresh belt of ammunition, and resumed shooting at the oncoming fighters.

While we were fighting off these attacks the bombardier said he had to relieve himself; but he didn't want to climb up to the pilot's compartment and use the tube that drained out the bomb bay. I suggested that he use his steel helmet as a container. He thought that was a good idea. A little later, as we flew over the edge of the Ruhr Valley, the flak and fighters became more intense. The bombardier reached for his steel helmet but hesitated when he saw that the urine had frozen solid. He looked back at me and pointed at his helmet. "What am I supposed to do with this?"

"That's your choice," I replied. "Perhaps it won't melt."

He put it on. A few minutes later he yelled at me: "Nutter, you son of a bitch! Now it's melting and dripping down my neck!"

Before I could reply, a large shell burst below the floor of our compartment, riddling it with shrapnel. Our parachutes, which had been lying on the floor, were now full of holes. I remember thinking that we'd be in a real fix if we had to use them. Our only hope would be that the holes weren't all in the wrong places.

Our gunners didn't stop shooting at the German fighters until we reached the Zuider Zee. We were fortunate that they didn't follow us across the North Sea. We had used up all our ammunition. As we started our descent, I discovered that the shell casings disrupted the accuracy of my magnetic compass, so I had to use my astrocompass to determine our course. After we landed at Chelveston, I dropped down through the nose hatch and looked back at the underside of the wings and the fuselage. They looked like a sieve. It was a miracle none of us had been wounded or killed.

Hansell attended the mission critique. I asked him about our losses and he told me that our wing had lost twenty-two of fifty-eight planes, not exactly a good percentage. I wondered if I made the correct decision to bomb the target when the others turned back. Colonel Wilson didn't mention the losses or his problem with oxygen. He told General Anderson we were only a minute beyond our scheduled arrival time over the target and that the bombing results were excellent. I asked Hansell why the fighters didn't rendezvous with us on the return flight. We had been told at the briefing that morning that the P-47s had finally obtained auxiliary fuel tanks and that we would have fighter support from the Dutch coast back to England. "The only fighters we saw had Nazi markings," I said. He didn't reply.

There was no mission scheduled for the next day, and Colonel Wilson told our crew to put on our best uniforms. We were to be honored with a visit by members of the Senate Armed Services Committee. He introduced me to three senators. I was pleased to shake hands with Sen. Henry Cabot Lodge Jr. from my home state of Massachusetts.

"You boys are really in the big leagues here," he told us.

He congratulated me for my navigation on the Kassel mission, and I was awarded the Distinguished Flying Cross. It was hardly a consolation. We had lost 38 percent of our force. After the presentation we had our picture taken with the senators. Lodge wrote a warm letter to my parents.

Our losses for the month of July had reached 10 percent. Kassel was a dress rehearsal for even greater disasters in August and September. The bloody summer was in full bloom. Starting with the Hamburg mission, we had attempted to hit ten major targets in five days. During that stretch we lost a hundred aircraft carrying a thousand men. It was about to get worse.

Despite our heavy losses on the Kassel mission, our bombing results gave Hansell's planning committee confidence that our planes could reach the German ball-bearing factories at Schweinfurt without fighter support and return with acceptable losses.

When Hansell returned to Washington from his earlier tour of duty in England as an observer of RAF operations, he had brought with him detailed RAF intelligence reports describing vital German war production centers. From those reports, air force operational analysts identified oil and ball bearings as bottlenecks in Germany's war industry. They believed that ball bearings and oil were Germany's Achilles' heel. All tanks, vehicles, aircraft, weapons, and submarines using moving parts were dependent upon ball bearings and oil. Without them, the German war machinery would be paralyzed.

There were two targets in Europe the committee considered to be critical: the ball-bearing factories at Schweinfurt in eastern Germany and the oil refineries in Ploesti, Romania. Hansell believed that their destruction could shorten the war by as much as a year. It would be the culmination of his theories about airpower and would justify his 1941 and 1942 war plans and projections.

Eaker and Hansell flew to Washington to present the Schweinfurt plan to the joint chiefs. General Arnold and Assistant Secretary of War Lovett enthusiastically approved the plan. Successful Schweinfurt and Ploesti missions would restore the joint chiefs' confidence in the faltering strategic bombing program. It would redeem promises of victory through airpower. Arnold told Eaker and Hansell that the attacks on Schweinfurt and Ploesti could not be delayed to wait for long-range fighter support. In an effort to get the joint chiefs to approve the raids, Arnold told them that the missions would help pave the way for the 1944 invasion of France. He promised them that the daylight bombing of key German targets would force Hitler to commit his fighters and that we would make the cost prohibitive. However, the bombers were not just bait, they would be destroying both German fighters and essential industries at the same time. Our aircrews were not being sacrificed. They were frontline troops preparing for an invasion. Without air superiority, an amphibious assault on France was certain to be a disaster. He ended by saying that the air battles over Germany could be won despite the current loss rate, because the United States had the population and resources to overwhelm the enemy.

Both Eaker and Hansell were sober during the flight back to England. Hansell's initial euphoria after obtaining authorization to bomb key German targets was tempered by the thought that the missions would have to be flown without long-range fighter support or enough bombers to destroy the targets. Both generals knew that the crews did not have sufficient defensive firepower to withstand determined German fighter attacks. Without escort fighters they were sure to sustain excessive losses. Knowing that, Hansell told Eaker that LeMay was the man to lead the first attack on Schweinfurt. He was the best and toughest of the bomber commanders. Whatever the odds, LeMay would never turn back from a target.

• • •

The city of Schweinfurt was an unlikely target, a city of fifty thousand people on the Main River in a bucolic area in eastern Germany. It was Germany's most important source of ball bearings, with five ball-bearing factories in the center of the city, two of them owned by a Swedish company. Although the citizens of Schweinfurt knew about the bombing of Hamburg and Kassel, no German leader had suggested that they might be a target.

Hansell's committee prepared the first draft of the plan to bomb Schweinfurt in June 1943. After the Kassel mission on 28 July, it modified the plan in an attempt to minimize the number of fighter attacks we would have to endure. On 2 August Hansell learned of the heavy losses B-24s flying from North Africa suffered in a low-level attack on the Ploesti oil refineries. That force lost fifty-six bombers—a staggering loss rate of 25 percent. The bombers that did get through failed to destroy the cracking plants and other facilities, and the Germans restored the refineries to full capacity within a few weeks of the mission.

Under ideal conditions, two hundred bombers might be able to destroy half of Schweinfurt's ball-bearing factories. Our B-17s could not carry more than six tons of bombs. We were forced to sacrifice bomb capacity in order to improve our defensive capability with sufficient ammunition for our thirteen .50-caliber machine guns. One other factor had an important limiting effect on the amount of bombs we could put on a target: abortions. Approximately 10 percent of the aircraft that took off on a mission failed to reach the target or turned back for a variety of reasons: weather, pilot or navigational error, enemy action, and mechanical failure.

A premature unsuccessful mission could be counterproductive. Once an important target was bombed, the enemy was on notice that they could expect a follow-up attack. Unless such a mission was scheduled immediately, the enemy's defensive preparations could make the return strike more hazardous than the first one. Delaying follow-up missions also gave the Germans time to disperse production facilities to other areas.

Hitler's production chief, Albert Speer, had done a remarkable job of repairing bombed German facilities. British intelligence informed Hansell that the Allied bombing had not seriously disrupted German production of war goods and materiel. In fact, the Germans managed to increase their aircraft production despite the Allied attacks on factories.

General Anderson, commander of the Eighth Air Force Bomber Command, asked Hansell to make the initial presentation at the wing briefings for the Schweinfurt mission. Hansell was not comfortable; he could not mention his concern about the lack of fighter support.

Present at the planning meeting were Generals Eaker, Anderson, Hansell, and Williams, Colonel LeMay, and the operations personnel of the wings and groups. I attended as group navigator of the 305th Group.

Hansell stepped up to the map of Germany and pointed to Schweinfurt. He told us that it was the most important strategic target in Germany. This mission would be our first attempt to destroy a key bottleneck industry. He then gave a short history of the importance of German ball-bearing production. Schweinfurt produced almost 50 percent of Germany's ball bearings, and he said that a successful mission might shorten or even win the war. Now came the difficult part. He paused and looked directly at us, his gaze sweeping over the audience. Many of us would be flying the mission. He knew that we were waiting to hear about fighter support.

"We have revised our plans for the mission since the recent mission to Kassel," he said. "On the Kassel mission we learned that the Germans have devised new procedures for coordinating their fighter attacks. We can expect them to use radar to alert their fighters as our planes reach the German coast. There will be no long-range fighter support. We're still waiting for larger belly tanks for the '47s. They'll accompany you to the German coast—the extent of their present range. We plan to confuse the German fighters with a diversionary mission. LeMay's wing is not going to bomb Schweinfurt. Ten minutes before it reaches the Schweinfurt area, they will change course and head east for Regensburg on the Danube River. Regensburg has Germany's largest Messerschmitt factory. It is a target almost as important as the ball bearings."

When he finished he looked around the room and asked if there were any questions. No one said a word. We were trying to absorb the implications of spending five hours over enemy territory without fighter support.

LeMay finally spoke up; "It sounds like ball bearings are an important target. As for Regensburg, I will be pleased to bomb Me109 and Me110 factories. I have a question about Schweinfurt, though. How do we know that it is the bottleneck target that your operational analysts think it is? I guess they must think there's an easy way to win a war. What are their qualifications? Have they ever heard a shot fired in anger?

"Nutter told me that one of the leaders of this operational analysis committee was his property professor at Harvard Law School. What does a law professor know about selecting targets? If this target is as important as you say, shouldn't we be hitting it with our entire force, rather than splitting our force with this diversion? The 1st Wing can't destroy those factories alone. Even if they could, which I doubt, what other sources do the Germans have for ball bearings?"

Hansell didn't answer. He knew that the Germans had other ball-bearing plants in Stuttgart, Erkner, Steyr, Canstaltant, and Weiner-Neurstadt, plus factories in other parts of occupied Europe. A member of Arnold's staff had told him that the Swedes and Swiss were selling ball bearings to the Germans. If LeMay was going to fly on the mission, there was no way he could tell him that our State Department was negotiating with the Swedes to provide them P-51s if they would stop selling ball bearings to the Germans.

LeMay paused for a moment, then said: "If the Germans are now coordinating their fighters over central Germany, it will be difficult for a diversion to work, even if our timing is perfect. The only way a diversion can possibly work is for both wings to take off on time. If either wing is late, we might as well be flying separate missions. If we fly separately, we'll split our firepower in half. Each wing will get the full force of all the German fighters."

When Hansell offered no response, LeMay asked if the RAF was going to bomb Schweinfurt at night before we attacked.

Hansell replied that the RAF members of his planning committee had recommended a round-the-clock effort to Air Marshal Harris, but Harris thought a mission to Schweinfurt was premature.

LeMay said that specific targets would be difficult to locate in a small city in the middle of a residential area.

Hansell had avoided discussing Schweinfurt with Air Marshal Harris because he knew Harris believed our precision daylight bombing campaign was impractical. The RAF members of Hansell's committee told him that Harris had said the experts who recommended bombing Schweinfurt were mad. He didn't believe in what he called the "panacea" theories of armchair intellectuals.

Hansell wasn't about to tell LeMay about Harris's sarcastic comments. He knew that LeMay admired Harris, and the tenor of LeMay's remarks disturbed him. LeMay seemed to have tunnel vision, so Hansell gave him a mild rebuke, saying that he should not repeat any of his critical remarks to his staff or crews.

LeMay looked directly at Hansell, his eyes flashing. "Possum, you should know me better than that," he said. "I thought I should raise those questions during the planning stage. Once the mission is scheduled you don't have to worry about me. If Eaker and Anderson have decided that my wing should go to Regensburg, I want to lead the mission."

Anderson decided that he'd better take over the meeting. He and LeMay had been friends ever since they were aviation cadets together in Texas. He told him he was pleased that he had volunteered to lead the mission to Regensburg. The city housed Germany's most important and productive aircraft factories. Hitting the fighters and fighter production there was as important as the ball-bearing plants at Schweinfurt. Every time our bombers flew over Germany in daylight, we destroyed some German fighters. By going to Regensburg we would be hitting their fighters both in the air and on the ground.

LeMay then asked Anderson about the return route to England from Regensburg. Anderson explained that LeMay's wing was not going back to England; it would turn south and continue on to North Africa. LeMay's expression didn't change. He had to know that there would be serious problems flying to a strange base in North Africa and landing at night, with only a small fuel reserve. But Anderson was confident that whatever personal reservations LeMay might have about the mission, once it was scheduled, he would do his best to make it a success.

Outwardly unruffled, LeMay rattled off a series of questions. Would there be landing lights on the field? What facilities were available for maintenance and repair of combat damage? Would his crews be living in tents? What medical and hospital facilities would be available for the wounded?

Eaker spoke up and said that Brig. Gen. Lauris Norstad, the air operations officer in the Mediterranean theater, would handle those matters. He thought it was time to terminate the meeting. Although LeMay's questions were proper, he could have phrased them with more finesse and diplomacy. He should have taken it a little easier on Hansell. Hansell was close to Arnold and he reflected Arnold's thinking that a mission to Schweinfurt had to be undertaken no matter what the risks.

LeMay returned to his wing headquarters at Elvedon to prepare for the mission. He met with his group commanders. He ordered his pilots to practice instrument takeoffs. He made it clear that, if at all possible, the takeoffs for the mission would not be delayed because of bad weather. He informed his pilots and navigators that the mission's success depended on precise compliance with time schedules for takeoff, assembly, and arrival at the target areas. There could not be more than a ten-minute difference in the time between the arrival of the 4th Wing at Regensburg and the 1st Wing at Schweinfurt. A delay of even five minutes would make it unlikely that the groups would have any fighter escort by the P-47s to and from the occupied coast. LeMay ordered extra fuel tanks for his planes. This would be the longest B-17 mission of the war.

The Schweinfurt-Regensburg mission was first scheduled for 10 August. After two cancellations, Eaker and Anderson were determined to permit no further delays and rescheduled the mission for 17 August.

The seventeenth was a historic day for the Eighth Air Force. It was the anniversary of the Eighth's first mission over occupied Europe. Only twelve planes flew on that mission. Now, General Eaker planned to send 376 planes deep into Germany. It would demonstrate that the Eighth Air Force had come of age; it would be a potent force to achieve victory in Europe.

On 16 August, the Bomber Command weather officers predicted reasonably clear weather over eastern Germany, but they expected a thick fog over all our bases in East Anglia. Eaker and Anderson were apprehensive about the weather forecast. They knew that LeMay had trained his pilots for instrument takeoffs in bad weather. However, they were not as confident about the 1st Wing.

General Williams did not have LeMay's experience with English weather, and he allowed his group commanders to exercise their own discretion in training their crews. Although Williams had promised Anderson he would have 230 planes ready for the mission, with a projected abortion rate of at least 10 percent, it was doubtful that such a small force would have enough bomb tonnage to inflict major damage on Schweinfurt.

Anderson looked out the window into a swirling mist. If the fog was this thick all over East Anglia, he doubted the 1st Wing could get all of its planes in the air. As he looked out at the fog, Anderson asked Eaker if he should recall LeMay and cancel the mission. Williams's wing still had not taken off.

Eaker tried not to show his concern. He felt he had no choice. Arnold wanted the mission to go. He told Anderson it was his call.

Anderson said he would let LeMay go and hope for the best. However, if Williams didn't get his force in the air within the next twenty minutes, the diversion wouldn't work.

An hour later Eaker still had received no reports of any 1st Wing units or P-47 fighters taking off. That meant LeMay's wing would have to face the German fighters alone, and that the Germans would be able to land, refuel and rearm, and hit Williams's units separately.

The P-47s that did take off had to turn back at the Dutch coast. It was two hours before any 1st Wing units were airborne. Each wing would receive the full brunt of the Nazi fighters alone.

More than five hundred German fighters attacked the two bomber formations. The losses were catastrophic for both wings. LeMay lost twenty-four of his 146 aircraft. Eight of his crews ran out of fuel and were obliged to ditch in the Mediterranean. Fifty more B-17s were so badly damaged that it took weeks to repair them for the return trip to England. Only the group that LeMay flew with suffered no losses. The planes in that group had the most disciplined and tightest formations.

All 230 of the 1st Wing's aircraft took off, but only eighty-three made it to Schweinfurt, and no more than fifty hit the ball-bearing factories. Flak and fighters shot down thirty-six aircraft, and two crews had to ditch in the North Sea. An additional 121 planes were badly damaged. The total losses from both wings were sixty aircraft and six hundred airmen. Many more were seriously wounded.

The Eighth Air Force could not continue hitting targets deep inside Germany with loss rates approaching 20 percent. The price paid was too great for the results achieved. No more than a third of the five ball-bearing factories at Schweinfurt had been damaged. Many bombs landed in residential areas causing extensive civilian casualties. Repair of the damaged factories was completed in mid-September, and Schweinfurt's October ball-bearing production exceeded August's.

LeMay's groups experienced greater success at Regensburg, where they destroyed 60 percent of the aircraft plants. Although the RAF and Eaker commended LeMay for the precision of his bombing, Eaker refrained from mentioning Schweinfurt. He later was embarrassed when General Arnold held a news conference in Washington and told reporters the bombing at Schweinfurt was executed with the precision of a rifleman firing at a bulls-eye. Arnold added that it would not be necessary to return to Schweinfurt.

After a year of bombing targets in Germany and occupied Europe, the Eighth Air Force had yet to destroy any key military industries. The future was ominous. The Germans had increased their annual aircraft production to seventy-five hundred fighters. Hansell knew that LeMay was correct when he said the Eighth Air Force was headed for the garbage can if another Schweinfurt mission was scheduled without fighter support.

In late August, shortly after the Schweinfurt-Regensburg mission, Hansell accompanied General Arnold to a meeting of Allied leaders in Quebec, Canada. When General Marshall and Admiral King questioned Arnold about the losses at Schweinfurt, Arnold said they were an aberration.

Hansell was discouraged. Although he had known that heavy losses would be inevitable without fighter support, he had not ex-

pected a disaster of such magnitude. It appeared from the reconnaissance photos that the 1st Wing had destroyed only a fraction of
Schweinfurt's ball-bearing production. He knew Arnold would soon
demand a follow-up mission, his comments to the press notwith-
standing.

Eaker was anxious to learn the extent of LeMay's losses and when
he would be able to return from North Africa. He and Hansell had
planned for LeMay's units to bomb German airfields at Bordeaux,
France, when they returned to England. Eaker felt that although
LeMay might not complain about the extent of his losses, his depleted units would be in no condition to encounter German fighters on a mission to Bordeaux. He decided to confer with LeMay in
person. He flew to North Africa and, after arriving at Telergama, met
with the 4th Wing commander in his tent. He started the conversation by expressing his concern about LeMay's losses and damaged
aircraft.

LeMay said he had no complaints. He had done the best he could
under the circumstances. He then told Eaker that the diversion was
a disaster. There had been no fighter support over the Channel. His
wing had been left to meet the full force of the Luftwaffe attacks
alone.

Eaker did not reply, except to complain about the weather.

Bad weather was to be expected, said LeMay. His wing planned
and trained for it. It would be several days before his planes were in
condition to return and hit Bordeaux. There were no mechanics or
parts with which to repair damaged planes, as he had been promised.
He had been out on the flight line, personally working on the aircraft with the flight engineers. They were cannibalizing parts from
the most badly damaged planes. He told Eaker that he hoped to put
up sixty aircraft for the return mission to Bordeaux.

Eaker said it wasn't necessary for LeMay to bomb Bordeaux on
the way back. His crews deserved a rest after the job they had done
at Regensburg.

LeMay said that it would be stupid not to hit the Germans on the
way home. He said he wanted to make the Nazis think there would
be more shuttle missions to come. In the next breath he told Eaker
that unless he could provide adequate rest facilities for the crews and

maintenance for the aircraft, it would be a mistake to plan further shuttle missions.

Eaker returned to England without further comment.

The Regensburg force was the only one that flew to North Africa. However, the Eighth flew several shuttle missions between England and Russia in 1944. As LeMay had predicted, they were unsuccessful.

It was a week before LeMay was able to complete repairs on his damaged aircraft. On 24 August he led a force of fifty-seven B-17s north to Bordeaux. They bombed the German fighter base there with the loss of three more aircraft.

Eaker and Hansell knew it would be impossible for the Eighth to conduct another mission deep in Germany for at least two weeks. Assuming that 150 aircraft took off and the abortion rate was 10 to 15 percent, only 135 aircraft or so would get to the target—not enough to make the effort worthwhile.

For the next two weeks, VIII Bomber Command flew "milk runs" to coastal targets. Hansell knew that this was a critical period for the daylight strategic bombing program. Intelligence officers informed him that German war production was increasing. Hitler was transferring fighters to central Germany to meet the American daylight attacks; he was willing to sacrifice support for his ground forces in Russia and the Mediterranean to stop the American daylight missions.

In the last week of August 1943, Eisenhower was in Sicily preparing to invade the Italian mainland. He requested tactical support from the Eighth Air Force. Arnold was concerned. Admiral King had asked him if the Eighth could continue daylight operations over Germany after the losses it had suffered on the Schweinfurt-Regensburg mission. Arnold assured King that the missions would continue, but said that a brief stand-down was needed.

King said the bomber forces in England still had not shown that strategic bombing was effective, and he recommended that the Eighth Air Force's groups be dispersed to support Eisenhower in Italy, the navy in the Pacific, and to prepare for the invasion of France in the spring of 1944.

Arnold asked General Marshall to defer any decision about diverting bombers to either Italy or the Pacific until he could make a personal visit to England.

Arnold was stunned by the intensity of the criticism. He recalled Churchill's memo to the president in October 1942 stating that the Eighth Air Force would suffer heavy losses in daylight missions over Germany without fighter support, and Churchill's comment to Eaker at Casablanca that he would support daylight bombing for a time. He wondered if Churchill was about to tell the president that the time was up.

Arnold decided that he should go to England. That would be less stressful than answering his critics in Washington. He had a sickening feeling that he should not have ignored Churchill's and Eaker's pleas for the P-51. Hansell had cabled him that the bombing results of LeMay's Regensburg mission had been outstanding. If the RAF was congratulating LeMay, it was time that he sat down with him. Perhaps LeMay was the man who could make daylight bombing work without fighter support.

Hansell and Arnold flew back to England on 31 August. An ambitious young colonel on Arnold's staff, Robert Travis, pleaded with Arnold to take him along. Travis had heard Arnold suggest that Eaker was not tough enough with his combat crews: he wasn't flying enough missions and he didn't seem to know how to get maximum results from his combat crews or maintenance people. Travis hoped to persuade Arnold to permit him to lead a mission; he would show the Eighth Air Force what tough leadership could accomplish. He could be as tough as LeMay. He needed the combat experience if he were to have a command future in the air force.

Travis knew that Arnold was going to have an important policy meeting with Eaker's key personnel. This would be his chance to lead a mission while the top brass were having their meeting. Shortly after their arrival, Arnold ordered Eaker to give Travis temporary command of the 41st Wing for a mission to Stuttgart.

Stuttgart was a leading German war production center, with a ball-bearing factory and several aircraft plants. Like Schweinfurt, it was deep in central Germany. Although Hansell had identified its factories as bottleneck targets, he and LeMay questioned whether a mission was appropriate so soon after the disaster at Schweinfurt. It would be another long mission without fighter support. Moreover, the 41st's aircraft had no auxiliary fuel tanks, so a mission to Stuttgart would require precise execution. Crews would be in danger of running out of fuel if they strayed off course or encountered adverse weather conditions.

The 1st Wing navigator was on leave and I was assigned to participate in the mission briefing on 6 September. General Williams, the wing commander, was on leave. Hansell, the only general present, introduced Travis, who told us that General Arnold had designated him to lead the mission. After Hansell gave us a brief description of the Stuttgart targets, Travis asked Col. Jim Seaver, the division weather officer, to brief us. Seaver predicted dismal weather conditions in both England and the Stuttgart area, with at least seven-tenths cloud cover over the target. I suggested that the lead crews might have difficulty sighting the targets visually in heavy cloud cover. Seaver wasn't sure about weather conditions for the planes returning from the mission.

Travis, upset by our negative comments, asked Seaver if the weather would clear. Seaver replied that it was unlikely. Travis scowled and said that you couldn't win a war without taking chances. "Maybe that's why you don't have better results," he added.

I looked at Hansell. He frowned but made no comment. His responsibility was planning, not tactical operations. No one else spoke. Travis ordered the mission to proceed.

The wing had received several replacement crews the previous week, but the veteran crews were only partially rested. In all, 338 aircraft were made available for the mission. More than a third of the new crews had never been in combat. I was concerned that the shortage of fuel and lousy weather were going to be serious problems. Travis rode as copilot in the lead aircraft. When they arrived in the Stuttgart area, the thick overcast prevented his navigator and bombardier from locating the initial point of the planned bomb run. They continued on over the target area, but Travis's crew could not locate any of the designated targets. They flew over Stuttgart without dropping any bombs. Travis was furious. He ordered another bomb run. This was an unexpected bonus for the German fighters, and they took advantage of Travis's unexpected heroics.

As Travis and his pilot looked for a hole in the clouds, the mission commander first ordered a frantic turn to the left, and then to the right. The leaders of the groups following him were astonished. Many planes broke formation. They became disorganized and were all over the sky. After again failing to identify any targets, Travis ordered a third bomb run. The second and third bomb runs were a disaster. They consumed precious fuel needed for the return flight and exposed the crews to more fighter attacks. Unable to spot any military targets on the third run, Travis ordered that they drop their bombs over the center of the city. It was area bombing at its worst.

With their meager fuel reserves depleted, several crews sought refuge in Switzerland. The mission lasted seven and a half hours. Forty-six aircraft were lost, twelve ditched in the English Channel, and many more landed with little more than fumes in their fuel tanks. Ten aircraft were damaged beyond repair.

Travis's attempt to lead the Eighth Air Force on a successful mission was a pathetic failure. General Williams, furious about the miserable bomb results and severe casualties, ordered a hearing the next day at his headquarters. He asked about the weather briefing. Colonel Seaver repeated his prediction of unfavorable weather conditions and heavy cloud cover. Williams then turned to me and asked if Seaver was correct.

Travis stared at me. I knew I was on the spot.

I turned, looked directly at Williams, and said, "Yes, sir."

Williams made no comment and terminated the meeting. Travis told Arnold the bombing results were excellent. Arnold didn't learn until later that the mission had been a disaster. Eaker was bitter; he thought they would have been better off returning to Schweinfurt.

Ten days later, Travis led 140 aircraft from the 1st Bomb Wing on a mission to Nantes, France. The target was a submarine supply ship, the *Kortosina,* on the Loire River. The bombs missed the target and hit commercial and residential areas in Nantes, including a hospital, movie theater, parks, and a sports stadium. More than a thousand French civilians and children were killed. Thousands more were wounded. Again there was a bitter postmortem.

Travis led a third disastrous mission on 11 January 1944. The target was a German aircraft factory in Oschersleben that produced 50 percent of Germany's FW190s. Travis reported that German fighters attacked his formation in bunches as soon as they crossed the Dutch coast. He showed the same disregard of adverse weather conditions as he had on the Stuttgart mission. After receiving a radio report advising him that the weather over England was deteriorating rapidly and the 2d and 3d Bomb Divisions (the bomb divisions were organized in late September 1943) and the fighter escorts were being recalled, he elected to continue on and attempt to bomb Oschersleben. The result was even worse than the Stuttgart disaster: sixty bombers were lost and five more were damaged so badly they had to be scrapped. Many of the combat crews blamed Travis for not turning back. I attended the mission debriefing at our division headquarters. He denied hearing the recall order and that the weather was impossible.

Travis flew a total of thirty-five missions. Always a gung-ho leader, he was promoted to brigadier general in 1944. He was killed in a B-29 accident in 1950. In 1951 the air force base at Fairfield, California, northeast of San Francisco, was named in his honor.

General Arnold arrived at Eaker's headquarters on 1 September 1943 and remained there until the planes took off for Stuttgart. He requested that Eaker and Hansell accompany him to meet LeMay at his wing headquarters at Elvedon. Eaker told him that LeMay would give him straight and candid answers about the problems of the VIII Bomber Command.

After the heavy losses at Stuttgart, Arnold knew that although Eaker was reluctant to send his crews to Schweinfurt a second time without fighter support, they would have to return if he was to keep his promises to the joint chiefs. He examined the strike photos of LeMay's bombing at Regensburg. The results were much better than at Schweinfurt and with a smaller force. He also noted that the group LeMay led on the mission had no losses. LeMay had demonstrated that daylight precision bombing could be successful if the groups had competent leadership.

Eaker told Arnold that LeMay was an "iron ass" who got results and had the respect of his men. LeMay would give Arnold a practical analysis of our problems.

The air force's precision daylight bombing program was in jeopardy. The press was beginning to question the extent of the Eighth Air Force's losses. Fred Anderson had even suggested that the 305th Group fly experimental night missions with the RAF until the groups could recover from their losses.

Arnold told LeMay that Eaker and Hansell said he was their most successful combat commander. He asked LeMay whether daylight operations could be continued over Germany without long-range fighter support.

LeMay replied that he still believed daylight precision bombing was the best way to hit military targets in Germany. He acknowledged, however, that the RAF's night bombing accuracy had been improving ever since it began using Pathfinder aircraft and new air-to-ground radar equipment. He said he was planning to install the same radar equipment in one of his groups and that he believed that as soon as the crews learned how to use it and were given long-range fighter support, bombing accuracy would improve. He explained that having fighter escort to and from targets would do more than protect crews, it would allow bombardiers to focus better on the task at hand and thus increase their accuracy.

In the meantime, while they were waiting for long-range fighters, LeMay said he liked General Anderson's idea of sending some of the best crews from the 305th to fly night missions with the RAF. He said having us drop bombs both night and day would confuse the Germans.

Arnold was impressed with LeMay's self-confidence and determination. His units had the best bombing record in the Eighth Air Force and the fewest losses. Arnold had no objection to experimental night missions with the RAF. That would show the president and Churchill that he was flexible. Fighter support was useless and unnecessary at night. At night they could put their planes in the air without regard to the weather over Germany.

The joint chiefs had compelled Arnold to hold back the P-51s from the Eighth while the negotiations with the Swedes were pending. Those negotiations had failed, so there was no reason not to give them to the Eighth Air Force. Long-range fighters would kill two birds with one stone: They would protect the bombers and destroy German fighters.

He wound up the meeting and told Eaker, Hansell, and LeMay that he would get them fighter support as soon as possible. Until they were available we would have to continue hitting Germany in daylight. We could take the losses; the Germans could not. Experimental night bombing did not represent a policy change. Arnold wanted to bomb Germany to a pulp, and it didn't matter to him whether it was in the day or at night. Hansell wasn't pleased about the proposed night missions with the RAF, but LeMay had convinced him that he was sincere about making precision daylight bombing work. His bombing results at Regensburg proved that. Besides, Hansell was sure he would have a chance to talk to Arnold before there would be any shift to daylight area bombing. LeMay had made a strong and favorable impression on Arnold. As usual, he did not exhibit social grace. It was apparent, however, that Arnold liked his candid and direct approach.

On the trip back to Eaker's headquarters, Arnold reviewed the meeting. LeMay's evaluation of the problems on the Schweinfurt-Regensburg mission had been impressive. Eaker and Hansell had been telling him about the need for long-range fighter support for months. But they had not described it in the context of bombing efficiency and accuracy. He liked LeMay's tough approach. He didn't seem discouraged about the losses. He liked his comment that the Nazis had started the war and we should give it back to them in spades. We have never been turned back from a target and we never will.

Arnold noticed that Hansell's face had darkened when LeMay praised the use of incendiaries by the RAF at Hamburg. Yet he had raised an interesting point: the RAF's area bombing at night had destroyed important German military facilities at Hamburg, whereas Eighth Air Force bombers failed to destroy any military targets there because of the cloud cover. LeMay seemed to be suggesting that we should use RAF tactics if that was the only way to destroy targets.

Arnold was aware that 1944 would be the most important year in the air war against Germany. When the Eighth started bombing Berlin, he would have to make a decision about area bombing. The Casablanca directive was ambiguous. It stated that at an appropriate time, an air offensive could be used to undermine the morale of the German people and their support of the war. This seemed to give the air force the discretion to engage in area bombing if it believed that it would win the war. On the flight back to Washington, Arnold felt that his visit to England had been worthwhile. LeMay had given him some promise of success for the coming months. He wasn't a pie-in-the-sky staff type. In his last meeting with the president, Arnold noticed that when he reported the firestorms and civilian casualties at Hamburg, the president had not raised any objections. He was becoming more realistic and flexible about bombing policy.

During his visit to LeMay's headquarters, Arnold noted that LeMay's people were self-confident and had excellent morale. Eaker told him that LeMay worked his men hard, but his crews were sure he would never ask them to do anything that he would not do himself. He had put together a competent team, building up the 3d Bomb Division with the same tough training methods and discipline that he had used in the 305th Group. Arnold had at last found a realistic combat commander. He decided that as soon as he returned to Washington, he would recommend LeMay for promotion to brigadier general and a medal for his personal leadership at Regensburg.

He decided to keep an open mind about Eaker. He should schedule another mission to Schweinfurt as soon as the weather cleared. If the situation didn't improve, perhaps he would have to make a change. He and Eaker had been close friends for many years. Eaker was an excellent military diplomat. His diplomatic skills had saved the Eighth Air Force's daylight bombing program at Casablanca. Eaker continued to have cordial relations with the RAF. Arnold had to think of the future. He knew that the Allies were determined to invade France in the spring of 1944.

The Nazis continued to maintain air superiority over Germany. Eaker's supervision of his maintenance program was almost nonexistent. He had not made effective use of the planes and crews available to him. He didn't seem to understand the meaning of the words, "maximum effort." The RAF was getting all the favorable headlines about their massive night missions against the German cities. They had dropped five times more bombs on the Germans than the Eighth Air Force. In the minds of the American people, the president, and the joint chiefs, the RAF was more successful. The American people didn't understand and probably didn't care about the difference between area bombing and precision bombing; they were satisfied if our bombers inflicted massive damage anywhere on Germany.

There was another thing about Eaker that bothered Arnold. He not only didn't get enough planes and bomb tonnage on targets, he didn't involve himself in the tactical planning and execution of the missions. Arnold had received a report that at the Schweinfurt planning meeting, LeMay had questioned the purpose and value of the diversion to Regensburg and shuttle to North Africa. In approving it, Eaker had ignored LeMay's criticism and blessed a plan that cut the bomb tonnage on Schweinfurt in half. Eaker had to know that with less than two hundred planes bombing Schweinfurt, they could not destroy the targets.

If LeMay's units had bombed Schweinfurt on 17 August with the 1st Wing as originally planned, the mission might have been successful, or at least destroyed a major part of the targets. The entire diversion and shuttle concept to Africa was too cute. The Germans now knew that the Eighth Air Force believed Schweinfurt to be an important target. The defenses would be stronger the next time around.

The Stuttgart mission was doomed from the start. Eaker should have insisted that if they were going to put that many planes in the air and fly that distance, it should be to Schweinfurt. Not only was the planning bad, the mission itself was hopelessly disorganized and poorly executed. None of the units hit the target. They scattered their bombs all over the countryside, without hitting a single military target in Stuttgart.

Arnold knew that Eaker did not support his intention to bomb Germany to a pulp. Eaker wanted the fighters to defend the bombers rather than use proactive tactics against the Luftwaffe. Instead of having his fighters go after the German fighters, Eaker instructed them to stay close and protect the bombers. The Allies now had overwhelming superiority in terms of manpower and aircraft in the pipeline. Every pilot the Luftwaffe lost was irreplaceable. The United States could afford to lose pilots and aircrews; the Germans could not. It was a matter of simple mathematics. Even if U.S. aircraft losses were equal to the Germans', the United States was winning the battle of attrition.

Arnold thought about the military history course he had taken at West Point. He had always been fascinated by the Civil War. He recalled how Lincoln and Grant had been criticized as "butchers" for engaging in a battle of attrition against Lee in 1864 and northern Virginia in 1865. Their critics claimed that thousands of Union troops had been sacrificed in those campaigns. But Lincoln and Grant had won the war.

This was total war. It took guts to knowingly send men to their deaths. Unfortunately casualties are necessary if a war is to be won. He recalled the bitter criticism of Sherman's march through Georgia. It was Sherman's mass destruction of the South's lifeline that made Union victory inevitable. Killing and mass destruction were the price for winning a war. If necessary, the United States would have to wear down the Germans like Grant and Sherman did the Confederates. He thought about LeMay and another warrior, Justice Oliver Wendell Holmes, who had been a colonel in the Civil War. Holmes said that a good soldier had to have a fire in his belly.

LeMay had that fire. Maybe he had something more important: a hard-hearted determination to win no matter what the odds. His self-confidence and dedication to winning seemed almost inhuman. You took one look at LeMay's face, and there was no doubt about his priorities. He didn't whine about tough assignments. When he told his men they could shoot their way in and back to targets, they knew he meant it; he would lead them personally.

LeMay was the toughest person mentally that Arnold had ever met. He had to get to know him better. The press had finally discovered LeMay. He didn't have a glamorous personality like MacArthur and Patton; there were no press conferences, props, or fancy uniforms. He was a different kind of hero for a different kind of war. He would bring LeMay back to Washington, telling him it was for a war-bond tour. They would talk tactics and strategy with his staff. There would be no bullshit. He was the man to lead long-distance missions against Germany. In the spring, LeMay might be just the man to lead the B-29s against Japan. Arnold needed someone to take that monkey off his back.

On 1 October 1943, Arnold received good news from Fred Anderson at the VIII Bomber Command. On 27 September, over the port city of Emden, the 1st and 3d Bomb Divisions successfully employed the British H2S air-to-ground radar system. The radar was able to pick out the targets in the city by picking out sharp land-water contrasts on the radar set. It could also be used to pick out target areas at night. Another highlight of the mission was that the P-47s were able to accompany the bombers all the way to the German coast.

We flew a most unusual and unexpected mission in the last week of August. Colonel Wilson called an emergency meeting of the group operations officers and squadron commanders. He told us that Eaker's headquarters had received intelligence reports that the Germans were planning some type of aggressive activity with their battleships. The German battleships had been operating out of occupied French naval ports against Allied shipping. We had not seen any battleships on our missions to Wilhelmshaven.

The British believed the Germans might attempt to move their battleships to Norway's fjords. There they would be a serious threat to Allied convoys carrying war materiel for the Soviets along the coast of Norway to the Russian arctic port of Murmansk. Eaker selected the 305th Group to lead the search for the warships from the English Channel, along the Frisian Islands and, if necessary, along the coast of Denmark to the Norwegian fjords. Colonel Wilson selected Maj. Jerry Price, commander of the 422d Squadron, to lead our group. He appointed me to be lead navigator and ordered us to be ready for takeoff in an hour.

Price and I studied our maps and planned a tentative route. Wilson ordered the armament crews to load the bombs without delay. Maintenance crews filled our fuel tanks to capacity. I had a short meeting with our navigators and told them the area of our proposed search. We had no precise route. It would be a game of follow the leader.

As we rode to our aircraft, I noted that there was low cloud cover and limited visibility. I was concerned about fog and visibility around the German naval ports. We went to our revetment. Jerry had no problem starting engines one, two, and four, then spent ten minutes grinding the third engine. It wouldn't start. He pulled out and headed for our takeoff position on three engines. The remainder of the group followed us. At the end of the runway we stopped, and for another ten minutes, Price continued his futile efforts to start engine three.

His voice came over the interphone: "I'm going to try this for one more minute. If it doesn't start, we'll take off on three engines. I should be able to start number three in the air. Everybody get in a secure position for takeoff."

Chuck Malec, the bombardier, turned to me and said, "What the hell is a secure position in a takeoff on three engines with a full bomb and fuel load? I'm going back in the tail."

"Good luck," I replied. "If we crash on takeoff I'll die ten seconds ahead of you."

As he left to go back to the rear, I climbed into his seat. I thought I might as well watch from up front.

The takeoff was hairy, to say the least. Jerry gave our three engines full power and with a roar we started down the runway. I knew that Jerry would use every inch of it. As we approached the end he pulled back on the wheel. I looked down through the Plexiglas nose at a stone wall. Jerry retracted the wheels and they seemed to brush across the stones. No one spoke. We leveled off at three thousand feet and headed for the English Channel. Jerry was correct. He started engine number three right after we leveled off.

At the Belgian coast we headed north. We flew over several German merchant ships and edged along the Frisian Islands past Wilhelmshaven. They filled the air with flak. We ignored them. There were no battleships in the harbor. Except for what looked like fishing boats, the Danish coast was deserted. Then we turned and headed toward Stavanger and Trondheim in Norway. There were a few fishing boats in the fjords but no sign of any battleships. We were running low on fuel. We turned south toward Scotland, then to the English Wash, Peterborough, and finally home to Chelveston.

Our search had been futile. In October, a British midget submarine disabled the huge German battleship *Tirpitz*, sister ship of the vaunted *Bismarck*. The battle cruiser *Scharnhorst* was sunk off the coast of Norway by British warships the day after Christmas. I didn't visit Norway again until my honeymoon.

11: Munich by Night, Schweinfurt by Day

Our losses during the bloody summer of 1943 made it clear that daylight bombing without fighter support was in serious trouble. The doctrine that fighter support was unnecessary had been proved to be tragically incorrect. In early September our group commander, Lt. Col. Don Fargo, called me to a meeting in his office. I was surprised to see the VIII Bomber Command's top brass there: Generals Anderson, Hansell, Williams, and LeMay. In addition to Fargo and me, our group bombardier and Maj. Jerry Price of the 422d Squadron represented the 305th.

Anderson spoke first and warned us that the meeting was a matter of the highest security. He then summarized our losses for the summer. We had lost nearly three hundred planes and more than three thousand crewmen. Our losses on the Schweinfurt-Regensburg and Stuttgart missions alone made it clear that until we obtained long-range fighter support we would have similar losses every time we sent our crews deep inside Germany. During the previous three months we'd flown only fifteen missions to inland targets, and with the exception of Kassel and Regensburg, our bombing results had been less than satisfactory. The Germans still had air superiority over us in daylight, and in spite of our bombing they appeared to be increasing their aircraft production.

He told us that LeMay had been talking to Air Marshal Harris of the RAF's Bomber Command. He said Harris told LeMay that the RAF hit more military targets in Hamburg and Peenemünde than we did all summer. In August, Eaker began considering sending some of us on night missions, and on 22 July Lt. Gen. Jacob Devers sent a memo to General Arnold recommending that we consider night missions. Anderson said he personally had flown on night missions to Hamburg and Essen as an observer and that their navigators were now using the H2S radar to pick up landmarks such as rivers, harbors, and large buildings in urban areas. With winter approaching, the weather would only get worse. We couldn't limit our missions to days when there was no cloud cover. The British radar was now more effective. If we used radar and flew at lower altitudes at night, we would be more independent of weather and wouldn't need fighter escort.

Anderson then asked Hansell and LeMay if they had anything further to add.

"I have never liked night missions or any type of area bombing," said Hansell. "Daylight precision bombing has been the foundation of our strategic bombing theories. I don't think radar will ever replace a visual sighting of the targets."

"You are correct," replied Anderson. "But we have to face the reality of our heavy losses and the fact that our bombing has been generally unproductive. If the RAF starts fires and the area is lit up at night there's nothing wrong with hitting military targets if our crews can locate them visually with the assistance of radar. I want to emphasize that this is not a change of policy."

LeMay said he didn't disagree with Hansell's remarks, but he wanted to recommend that the 305th be used to fly any night experimental missions. He said that Major Price, commander of the 422d Squadron, had the initiative and flexibility to command night missions. Then he said I could train the navigators. He reminded General Anderson that I had flown as lead navigator for him on a mission to Bremen and that I had been on night missions with the RAF, learning how to use the H2S, Loran, and Gee radar systems. He then expressed concerned about security at Chelveston, especially the civilian workers who maintained the runways. He said the Germans may have had advance notice about the Schweinfurt-Regensburg mission, and he warned that if there were spies on the base, they would expect night operations when they saw covers being installed on the superchargers.

He also was concerned about the accuracy of navigation for a night mission to Munich, which the RAF was planning to hit soon. It would be the longest mission of the war to date, and even with extra fuel tanks in the wings our planes would have only half an hour's fuel reserve.

The mention of Munich piqued my interest. I knew that Munich had been the birthplace of Hitler's Nazi party. There were more

Nazis there than anywhere else in Germany. It had been the site of Prime Minister Chamberlain's failed umbrella diplomacy and his surrender to Hitler. A mission to Munich was an opportunity for me to make a personal statement to the Nazis. If Jerry Price was going there, I wanted to go with him. After my old crew and Doug Venable were lost, Jerry had become my closest friend.

As soon as the meeting broke up I called a meeting of the 422d Squadron's navigators. After reviewing night celestial procedures, we took out our long-unused sextants and went to a secure location where we practiced with them late into the night. After a few more practice sessions, Jerry and I felt reasonably confident that the 422d was ready for night operations.

A week later, several planes from the 422d Squadron accompanied the RAF on a night mission to some coastal targets. There were no losses. After four short missions, it was time to schedule longer missions into Germany. By the end of the month, planes from the squadron had dropped sixty tons of bombs at night with only two losses. On 2 October, Jerry came to my desk at headquarters and said, "Ralph, the RAF is going to Munich tomorrow night. We're going with them."

I studied my maps and prepared a route and bombing run. One other plane from the 422d would accompany us. That evening, Jerry and I went to the officers' club for a drink. We often listened to a British traitor known as "Lord Haw Haw," who made nightly propaganda broadcasts for the Nazis. We had always considered him to be a joke, but we were concerned about his comments if they related to security.

On one occasion, while bragging about his knowledge of our base operations, he suggested that we correct the clock in our officers' club, which was five minutes slow. He was precisely right. We wondered what else the Germans knew about our plans and operations. Who, and where, were the spies on our base? Security was exceedingly important on night missions. Surprise was our most important defense because our gunners could not see enemy fighters in the dark.

In any event, Jerry and I were eating dinner and listening to the radio on the night of our mission to Munich when Lord Haw Haw came on with his nightly broadcast.

"Good evening," he intoned in his cultured British accent. "I have a special message for you Yanks in the 305th Group at Chelveston. I won't hurt your feelings and talk about your recent losses at Regensburg and Stuttgart. We are, of course, pleased we have been able to teach you a lesson in daylight that you should have learned a long time ago. We have destroyed you and the RAF in daylight. Now, we have another lesson for you. You are trying night operations, and you are so stupid and so brazen to think that you can bomb Munich. The RAF hit-and-run night missions are a sad joke. They kill innocent civilians but never hit any military targets.

"Now you are going to try to join them in attempting to terrorize our people at night. It won't work. We think it only appropriate that we should give you a special greeting at Munich. It would be most disrespectful if we didn't give you a warm welcome; one that you so richly deserve. I can't wish you good luck, because I know you won't have any. We will be waiting for you. I will sign off now. This will be the last time you will hear my voice, or, I might add, any others after tonight."

I looked at Jerry. "I guess Lord Haw Haw thinks our numbers are up," he said.

"That bastard," I replied. "We'll see about that."

I went back to my Quonset hut and put on my best uniform. I figured if the Germans were going to give us a special greeting I should at least dress up for the party. I had a friend take my picture as I climbed into the plane.

We took off at 7:55 P.M. I felt very much alone as we crossed the coast south of Antwerp in German-occupied Belgium. I knew the Germans would make a concerted effort to use every weapon in their arsenal and spare no fighter and flak attacks on our long, lonely flight to Munich. After the damage the Germans inflicted on the Eighth Air Force in August, they had good reason to believe they had air superiority in daylight. Now, if they could prevent us from bombing Munich, they hoped to persuade our leaders that we would fail in night operations.

We did not have to wait long for the German response. As we crossed the Belgian coastline I looked down and saw German searchlights sweeping the skies. They seemed to be looking for us. Was this the greeting that Lord Haw Haw had been speaking about? Suddenly we were blinded by a bright light that seemed to penetrate every part of our aircraft. There was a loud crash and the plane shuddered. They definitely had our range. Jerry took evasive action, but we were unable to escape the blinding glare of the searchlights. We were in the center of cones of light.

I knew that others would soon follow the first shell. We were like a moth in the center of a flame of candlelight. I saw tracers coming at us from all directions. The flak guns were withholding their fire so that the night fighters could give us a different type of greeting. There was no way our gunners could respond to the attacks of the German fighters. It was like fireworks on the Fourth of July. I felt they were shredding every inch of our plane. It seemed impossible that they would not hit us in a vulnerable spot.

"There's a fighter behind us," yelled the tail gunner. "Corkscrew, left!"

Jerry reacted immediately. He went into a series of dives and climbs, twisting and turning to escape both tracers and flashes of light. It appeared that the fighters were firing both machine guns and cannon. I wondered if our wings could withstand our violent twisting and turning. We had been told that violent evasive action could pop the rivets holding our aircraft together.

After what seemed like hours, we escaped the cones of the searchlights and leveled off in the darkness. Jerry called the roll of our crewmembers. Miraculously, no one had been hurt and there was no indication of any serious damage to our aircraft. We still had two hours to go before we reached Munich. We passed over Sedan on the French border, then flew north of Strasbourg and past Mannheim in Germany.

We had received our first lesson in night combat, where we were a blind prey, unable to see our enemy. There was no way we could anticipate the hit-and-run tactics of the fighters and flak. When our gunners did fire at the approaching fighters, it was usually too late. Even worse, our tracers and the muzzle flashes from the machine guns pinpointed our location. We were sitting ducks in a shooting gallery, the apex and center of great beams of light. Before we left Los Angeles I saw searchlights crisscrossing the sky announcing the debut of motion pictures, but this was one debut I did not enjoy. I wished we could have been a shrinking flower and not the center of a Nazi stage. I had just started to relax for a moment, when I heard a tremendous crash above and behind me in the pilot's compartment.

"Are you guys all right?" I called to Jerry.

He said nobody had been wounded, but the instrument panel was in terrible shape. Most of his instruments had been shattered. I asked him about his compass. He said it was useless, but the gyro seemed to be working. I looked at my own compass. It appeared to have been hit by a shell fragment. The needle was fluctuating erratically. I told Jerry we had no choice. I would try to use my astro compass and set a course with celestial shots.

Jerry suggested I take an immediate celestial fix. I wasn't happy about putting my head in the Plexiglas astrodome, where it would stand out as a target for the fighters if the searchlights found us again. I was also concerned about being able to get an accurate reading while Jerry was taking evasive action. I would concentrate on a star when there was no roll of the aircraft and try to get more than one reading in thirty seconds. I was finally able to take three celestial shots. I quickly plotted our location and was pleased that we were still on course to Munich.

Suddenly, we heard an emotional cry over the interphone: "Let's turn back. We're never going to make it. If we don't turn back, I'm going to bail out."

"Shut up," Jerry said. "If you bail out, you'll be a deserter."

The interphone was quiet. I looked above at my astrodome and decided to try to take another fix and give Jerry a new course to set in his gyrocompass. Suddenly, the cabin was once again flooded with light. I was sure the fighters were waiting to see my head in the astrodome. These were conditions that I had not anticipated in navigation school.

After a few false starts, I was able to adjust to the light, zero in on some stars, and make some additional celestial sightings, limiting my time in the astrodome. I probably set a record for celestial sightings. After computing our position I gave Jerry a new heading for Munich. Fatigue was setting in, and I was concerned that my computations might be incorrect.

I was about to relax when I heard another tremendous crash and felt the plane shudder. The number-three engine stopped. Jerry feathered the windmilling propeller and reminded me that the force of the explosion and his evasive action had probably driven us off course. I again put my head in the astrodome, taking more celestial sightings until we could see fires from the RAF incendiaries at Munich. We were still nearly a hundred miles away and there was no let-up from the flak and fighters. The attacks seemed to increase.

Miraculously, no one in our crew was hurt. Once again we heard from our protesting crewmember. He pleaded with Jerry to turn back. He cried and said there was no way we could make it to the target and return to England on three engines.

Jerry again told him to shut up, and then added, "That looks like Munich ahead."

Our target was a converted BMW automobile plant, which we were supposed to identify in the light of flares dropped by the RAF pathfinders. Jerry asked me to give him an initial point from which to start our bomb run. We were flying at twenty thousand feet, and explosions from flak and fighter cannon continued to rock our aircraft. I said it was unlikely that we could fly straight and level for a precise bomb run on a military target and recommended that we aim for the center of the city. I could see the outline of large buildings in flames. Suddenly, I saw what appeared to be a flare dropping from an RAF pathfinder. I told the bombardier to aim for the flare as it hit the ground.

At 10:58 P.M. the bombardier yelled, "Bombs away!"

I immediately started giving Jerry a course that would take us south toward Switzerland.

"We should be heading northwest," he said, cutting me off.

"Normally I would agree," I replied. "But if we take a direct route toward England, the fighters will be hitting us all the way back to the coast."

"So what do you suggest?" he asked.

"Let's head toward Switzerland. Several of our planes landed there after the Stuttgart mission. We can still try to make it back to England by skirting the edge of the Swiss border. That may be the only chance we have to avoid fighters."

Jerry agreed. As we turned to the right, away from the burning city of Munich, I took a last look at the tremendous conflagration. I had no way of knowing if our bombs had hit a military target. I didn't really care. I wasn't worried about our policy against area bombing. One thing was certain: we had done some damage to the birthplace of Nazism. We had brought a piece of the war to people who either supported Hitler or made him possible. Perhaps some of them would understand the pain and suffering their country had inflicted on the residents of Warsaw, Rotterdam, and London.

We had made the deepest penetration of Germany by any American bomber to date, but for the mission to be deemed a success, we had to make it back to England. As we headed south toward Switzerland, I was at last able to relax for a short time. In the distance we could see lights beyond the Swiss border. I had not seen any city lights at night since we had been in England. I thought a moment about what I considered to be the neutral Swiss. I did not know then that they were making huge profits by manufacturing war goods, including ball bearings, for the Germans and Italians, or that those goods had been paid for with the money and gold the Germans had stolen from Jews and the occupied countries. I thought about our crews who had landed in Switzerland after the Stuttgart disaster. Maybe they heard us. I gave them a silent salute and said to myself, "Best of luck, fellas." We could use a little of that luck.

As we passed over Schaffausen on the Swiss border, the German searchlights no longer probed the sky looking for us. Nor were any fighters following us. Apparently they expected us to land in Switzerland. Suddenly we faced a new and potentially more dangerous problem. The rhythm of our three engines was broken by a new sound. Engine number two began to run rough.

This lasted for about a minute, and then it shuddered and stopped. Jerry feathered it. No one spoke. Now, with only two engines, we all knew we would need another large serving of luck to make it to the English Channel and England. I'm sure most of the crew was thinking, "Here we are at the Swiss border on two engines. Let's land in Switzerland. It's going to be touch and go whether we can avoid ditching in the Channel even if we do avoid the German flak and fighters."

A B-17 could make it back on two engines, as we had demonstrated halfway across the Atlantic. But we didn't know the full extent of the damage to our plane. What else could go wrong? Would the two remaining engines keep going? If we were going to land in Switzerland, it was now or never.

Jerry was not the kind of leader to poll the crew. I knew he had made a decision when he asked me to give him a route across France, and then to England. The trip toward France was almost a pleasure. We crossed the French Border at Mulhouse and headed toward Reims. There were no searchlights blinding me in the astrodome. I took some quick star sightings and gave Jerry a course.

Incredibly, we encountered no further flak or fighters as we flew over Dieppe and began to cross the English Channel. Jerry informed me that we might have enough fuel to reach our base if all went well with our remaining two engines. We arrived at the English coast just before dawn. It looked like we were going to make it. Suddenly, we had a new problem.

All of our bombers carried a radio identification system called Identification, Friend or Foe (IFF). Ours had been damaged by flak. The British, thinking we were an approaching German bomber, fired a barrage of flak that was equivalent to what we had been receiving from the Germans for the last several hours. Once again it was like the Fourth of July in October. I thought that it would indeed be ironic if the British shot us down. We had managed to survive the special greeting promised by Lord Haw Haw, but we never expected the same hostility from the British. As usual, Jerry pulled us through. He broke radio silence and gave the British our unit and aircraft number. They turned off their searchlights and the antiaircraft guns ceased firing.

But there was still the problem of fuel: Did we have enough to get us home? As we made our final approach to Chelveston, one of our two remaining engines started to sputter. It kept going until our wheels touched the runway. The squeal of our tires was one of the most pleasant sounds I'd ever heard. After taxiing to our hardstand, we climbed wearily out of the plane. We were exhausted. Our mission had lasted seven hours. We skipped the mission debriefing and headed for our barracks.

I stumbled into my Quonset hut and dropped, exhausted, on my bed, too tired to sleep. I opened my eyes and looked around the room. It looked different. I had been "rat holed." When a crewmember didn't return from a mission, it was customary to clean his room for a replacement. His possessions were divided among the survivors. We called this practice "rat holing." Getting my things back was difficult. None of my friends wanted to admit that they had not expected us to return. I did better than most, though. I got my radio back. Later, I was given a special commendation for this Munich mission.

A few days after the Munich mission, Jerry asked me if I would like to join him in a bit of R&R in our headquarters-assigned A-20. We enjoyed taking the A-20, a twin-engine medium bomber, to the English Channel off the Straits of Dover. We would fly halfway across the straits at an altitude of twelve thousand feet in a deliberate attempt to alert the German fighters along the French and Belgian coast. When we saw German fighters taking off to engage us, Jerry would put our plane in a dive for the cliffs of Dover. If they followed us closely they would be vulnerable to attacks from English fighters.

I told Jerry I was sorry, but I was too busy and couldn't make this flight with him. He went alone and did not return. We never learned whether he had been shot down by a German fighter or had experienced some mechanical problem. As with Doug Venable, I had the sad task of packing his footlocker to return to his family in Colorado.

On 5 October I was told to report to wing headquarters. I was prepared to recommend that we continue night bombing until we obtained fighter escort. The 305th had proven that night operations could be successful. I was told that Anderson agreed but General Arnold had ordered another daylight mission to Schweinfurt.

The night bombing experiment was over. The 305th flew eight night missions with the RAF and dropped sixty-eight tons of bombs on the Germans. Our losses had been low. We had proven that Eighth Air Force crews could bomb successfully at night. I had learned about incendiary night bombing. My experience was not a total waste, however, because we used the same tactics against Tokyo in night missions during March 1945.

The next few weeks almost destroyed the Eighth Air Force. Eaker was desperate to demonstrate to Arnold that high-altitude daylight precision bombing could succeed. Crew losses were catastrophic. There was to be no rest for the weary aircrews. We lost 58 bombers on 8 and 9 October, and a maximum effort was mounted against Münster, an important railway center at the edge of the Ruhr Valley, on the tenth. For the first time the aiming point of the mission was a civilian target. It was to be the most prominent building there, a thousand-year-old cathedral in the center of a residential area. VIII Bomber Command hoped that we would destroy the workers' homes and their morale. General Hansell was aghast. His protests about using the cathedral as an aiming point were ignored. Fighter escort did not get off the ground due to fog. The 100th Bomb Group lost all but one of the thirteen B-17s it sent out that day. Bombs were scattered all over the city. Thirty bombers were lost. Four days later the Eighth was to double that loss at Schweinfurt.

Earlier that month, General Arnold had attended a meeting in Washington with the joint chiefs. When Admiral King learned about our experimental night missions with the RAF, he asked Arnold if he was contemplating giving up daylight bombing because of our heavy losses at Schweinfurt and Stuttgart. King said if that was the case, Arnold should assign a few more planes to fly at night with the RAF and disperse the remainder of his heavy bombers to support Eisenhower in Italy and the navy in the Pacific.

Arnold made no attempt to minimize the problems of the past summer. He argued that this was not the time to retreat. The battle for air supremacy over Germany had been joined. Hitler was committing the bulk of the Luftwaffe against U.S. daylight bombing, not the RAF at night, and he was losing his best pilots as a result. He assured the joint chiefs we would win the battle of attrition. The Eighth Air Force now had enough aircraft to bomb Germany to a pulp, and we were ready to resume missions to central and eastern Germany. One more mission to Schweinfurt would knock out most of the German ball-bearing industry.

Arnold left the meeting knowing that he could not delay a second mission to Schweinfurt any longer. A successful fall air offensive was absolutely necessary. The army and navy were waiting for the Eighth Air Force to fail.

Responding to the pressure from Arnold, General Eaker called a meeting to plan for a second mission to Schweinfurt, with each wing represented by its senior operations personnel. Eaker told us that Arnold wanted us to hit Schweinfurt again as soon as possible. British intelligence informed him that the Schweinfurt factories damaged in August were operating at 90 percent capacity and that the Germans had taken no steps to disburse these factories. The two B-17 wings and the 2d Wing, which was composed of B-24s, should be able to put at least 330 aircraft over Schweinfurt. This time there would be no diversion. General Williams asked if the P-47s would have larger belly tanks so they could stay with us longer. Eaker replied that he didn't expect any increase in fighter support before the next mission.

His instructions from Arnold were clear and unmistakable. The mission had to go as soon as the weather cleared. Arnold believed that the future of strategic bombing and an independent air force was on the line.

Eaker told us that things would be different this time. With more than three hundred planes, we should be able to damage the ball-bearing factories enough that we wouldn't have to go back again. He reminded us that the Eighth Air Force was part of a bigger picture, a substitute for a second front in Europe. If German ball bearings were cut off they would not have the vehicles and weapons they needed to resist an invasion.

The room was silent. I looked around. I doubted that anyone had been reassured by Eaker's brave words. I returned to Chelveston. I was concerned how our crews would react to news of a second mission to Schweinfurt without fighter support. Ever since LeMay left us to assume command of a wing, our group's morale had been deteriorating. We had suffered heavy losses and gone through a series of temporary group commanders.

As I walked to the briefing room in the early-morning darkness on 14 October, the weather seemed a carbon copy of 17 August. It was the same suffocating fog and low cloud cover. I hoped that VIII

Bomber Command would be more decisive about the weather and do a better job of coordinating the wings and groups than it had done in August. At least today, all of the units would be flying to Schweinfurt.

I pulled back the curtain covering the map and the route across Germany. The crews looked at the red string leading to Schweinfurt. No one had to be reminded of the losses we'd suffered on 17 August. There was a loud groan in the back of the room and someone called out: "Goddamn, not that hellhole again. We've had enough of German balls. What about ours?"

Colonel Fargo stepped up to the map. He ignored the sarcastic comments and began outlining the plans for the mission. When he finished, he read a message from General Anderson, commander of VIII Bomber Command: "This air operation today is the most important air operation yet conducted in this war. The target must be destroyed. It is of vital importance to the enemy. Your friends and comrades that have been lost and that will be lost today are depending on you. Their sacrifice must not be in vain. Good luck, good shooting, and good bombing."

Colonel Fargo had no personal comments to add to the statement. I looked out across the room. The wording and the tone of the message did not encourage the crews, who believed that all our targets were important. Anderson didn't have to remind us that some of our friends would be lost today. Anyone who'd been in the group for more than a week knew that our losses were heavy. They knew that any mission deep into Germany was dangerous. I thought a more upbeat message might have been more appropriate. Reality would come soon enough.

The group meeting broke up and I stayed with the navigators. I explained the route in more detail, discussed landmarks in the target area, and pointed out the location of a possible concentration of flak guns. We spent an hour studying models of the ball-bearing factories and photos of the Schweinfurt area.

This was to be my last day with the 305th. I had done a full tour of twenty-five missions plus a night mission to Munich and some missions with the RAF. I had a new assignment as division navigator at Brampton. I was reluctant to say good-bye to my old comrades, so I didn't tell them I was leaving. I wished each of them good luck as they left for their planes.

Most said, "Thanks, Ralph, we'll need every bit you can give us."

They were sober and preoccupied. There was none of the usual gallows humor of our earlier missions.

I decided to return to the weather office for a last-minute projection of conditions over the continent. The weather was clearing. There were no changes in the forecast. It was not necessary for me to alter the times specified in the flight plan.

The 305th was scheduled to take off at 10 A.M., but got off seven minutes late. It was an inauspicious start. Things got worse—much worse. The three wings launched 377 bombers, including, for the first time, sixty B-24 Liberators. The B-24s had not yet accompanied the B-17s into Germany's interior because they had difficulty keeping up with the Fortress at high altitude. The inclusion of the B-24s made it apparent that Eaker and Anderson were scheduling every available aircraft for this second Schweinfurt mission.

The B-24s were lucky. Because of the thick overcast in their assembly area, they were unable to locate and join the two B-17 wings. They were recalled and their mission was canceled. Anderson's projected strike force of nearly four hundred planes was now reduced to 317—and it hadn't even left England. The mission was doomed to failure long before any planes reached Schweinfurt.

A new squadron commander, Maj. G. G. Y. Normand, was leading the 305th that day. It was his first experience as a mission commander. The group had become a different organization after LeMay left for his new assignment. More than half our crews were replacements. The remaining veterans felt that no one could replace LeMay, and they lacked confidence in the new group leaders. Their low morale was made worse by the heavy losses during the summer.

After the late takeoff, Major Normand led the group in search of the wing assembly area. Because he was late, he was unable to find the group's assigned position in the wing formation and finally led the group to the lowest position in another formation, a favorite target for German fighters. Before leaving England, three planes dropped out and returned to base, claiming engine trouble. The 305th now had only fifteen aircraft. I never did find out why those planes aborted. I hoped it was not in anticipation of trouble at Schweinfurt.

After waiting for the 305th to join its formation, the 1st Division was twenty minutes late for its linkup with the P-47s. The fighters headed toward the Dutch coastline without them. As the groups approached the coast they were attacked by hundreds of FW190s, Me109s, and twin-engine Me110s, Me210s, and Ju88s.

The Germans' first target was the 305th, which was flying in "Purple Heart Corner." Within a matter of minutes the group lost twelve of its fifteen aircraft. The commander of the group flying above Normand called him on the radio and told him to join their formation for the bomb run. Incredibly, he replied that his three planes would make their own bomb run. Before reaching the IP, the 305th lost one more aircraft. Then, instead of lining up behind the leader of the other groups on the bomb run, Normand flew beside it on the left. The bombs from the two 305th aircraft inevitably missed the target and hit the center of the city. Although 227 B-17s reached the Schweinfurt area, only a few hit the ball-bearing factories. The 1st Division lost forty-five aircraft, and LeMay's 3d Division lost fifteen. The loss of sixty B-17s equaled that of the 17 August mission. The reconnaissance photos made it clear that only 40 percent of the ball-bearing factories had been destroyed. Further missions to Schweinfurt would be required.

Before leaving for my new assignment as division navigator at Brampton, I decided to wait in the control tower for the 305th's planes to return. I stood there at the railing on the top deck with Colonel Fargo. By late afternoon we knew that our planes were close to the limit of their fuel reserve. I was about to leave when we saw a red flare coming from Barney Farrell's plane as it approached the runway. The signal meant he had wounded aboard. Fargo and I rushed to his plane as it rolled to a stop. The navigator was wounded and unconscious. Farrell was in shock. Major Normand landed a minute later. I asked him what had happened to the remainder of the group.

"You're looking at them," he said.

I turned away. I could see that Normand and his crew were in no condition for a debriefing. I walked slowly to my jeep. I decided I needed a stiff drink, probably more than one. I went to the officers' club and sat alone. The bar was empty except for the chaplain. We didn't talk. There was nothing to say.

I felt that sitting at a bar alone was a hell of a way to spend my last day with the group. I reviewed the last year. I had lost almost all of my friends, the men I had fought and lived with for more than a year. I knew it would be a long time before the war ended. If I survived, 14 October 1943 would be a day I would never forget as long as I lived. My promotion to major, which became effective that day, seemed irrelevant.

I was in no mood to say good-bye to Fargo or Normand. I drove to my new quarters at Brampton, where I was unable to sleep. For the first time I thought about a subject that none of us had ever mentioned. Why was a second mission scheduled to Schweinfurt without fighter support? Who was responsible for these losses? Could we keep going after Schweinfurt? Was the risk to the crews worth the damage we were inflicting on the enemy?

The Eighth Air Force had lost 454 bombers and 4,940 men from July through October 1943. Should we resume daylight missions into central Germany without fighter escort? We had proven that the Eighth Air Force could fly night missions. It seemed reasonable and prudent to schedule only night missions—at least until the P-51s arrived in December. I thought about our losses in the 305th. Of the thirty-five B-17s and their crews that left Gander Lake, twenty-one were shot down, a 60 percent loss rate. Less than a third of the original crews finished their missions. Thirty percent had been killed. For the first time I wondered why fate had been so kind to me. As a division staff officer, presumably, I would not have to fly any more missions over Germany. I had already flown more than were required in a full tour. I could be relatively safe. I thought about the war against Japan. We had heard rumors about the new B-29 Superfortress that Boeing was building for long overwater flights. They would be the ultimate test for a navigator.

The next morning I went to the division operations center for the latest reports on our losses at Schweinfurt. I entered the room as General Hansell was saying good-bye to General Williams.

He turned to me and shook my hand. "I'm leaving for Washington, Ralph," he said. "I'm going to work on planning for the new B-29 program. After you've worked here a while for General Williams, I hope you'll consider coming to work for me. We start training next year in the States. It will be quite a challenge for our navigators. I hope you'll think about joining us."

I paused a moment and then told him I would think about it. We shook hands and he gave me his warmest smile.

12: Hansell and LeMay in Washington

Hansell was up at 5 A.M. on 15 October 1943. He was scheduled to fly back to Washington and resume his former position as General Arnold's chief plans officer. After an early breakfast he decided to stop and say good-bye to General Eaker. As he entered Eaker's office he saw that the Eighth Air Force commander was studying the previous day's strike photographs and casualty figures and was visibly upset.

Eaker told Hansell that the bombing results were slightly better than in August, but the ball-bearing factories still had not been destroyed. Hansell asked if the final reports had come in from Williams's and LeMay's divisions. Eaker said that LeMay's division had achieved better bombing results and suffered only a third as many losses as the 1st Division. He said he thought it was time the 1st Division adopted LeMay's tactics and procedures. He added that preliminary reports indicated that so many had been badly damaged that it would be weeks before they could mount a force large enough to risk another mission over Germany without fighter support.

Eaker pondered what message he could give Hansell to carry back to Arnold, then told him he thought it best to give Arnold a forthright and candid explanation of the situation, and then stress that they had to have fighter support to and from inland German targets. It would be weeks before the damage to more than 140 of our aircraft could be repaired, so priority should also be given to getting replacements for the lost aircraft and crews. Although American losses were severe, the German pilots lost were irreplaceable. And although Schweinfurt had not been destroyed, ball-bearing production had been cut significantly.

Eaker emphasized that Hansell should tell Arnold that he was not discouraged. He still believed in daylight precision bombing. With fighter support, a daylight program could be successful. The strike photos showed that the incendiaries dropped on the Schweinfurt mission did the most damage to the targets.

Hansell agreed with Eaker's entire message to Arnold except his reference to incendiaries. He was still convinced that it was impossible to engage in high-altitude daylight precision bombing with incendiaries because the fires they started would kill innocent civilians. Eaker knew that this message was not going to inspire Arnold to have confidence in him.

Hansell reported to Arnold as soon as he arrived in Washington. He summarized Eaker's verbal report of the 14 October Schweinfurt mission and suggested that it was too early to determine the extent of the damage to the ball-bearing factories. He knew that Arnold was being pressed by the media to describe the bombing results and confirm the reports that sixty crews had been lost. There was already talk that the loss of twelve hundred men on the two Schweinfurt missions was too high. Arnold, believing it was necessary to prepare an optimistic press release, asked Hansell to draft one for him.

"The losses were moderate," Hansell wrote. "They were no greater than expected for so important a target. The bombs hit the target like a rifle hitting a bull's eye. Our planes 'got' Schweinfurt on this second mission. Their factories are completely useless. No ball bearings will come from the ruins. Our gunners shot down over 100 German fighters. We are gaining air superiority and control of the air over Germany. Daylight precision bombing is a success."

Arnold was pleased.

Hansell decided that this might be an opportune time to remind the Air Corps's chief of the promise he had made about providing long-range fighter support. He told Arnold that Eaker, Williams, and LeMay agreed that precision bombing could work if they had long-range fighter support.

Arnold replied that he had ordered North American Aviation in California to deliver all its P-51s to the Eighth Air Force. With fighter support, it wouldn't be necessary for the Americans to join the RAF in night area bombing. Then he asked Hansell how LeMay achieved such good bombing results and why Eaker wasn't as tough as LeMay? Hansell thought it best not to respond. He had been unhappy when Eaker replaced him as commander of the 1st Bomb Wing. But Hansell had never spoken ill of his colleagues, and Eaker had been true to his word. He had approved the strategic targets Hansell selected.

On balance, things had worked out for the best. Hansell did not wish to return to England. His future was in Washington, working for Arnold in planning the B-29 campaign.

Hansell, seeing that Arnold had gotten upset when he mentioned Eaker, asked if he was all right. Arnold replied that he knew he shouldn't get so worked up, that this was not the time to give up on precision daylight bombing. Moreover, as long as his health held up, he *wouldn't* give up. He then commended Hansell for his work in planning the bombing of Germany for the Eighth Air Force. Now, he said, he needed his help in the B-29 program. The plan for the B-29s would be discussed at the Allies' next strategy conference in Cairo in November. He wanted Hansell and Col. Emmett "Rosie" O'Donnell Jr. to attend that conference. Churchill and Chiang Kai-shek would also be there.

Hansell was pleased because the Cairo conference would be the first step in making precision daylight bombing succeed against Japan with B-29s. He didn't like going with O'Donnell, however, because he had been critical of Hansell's planning for attacking Germany. Hansell also had doubted O'Donnell's devotion to high-altitude daylight precision bombing. He wondered whether Arnold was planning to give O'Donnell a command in the B-29 program.

As for LeMay, it was apparent that Arnold had a great deal of confidence in him. He was bringing him back home for a bond tour, but LeMay was the last person Hansell would have selected for a public relations tour. He knew that LeMay hated making speeches. Hansell had heard members of Arnold's staff jokingly call LeMay "the diplomat" because of his sometimes brutal and tactless statements. On the other hand, he thought that perhaps the American people needed a hero like LeMay. The war was far from over; there were still some tough years ahead.

During the next two weeks, Hansell worked on plans for the Cairo summit meeting. He studied maps of the Pacific, China, and Japan. The B-29s would need bases within at least fifteen hundred miles of the Japanese home islands. He studied the Chengtu area in China and another in the Mariana Islands in the central Pacific. He expected General MacArthur to push for B-29 support for his Philippines campaign. He also knew it was going to be difficult to persuade the army and navy to commit resources for B-29 bases on Guam, Tinian, and Saipan in the Marianas. The Japanese had heavily fortified all of them. Were the army, marines, and navy willing to risk huge losses of men and materiel to capture these islands to serve as bases for a strategic bombing campaign?

After consulting with senior army, navy, and marine planning officers, Hansell summarized his conclusions for Arnold, pleasing him. Arnold said that he would discuss the plans with General Marshall and, with his support, brief the president. Arnold knew that Roosevelt wanted to establish a tangible U.S. presence in China for Chiang Kai-shek's benefit. The immense B-29s on Chinese bases would show him that America was behind them in a maximum effort to defeat the Japanese. Since LeMay was also in town, he invited him to go to lunch. Hansell decided to recommend to Arnold that LeMay be given command of B-29 operations in the China-Burma-India (CBI) theater. He knew that Arnold believed LeMay was his toughest bomber commander and the most technically able flier in the air force.

Hansell had never considered LeMay to be a potential rival for a top command in the air force; he simply didn't have the necessary diplomatic skills. The CBI would be a good place for him. It would be impossible for him to bomb Japan's most important targets from remote bases in western China. He would be required to fly every bomb, as well as all of his equipment and fuel, a thousand miles over the Himalayas. Hansell doubted LeMay could do any real damage to the Japanese war effort from China. On the other hand, the strategic air war could be won by B-29s flying from the Marianas. It would be the most important command in the air force, and Arnold had promised it to him. If he handled it successfully, Hansell was confident that his future as a postwar leader in an independent air force would be assured.

LeMay was not interested in small talk. True to form, he started the luncheon with Hansell by asking him tough questions, such as why the groups were sent to Stuttgart in September when it was about the same distance as Schweinfurt. By delaying the second Schweinfurt mission to 14 October they had given the Germans a chance to disperse, rebuild, and strengthen their defenses. On the Stuttgart raid, 407 planes, the largest force of the war to date, had bombed a few ball-bearing factories. But Schweinfurt was Germany's main source of ball bearings, and the Germans could not have diverted or dispersed their production machinery from Schweinfurt in just three weeks.

Hansell replied that he had been opposed to the Stuttgart mission. Colonel Travis had played a large part in that decision. None of the staff was pleased about his influence with Arnold. Then he tried to explain to LeMay the original planning for the Schweinfurt mission. When it was first approved in April, he and Anderson thought they were going to have P-47s with belly tanks with sufficient fuel to accompany the bombers to the target. When that didn't happen, Arnold felt that he couldn't hold up either the Ploesti or Schweinfurt missions. He then warned LeMay to keep quiet about his criticisms of the Schweinfurt and Stuttgart missions. There was no way anyone could have persuaded Arnold to delay the strikes.

When they finished, Hansell stood up and told LeMay to enjoy the bond tour. He wished him luck. LeMay growled that he was the last man the air force should send to speak on a bond tour; the sooner he got back to his people in England, the better.

After meeting with Hansell and LeMay, Arnold thought that there was light at the end of the tunnel for the B-29 program. He would consider Hansell's recommendation that LeMay be given command of the B-29 program in the CBI. The entire B-29 program had been in a shambles since the first production unit in 1942. Arnold was concerned that the president was pressuring him to rush the B-29s and their crews into combat before they were ready. General Wolfe would be the first B-29 commander in the CBI. If he didn't get the job done, Arnold would replace him with LeMay. He would appoint Hansell chief of staff of the Twentieth Air Force until the B-29s were ready to begin flying from the Mariana Islands. Then he would give Hansell the XXI Bomber Command.

Arnold's other major problem was command of the Eighth and Ninth Air Forces in England and the Twelfth and Fifteenth Air Forces in the Mediterranean. LeMay was too young for a senior command position in Europe. He needed him to lead his bomber division on missions deep inside Germany. Hansell had told Arnold that Generals Lawrence Kuter and Hoyt Vandenberg thought the Air Corps chief should accept Eisenhower's recommendation to give Spaatz command of all U.S. Army Air Forces units in England and replace Eaker with Jimmie Doolittle. He could then promote Eaker and shift him to the less strategically important Mediterranean command.

Arnold knew that removing Eaker would be unpleasant. He was one of Arnold's oldest friends and strongest supporters, and he didn't disagree with Eaker's belief that bombing should not be directed at unarmed civilians. He did, however, wonder if Eaker would be tough enough to pull out all the stops when the invasion began. He knew that Marshall was not about to overrule Eisenhower's recommendation. He had to concede that it was not fair to blame Eaker for all of the Eighth Air Force's problems in 1943. Perhaps he might have done something about giving Eaker more fighter support if he hadn't had those heart attacks. He hoped that their friendship would not be another casualty of war. He knew Eaker would be upset and would characterize his new command in the Mediterranean as a kick upstairs. He was correct. Eaker later said that his banishment to the Mediterranean theater was his darkest hour.

While the Spaatz and Dolittle appointments were pending, Arnold decided that he should prepare Eaker for his new assignment. He suggested that Spaatz arrange a conference at Gibraltar with RAF Air Marshal Arthur Tedder and Eaker to coordinate the combined operations of the Eighth Air Force and the newly conquered air bases in Italy. He instructed Spaatz not to tell Eaker he was being replaced as commander.

On 5 November I received orders to report to General Eaker at his Pinetree headquarters. There he informed me that LeMay had recommended I serve as his navigator for a night flight to Gibraltar. He told me that the Germans had fighter bases in southwest France and, possibly, secret air bases in Spain. He also told me to bring a bathing suit, because in November the water would be warm enough for swimming.

We took off on 8 November, exactly one year since the invasion of North Africa. I had not been on a flight over the Atlantic since we'd left Newfoundland in October 1942, when I was a raw, inexperienced recruit. I was much more confident in my celestial navigation skills. Bad weather and cloud cover were now routine. After we broke out of the clouds I made some celestial sightings, plotted our location, and gave the pilot a new heading to the south. We had no unusual problems until we turned east toward Gibraltar.

I was concerned about descending over the mountains on both sides of the narrow straits between Spain and Spanish Morocco. There would be no room for error. I certainly didn't want to let down over Spanish territory. I had questions about Spain's supposed neutrality and the extent of Franco's support of Hitler. We circled down through heavy cloud cover. As we broke out of the clouds, I looked down on the famous rock of Gibraltar, which was engulfed in searchlights. I asked Eaker why there was no blackout. He told me that the English believed it was safer to risk bombing than the danger from the Spaniards beyond the barbed wire. If there were a blackout, they feared Nazi sympathizers might row out to ships in the harbor and attach bombs to their hulls.

As we circled the base preparing to land, Eaker looked at his watch and told me that my navigation was off. We were five minutes ahead of my estimated time of arrival. He told the pilot to circle the airfield for five minutes and land on time.

I looked down at the huge armada of naval and merchant ships anchored in the harbor and couldn't believe that they were safe from enemy bombers. We landed without incident and pulled up to a VIP greeting area where Air Marshal Tedder and General Spaatz were waiting to meet Eaker. Those of us in the crew were on our own.

I spent the next two days touring every corner of the "rock" and saw the famous monkeys of Gibraltar. I walked to the barbed-wire fence separating Gibraltar from Spain and stood a few feet away from uniformed Spanish troops whom I considered the enemy. I wondered what they were thinking as they looked at me in my American flight uniform. After that I walked down to the beach and took a dip in the Mediterranean.

On the tenth Eaker told us we would take off for England as soon as it was dark. We took the same route back. The trip was uneventful. He seemed to be in a good mood; no one had told him the conference was a prelude to his replacement and a change of command. The day before he had sent a memo to Arnold that he, Spaatz, and Tedder were in complete agreement on all matters. He didn't find out he was being replaced until early December.

When I returned to division headquarters at Brampton, the groups still had not recovered from the losses on the Stuttgart and Schweinfurt missions. Hitler was determined to avenge the Allied bombing of German cities. He ordered Göring to make indiscriminate terror attacks on southern England with the new V-1 flying bombs and V-2 missiles. Our strategic bombers were again diverted to support tactical operations, this time by conducting raids on the missile sites located on the French and Belgian coasts accompanied by fighters. Eaker and the crews were more than willing to delay the strategic bombing of German targets until the P-51s were available.

General Arnold and his staff were well aware that the Eighth Air Force was engaging in area bombing. He explained the change in policy by stating that the VIII Bomber Command engaged in area bombing whenever unforeseen weather conditions closed in on specific primary targets, whereas general industrial areas were attacked as targets of opportunity.

Adverse weather conditions over Germany were not unforeseen. They were expected. It was impossible for bomber crews to visually sight a military target for more than four or five days a month. Radar bombing was still in its infancy. It could not be counted on to locate specified military targets.

General Spaatz assumed command of the U.S. Strategic Air Forces and General Doolittle replaced Eaker as commander of the Eighth Air Force on 6 January 1944. After a brief transition period, General Eaker flew to Italy and took command of the Mediterranean Allied Air Forces. Arnold insisted that Spaatz and Doolittle conduct ten to fifteen missions a month without regard to weather conditions. In order to comply with this directive, they were obliged to schedule missions when there was a strong possibility that cloud cover would make it impossible to sight the targets visually.

Inevitably, bombing through clouds resulted in "collateral damage" to urban areas and an increase in civilian casualties. Spaatz and

Doolittle made another change. Eaker had instructed his fighter commanders that their first duty was to protect the bombers. The P-51 fighter pilots were no longer restricted to flying close escort for the bombers. They were instructed to seek out German fighters wherever they might be. They knew that the Nazi leaders would make every effort to stop us from bombing their cities in daylight. The bombers soon became the bait for luring up German fighters. While our bombers were hitting German airframe and aircraft engine factories, the fighters were destroying them in air battles and strafing them on the ground.

The air battle over Germany became a life and death struggle for air supremacy. Hitler had abandoned his invasion plans when he lost the Battle of Britain. Without air supremacy, an invasion of the continent by the Allies might not succeed. Arnold told Spaatz that Churchill had persuaded President Roosevelt to modify his earlier opposition to the area bombing of cities, and they were now authorized to do whatever was necessary to destroy German military production and the will of the German people to continue the war.

These new tactics did not reach full stride until February. With 750 bombers and P-51 support, the Eighth Air Force and the RAF planned a joint offensive called "Big Week." They launched six massive assaults on German cities between 20 and 25 February 1944. In that one week, the VIII Bomber Command dropped as many bombs as it had during the previous year. The losses were still heavy: the Eighth Air Force lost 226 bombers and twenty-eight fighters—6.6 percent of the attacking force. German fighter losses were also severe. The tide of the war was turning. The Germans were losing the battle of attrition.

Moreover, while the Americans were at last winning the daylight air war with larger forces and fighter support from the P-51, the RAF was losing its battle at night. The German night fighters, using vastly improved air-to-air radar systems, were able to inflict losses even greater than those suffered by the Eighth. On 8 March the RAF lost ninety-six bombers during a raid on Nuremberg. By the spring of 1944, the Eighth Air Force was dropping more bombs with a lower percentage of losses than the RAF.

As the tempo of Allied air missions increased over Germany, the cities began to suffer the same hardships the Germans had inflicted on the citizens of Warsaw, Rotterdam, London, and Coventry.

Shortly after the Big Week attacks, the war was finally brought to Berlin, the most important target in Germany. It was the administrative and communication center of the entire German war effort. In early March 1944, LeMay's division led a series of massive assaults on the German capital. Cloud cover made accurate visual bombing impossible on the first two missions, and no military targets were hit. Substantial damage was inflicted on 6 March, but it cost sixty-nine bombers and eleven fighters. Yet the loss of seven hundred airmen was a smaller percentage than our crews had suffered at Ploesti and Schweinfurt. However, that was hardly a consolation to the crews. My cousin Keith was a ball-turret gunner on the 6 March mission. His aircraft carried twelve five-hundred-pound bombs, three in each of its four racks. When they were released over the target, one became wedged in the bomb bay. Knowing the unreleased bomb was armed and could cause an explosion that would obliterate the plane, the radio operator yelled over the interphone, "We've had it. We'll have to bail out!"

Keith said that he would attempt to disarm the bomb and kick it free. He disconnected his oxygen mask, climbed out of his turret, and made his way to the bomb bay, where he bent down on the narrow catwalk between the racks and tried to disarm the fuse. His bulky parachute was in the way, so he removed it and stood there without oxygen, with nothing but twenty-five thousand feet of open space below him, as he disarmed the bomb. Then came the hard part: How would he dislodge it so it could fall free? He inched along the narrow catwalk and after several strong kicks knocked it loose. His mission complete, he clambered over to the open door into the radio room. He had been without oxygen for several minutes, and the radio operator hooked him up to a walk-around oxygen bottle, saving him from passing out and possibly falling out of the open bomb bay. Keith was awarded the Distinguished Flying Cross for his bravery.

Bomber losses continued to be heavy until May 1944, a few weeks before the Normandy invasion. The Eighth Air Force had gained air supremacy in the nick of time. They were almost bombing at will, sending more than seven hundred bombers over Germany on each mission. The attrition campaign had succeeded. The Germans had lost 50 percent of their fighter pilots, and they no longer posed a serious threat to the bombers or the invading ground forces.

Arnold was more impressed than ever by LeMay's combat leadership. In March 1944, he recommended LeMay for promotion to major general, making him one of the youngest to achieve that rank in U.S. military history. Although LeMay was three years younger than Hansell, he now outranked him. Arnold also recommended LeMay for the Distinguished Service Cross for his personal leadership of the Schweinfurt-Regensburg mission. The British awarded him the RAF's Distinguished Flying Cross.

By May, Arnold felt that Hansell and LeMay were ready and able to lead the B-29 campaign in the Pacific. LeMay received orders reassigning him to the CBI in early June. Before leaving Europe, however, he wanted to learn about the problems of ground warfare. He borrowed a P-47 from VIII Fighter Command and flew it to Normandy, where he landed in a barrage of enemy ground fire. It was an important lesson. He was determined to make the B-29 bombing program successful over Japan so that an invasion of the home islands would be unnecessary.

13: Reflections at Sea

I left England shortly after the massive Big Week attacks on Germany in late February 1944. I felt confident that the tide of the air war was at last turning. I was told that I would probably be assigned as an instructor for radar navigator-bombardiers in the B-29 program. As I said good-bye to Hansell in October, I didn't know that I would again be working for both him and LeMay in the Pacific.

Combat troops returning to the States for reassignment were given the option of flying home or going on a troopship sailing to New York to pick up ground troops for the forthcoming invasion. Never having been on an ocean liner, I chose to go by sea. I boarded the *Mauritania*, a pre–World War I ocean liner and sister ship of the famed *Lusitania*, which had been sunk by submarines off the coast of Ireland in 1916, an act that helped draw America into that conflict. The ship had no real defense against German submarines, and we had no naval escort.

In an effort to avoid submarines, the captain planned a route that would take us north of England to the coast of Iceland and Greenland, and then south and east of Newfoundland. We sailed north in an arctic snowstorm, with huge waves breaking over the bow. Visibility was limited. As we plowed through the heavy winter seas at full speed, I asked the British captain if we were in any danger of a collision with an iceberg. We were traveling at a speed of twenty knots, and I thought about the *Titanic* and its collision with an iceberg off the Grand Banks of Newfoundland while traveling at a similar speed. The captain agreed that the speed was dangerous, but said that we would have to take our chances as the submarines were more of a threat than icebergs. I wondered if I had made a mistake by choosing a sea voyage.

I told the captain I was a celestial navigator. He was still using an ancient British sextant. I asked him if he would join me in a contest to locate our position. He looked at my sextant and ordered me off the bridge. He said he didn't have time for games.

The passage took five days, and I spent many hours on deck looking out at the open sea, reflecting on my last two and a half years. I was a different person than the young law student who joined the Air Corps on 8 December 1941. I thought about a classmate who had told me I was a sucker to volunteer. I didn't regret my decision. He probably would not have understood the motives of our aircrews.

Almost all of my comrades who flew with our group across the North Atlantic were either dead, wounded, or prisoners of war. While I was flying and planning missions, I attempted to avoid thinking about our losses. Now I wondered how and why I had survived and if some of the losses of my friends could have reasonably been prevented.

After the war, General Eaker interviewed Albert Speer, Hitler's war production and armaments chief, while he was in prison. Speer asked him why he didn't defer the missions to Schweinfurt until he had sufficient bombers to inflict meaningful damage. Eaker replied that the missions were necessary to prove to the American public and the joint chiefs that daylight bombing was feasible and productive. The missions failed on both counts. No air force could continue with the losses we suffered in 1943. Our crews were sacrificed for an unproven theory. The Eighth Air Force had to return to Schweinfurt six times before it was no longer producing ball bearings.

I thought about my experiences working for Hansell and LeMay. I respected and admired them both. Hansell was a true intellectual, but it was apparent that he was not comfortable at our wing and division meetings. His approach to the problems of combat leadership was vastly different than LeMay's. LeMay accepted confrontation with group commanders as part of the territory. He analyzed every combat problem as an engineer. He considered every combat mission as if it were an engine with component parts, which had to mesh and interact perfectly. LeMay not only analyzed the performance of our crewmembers, the aircraft, and engines, but he studied the bombsights, armament, bomb trajectories, and bomb characteristics. He attempted to balance the cost and calculate the price of each mission. Those of us who flew with him knew that his rigid discipline and rigorous training program saved many lives.

I thought about how close we had come to giving up daylight bombing in the fall of 1943. I had a chance to discuss our failures in Europe with Hansell when we were on Saipan in 1944. We were waiting in the operations room for radio reports of a mission to Tokyo and he brought up the losses the 305th Group suffered at Schweinfurt.

"Ralph, that must have been a tough time for you in the 305th," he said. "I will never understand why someone on our planning committee didn't think of providing belly tanks for our fighters. It was luck, not planning, that gave us the P-51. We made some mistakes in planning those missions in 1943, but the experience laid the groundwork for the later success of the Eighth Air Force. If the groups and the 73d Wing will cooperate, we can duplicate the Eighth's success over Japan."

I thought about the future. It was the spring of 1944 and I was returning home for a brief interlude. The idea of a future life as a civilian didn't enter my head. I wondered how long the war would last. I didn't think in terms of months. I was certain it would be a long time before I could consider civilian life.

I enjoyed working for Hansell and LeMay. They both had suggested that I might be working for them in the B-29 program. Could I refuse if they asked me to use what I had learned for the benefit of new and untried people in the Pacific? I didn't think so. I owed too much to the friends I had lost over Germany.

I enlisted on 8 December 1941 because of the Japanese attack on Pearl Harbor. I didn't realize then that I would be obliged to fight in two wars, one in Europe and a second in the Pacific. I looked across the horizon to the west. In the distance I could see the tall spires of New York. I strained to see the Statue of Liberty. I understood how hopeful our precursors must have felt as they entered New York Harbor. Unlike them, I knew I would not be staying long.

When the *Mauritania* docked at the Brooklyn Navy Yard I was surprised to see a welcoming committee of military and civilian officials and a band. We were the first air force combat veterans to return home. As the senior officer of the troops about to disembark, I started to walk down the gangplank in the rain. I was wearing no rank insignia on my raincoat. An army captain approached me and ordered me to step aside. He said he was there to greet the commanding officer of the returning veterans.

"You're talking to him," I replied.

After a few words from the welcoming committee, I was approached by a civilian who identified himself as Austin Lake, a reporter for the Hearst newspaper in Boston. He questioned me about my future plans.

I told him that I hoped to spend some time with my family in the Boston area. After that it was up to the air force.

"Will you be going to the Pacific?" he inquired.

I told him I didn't know. That was classified information.

"We heard your broadcast from London last Christmas," he replied. "It sounded as if you expect to go out to the Pacific and bomb Japan with our new B-29 bomber."

I told him I couldn't discuss that.

He scowled and said, "If you aren't going to cooperate, I won't mention your name in the story I'm writing."

I turned to leave and said, "You do your job and I'll do mine."

All of us but the New York residents were transported by army vehicles to Grand Central Station. I took a train and was greeted by my parents at Boston's South Station. The next day the neighbors gave me a welcome home party. After most of the visitors had departed, members of the Jewish family that lived across the street asked me why we didn't bomb the crematoria and the railroad lines leading to the concentration camps in eastern Germany and Poland. I told them that I didn't know anything about the camps, and that they were never mentioned during our mission planning meetings. Moreover, the concentration camps were not military targets. Hitler would have been delighted if we had bombed them. We couldn't order crews to bomb the camps, knowing that it would kill many Jewish prisoners.

The air force's public relations officers had misled the American people. They claimed that we could drop our bombs in a pickle barrel from twenty thousand feet. Unfortunately, it wasn't true. If 5 percent of our bombs landed within a thousand feet of a target the mission was considered successful. The Germans did a remarkable job of repairing and rebuilding targets we bombed. Railroad tracks and marshalling yards were usually repaired within a matter of hours. During my tour of duty, the Eighth Air Force flew fifteen missions into central Germany. All of our missions were flown without fighter escort. On three occasions we lost sixty bombers. On one mission, my group lost all but two planes. When I left the 305th in October 1943, I was one of two survivors of the original group that had arrived in England in 1942.

After a short leave, I reported for duty as a radar navigator-bombardier at Salina, Kansas. I was about to become involved in a different war under vastly different conditions under the command of both Hansell and LeMay.

Part 2: The Air War Against Japan

14: General Arnold's $3 Billion Gamble

The B-29 was designed in 1940 by the Boeing Company as a larger and much improved version of their B-17. Boeing called it the "Superfortress. It weighed 140,000 pounds and was considered to be the Cadillac of World War II heavy bombers. Its many innovations included pressurized crew areas, improved radar, and a centralized, remotely controlled gun turret system. It could carry seventeen thousand pounds of bombs, almost three times the capacity of the B-17, and its ability to fly much longer distances at higher speeds and altitudes was thought to make it invulnerable to enemy fighters. It was never used against the Germans. Its complex innovations caused substantial production delays, and by the time it became available the air war in Europe was well in hand. The decision was made to send all B-29s to the Pacific, where its great range could be exploited. In its first operations against the Japanese it proved to be a design engineer's dream and a combat crew's nightmare.

The first B-29 prototype was flown in September 1942, and Brig. Gen. Kenneth B. Wolfe of the Wright Field Materiel Command supervised its technical development. General Arnold was confident that the air force at last had a heavy bomber that could achieve victory over Japan without the necessity of an invasion. He made extravagant promises to President Roosevelt and the Joint Chiefs of Staff about its capability.

The first production B-29s flew in June 1943 and the plans to use them in combat were developed at the Allies' Cairo conference in November. Hansell accompanied Arnold to Cairo. At the conference, Chiang Kai-shek complained to Roosevelt that the Americans had given him inadequate combat support against the Japanese. Chiang said that it was time for the Americans to make a tangible demonstration of their commitment. The president asked Arnold to develop a plan for bombing Japanese targets from China with the B-29. Arnold assigned the task to Hansell, who suggested that B-29s first be based in the vicinity of Calcutta, India. Advanced bases could then be built in the Chengtu area in western China, where they would be within range of targets in Manchuria and southern Japan. There were no land routes from India to China, so it would be necessary to fly all of their supplies over the Himalayas. Routine maintenance would be performed at the bases in India. Hansell recommended this India-China operation as a stopgap measure until air bases were captured closer to Japan.

Arnold doubted the logistical feasibility of basing B-29s in China, but Roosevelt and Churchill overruled him. They believed that even a partial effort would assist the Nationalists in the war against both Japan and Mao Tse-tung's communists. Churchill said the British would build B-29 bases in India, if Chiang would build the bases in the Chengtu. The president then told Arnold that he expected the B-29s to be available by January 1944. Arnold replied that neither the crews nor the aircraft could be ready to fly to India before the end of March, which provoked an angry response from the president, who said that the Nationalists were close to abandoning their defense of western China and couldn't wait that long. Arnold, knowing how disappointed Roosevelt had been with the Eighth Air Force's recent operations in Europe, was anxious to avoid disappointing the president again in the Pacific. Although he knew it would be many months before the B-29s would be ready for combat, he felt he had to agree to the January deadline. The cost of the B-29 program was approaching $3 billion, making it the most expensive war production project America had ever undertaken.

At the end of January 1944, the president called Arnold into the oval office and told him that the British bases were ready in India and that B-29s should be there within the next two weeks. Arnold was concerned. He knew that the crews and the B-29 were still not ready for combat. He decided to make a personal inspection of B-29 operations at Smoky Hill Field in Salina, Kansas. He would take Hansell with him. He knew he could relax with "Possum" along because he usually came up with a solution.

When Arnold and Hansell arrived in Kansas they were appalled at the mismanagement and lack of leadership of B-29 operations. Only four B-29s could fly. General Wolfe informed them that he had other B-29s on the base at Salina, but there were no parts available for maintenance and repair. Arnold lost his temper. If Wolfe was having trouble getting parts in the United States, how could he expect to operate in India and China? He ordered Wolfe to give him a written report concerning the missing parts by the following morning.

Hansell was worried about the future of the B-29 program and Arnold's health. He had never seen Arnold so out of control. On the way back to Washington he suggested that it was impossible for Arnold to control B-29 operations with the existing chain of command. He said that the joint chiefs would use any delay as an excuse to gut the entire B-29 program. There was only one way to prevent that: convince General Marshall to allow Arnold to report directly to the joint chiefs. That would prevent General MacArthur and Admiral Nimitz from exercising control of B-29 operations and using them to support their tactical operations in the Pacific.

Hansell offered to serve as chief of staff of a separate B-29 air force and administer the program under Arnold's direct supervision. He suggested that, inasmuch as the B-29 was not yet ready for combat, Wolfe should be the first commander of B-29s in China. He had been working with the development and production of the B-29 since 1940 and knew its mechanical problems better than anyone. After a few shakedown missions, if things didn't work out, Wolfe could be replaced by LeMay. Next to Wolfe, he was the most knowledgeable and the best technical man they had. He was the ideal man to operate out of those isolated bases in China.

Arnold relaxed. Hansell's plan would relieve some of the personal pressures on him. He told him he would discuss the matter with General Marshall. In the meantime, he ordered Hansell to investigate the entire B-29 program and attempt to determine if the aircraft had any serious design problems, or if the mechanical problems could be cured by improved production procedures.

Hansell first questioned Wolfe about the cause of the mechanical problems and production delays. Wolfe said that Sen. Harry Truman was chairman of a congressional committee investigating B-29 production problems. As he listened to Wolfe's explanation, Hansell couldn't understand how manufacturers and air force inspectors would intentionally risk the lives of airmen. He decided that it was better to leave that problem to the Truman Committee. If possible, he would limit his supervision to B-29 training and operations. The glare of publicity from the hearings might prevent further misconduct or gross negligence in the production of the big bomber's engines.

Wright Aeronautical produced the first B-29 engines in 1941. In the spring of 1943 the extensive production and mechanical problems of the aircraft and its RB-3350 engine came to public attention in testimony before Truman's Special Committee to Investigate the National Defense Program. The committee's investigation was triggered by the multibillion-dollar cost of the B-29 and its engines. The committee wanted to know why the B-29s and their engines were so expensive and had so many mechanical problems. Several crews had been lost in training accidents caused by a loss of engine power.

Truman was concerned that manufacturers were exploiting the combat needs of the troops at the expense of quality. Military contracts were usually fixed-price or cost-plus contracts. Each type had features enabling unscrupulous contractors to take advantage of the universal belief that no expense should be spared in the production of war equipment and supplies. Truman, remembering his experiences in World War I, was determined that the troops and airmen risking their lives in combat should have the best equipment available.

He subpoenaed company officials and air force inspectors to testify. The airmen informed the committee that several hundred engines had been condemned as defective. Wright officials countered that the speeded-up production schedule they were required to meet did not permit normal inspection procedures. The problems of B-29 production soon became a nationwide controversy, and Wright Aeronautical purchased newspaper advertisements condemning the Truman Committee hearings.

Hansell was aghast at this unfavorable publicity. He was concerned that the entire campaign for bombing Japan could be in jeopardy. The most knowledgeable and experienced engineering officers in the B-29 program were General Wolfe and Col. Clarence Irvine. They informed Hansell that they were confident that the Truman

Committee hearings would improve the inspection procedures for the B-29 engines. But that took care of only part of the problem. The B-29s incorporated many other novel improvements that had not been adequately tested or corrected before Hansell and LeMay were obliged to send their crews over Japan.

After returning from England in the winter of 1944, I was assigned to the B-29 base at Salina and began training as a radar navigator-bombardier.

Salina is in the center of Kansas wheat country. In April, the vast wheat fields were green and beautiful. My wife and I arrived from Boston on a cool spring day in a setting quite unlike the one that had greeted me in the Muroc desert in 1942. As we drove past the airfield I saw my first B-29. It was the most impressive and largest aircraft I had ever seen. At lunch I met some men assigned to the 58th Bomb Wing who were about to leave for India and China. I told them I was anxious to make my first flight in a B-29.

Their comments did not inspire confidence: "The B-29 is not the reliable B-17 you flew in Europe. . . . The name 'Superfortress' is for public relations purposes only. . . . Don't push your luck. . . . The B-29 can be your funeral pyre. . . . These are 'The Killing Fields' of Kansas. . . . The B-29 has more bugs than an African anthill. . . . The pressure system is a joke. We lost one of our gunners when the system blew out. His blister popped off and he was sucked out without a parachute. The same thing could happen to you. . . . You'd better hitch yourself to the gun turret before you take any celestial shots in the astrodome. You should also attach your oxygen mask to your helmet and be ready to use it at high altitude if the pressure system fails. . . . We call the engine 'the Beast.' . . . A takeoff is considered a success if an engine doesn't catch fire. . . . There are so many crashes on takeoff that Kansas farmers should pay the air force for spring plowing. . . . You can see the burned areas in the wheat fields where a B-29 lost power on takeoff and crashed. There have been nineteen incidents where a B-29 engine has failed on takeoff. . . . You'd have been safer if you'd stayed in England."

The 58th Wing had only four operational aircraft for training. The others had been grounded for repairs or sent back to the Wichita factory for modification. It was almost impossible for the crews to train or be checked out in a B-29. Most of the training was in B-17s.

When I asked if navigators were being trained for navigation over water I was told that the only water they had seen was the Mississippi and Missouri Rivers and the Gulf of Mexico between Florida and Cuba.

This greeting was hardly the welcome to B-29s I had expected. The situation at Salina was a repeat of our nonexistent training at Muroc in 1942. There were no living quarters on base available for married officers. After searching for several days, my wife and I finally rented a room in a converted county poor farm. It was an ancient brick building surrounded by miles of wheat fields.

The following day I began my training in radar navigation and bombing, beginning with a new, advanced radar set. Within a week I was making practice bomb runs in a B-17 on targets in Wichita, Kansas City, and St. Louis. I learned to pick up rivers and dock areas on the Mississippi River. The land-water contrast on the Japanese coast would be a great help in locating targets that could not be visually sighted with our Norden bombsight.

We never had enough B-29s for practicing the three-thousand-mile roundtrip flights we would be making in the Pacific. A few crews were scheduled for training missions from Salina to Cuba and return, but these usually ended with B-29s scattered all over the southeastern United States after experiencing engine and fuel shortage problems. The B-29's engine and other mechanical apparatus never improved while I was at Salina. They continued until LeMay mandated modifications and set up an entirely new system of maintenance in China.

Hansell visited Salina shortly after he was appointed chief of staff of the Twentieth Air Force. I told him the sad stories I had heard about the B-29's mechanical problems and the lack of training for the crews. He was reluctant to tell Arnold that he and LeMay were concerned about sending crews into combat before the mechanical problems had at least been partially rectified and the crews given more time to train. When he finally suggested a delay of a few weeks, Arnold replied that he had made commitments to the president, Churchill, and Chiang Kai-shek. Ready or not, the 58th Wing would have to go to India and China.

The B-29 campaign was not off to a good start, and things would get worse before they got better. The first two B-29s flew the "Hump" route over the Himalayas from India to China on 24 April 1944. The flight over the world's highest mountains added to the crews' problems. The weather was bad with high winds, and there was almost no maintenance support at the bases in Chengtu. Flight engineers and ground maintenance crews had to perform all repairs and maintenance.

Wolfe asked Hansell for permission to fly his first combat missions singly, at night, at low altitude. He told Hansell that the climb to high altitude in formation imposed an additional strain on the engines. Hansell replied that it was air force policy to bomb in formation during daylight at high altitude and that he expected Wolfe to comply with that policy.

15: Hansell and LeMay Lead the B-29s

Arnold evaded the Truman Committee hearings throughout the summer of 1943. He was anxious to avoid questions about the deficiencies of the B-29s and possible misconduct by air force inspectors. He knew that the president and General Marshall could not have been pleased about the testimony and unfavorable publicity coming from the hearings, and he was concerned that they would blame him for the mismanagement of the B-29 production program. They had both supported the multibillion-dollar B-29 budget over the strong opposition of the army and navy. They had relied on his representation that the B-29s could achieve victory over Japan without the necessity of invasion.

Arnold believed that the B-29 was his last opportunity to prove that victory could be achieved through strategic airpower, without an invasion by ground troops. If it should fail, Arnold knew he would be forced into early retirement.

General Marshall agreed to support Hansell's plan to put B-29 operations under the operational control of the joint chiefs with Arnold serving as the nominal commander. He did not have the time or the energy to manage the production or the operation of B-29 combat units. He would have to rely on Hansell and Wolfe, although he had questions about Wolfe's ability as a combat commander. Nevertheless, he felt compelled to use him in China because of his role in developing the B-29. If Wolfe proved unequal to the task of combat command in China, Arnold could replace him with LeMay.

Arnold believed that LeMay and Hansell would make a good team in the Pacific. They had worked well together in England. He knew that Hansell had limited experience as a combat commander, serving only a few months in that capacity before Eaker had removed him. Eaker had replaced him because he considered him to be too high-strung. Arnold hadn't noticed that trait while Hansell had been on his staff, but he knew he had no problems dealing with the joint chiefs and the RAF. If Hansell could get along with Admiral King, he could work with anyone.

Hansell had been invaluable at the Cairo Conference in November. He had come up with the plan for basing the B-29s in China, thus getting the president off the hook with the Chinese. The army and navy trusted him. He had even persuaded the navy to allow the air force to use the Mariana Islands as bases for the B-29s, rather than wait for the capture of Formosa and the Philippines. He felt he owed it to Hansell to give him a chance to command the most important air force combat unit of the war. His biggest test would be dealing with Wolfe and Rosie O'Donnell as wing commanders. He would have to convince them both that it was practical to bomb visually in daylight at high altitude.

The 58th Bomb Wing arrived in India in mid-May 1944, but the aircraft continued to be plagued with engine problems. Wolfe began bombing Japanese targets in Manchuria and southwest Asia in early June. He hit his first target in Japan—Yawata, located on Kyushu, the most southerly of the home islands—on the fourteenth. Only sixty-five bombers made it to the cloud-covered target area. Fifteen planes attempted visual bombing, and the remainder bombed through the clouds with the assistance of radar. Seven planes were lost but only one because of enemy action. The others had mechanical problems. The damage to the target was minimal.

Although Arnold's staff issued a glowing press release stating that the first B-29 mission to the Japan homeland was "the start of global warfare, which would end the war," Arnold did not conceal his displeasure with Wolfe. He was impatient for immediate results. He called Wolfe's combat leadership amateurish and made no allowances for the immense logistical task of flying all the fuel, bombs, ammunition, and other supplies a thousand miles over the Himalayas from India. After the Yawata mission, Wolfe could not schedule another mission to Japan until supplies could be transported from India by the same aircraft that had flown the mission to Japan.

Arnold would accept no excuses from Wolfe. He asked Hansell his opinion of Wolfe as a combat commander. Hansell was in a difficult position. Six months earlier, Arnold had asked him the same question about General Eaker's Eighth Air Force. Hansell told Arnold that Wolfe was trying to avoid high-altitude formation bombing in daylight because he believed the crews should bomb individually at night until they were better trained and had eliminated the B-29's mechanical problems.

After only three weeks of combat operations against Japanese targets, Arnold decided to replace Wolfe with LeMay. He would let Hansell give Wolfe the unpleasant news. On 5 July, Hansell ordered Wolfe to return to Washington. He asked LeMay to attend the meeting with Wolfe. It foreshadowed a later meeting involving Hansell and LeMay in January 1945. Hansell told Wolfe it appeared that he did not believe in high-altitude, precision, daylight bombing. In his defense, Wolfe described the problems he had encountered in China: the engines continued to overheat; there were repeated oil leaks and fuel problems; the pressurization system was not reliable; and the crews simply weren't ready to fly in formation at high altitude on daylight missions.

When he completed his tale of woe, Wolfe turned to LeMay and told him that the conditions in China were impossible. He would be pleased to return to his old job at the materiel command.

LeMay didn't reply.

Hansell thanked Wolfe for making a conscientious effort and informed him that he would receive a second star when he returned to Wright Field.

In August 1944, Col. Emmett "Rosie" O'Donnell arrived at Salina to assume command of the 73d Bomb Wing. O'Donnell encountered the same mechanical problems that had plagued Wolfe. He didn't have sufficient aircraft to practice daylight formation flying. Only a few crews were able to fly practice missions to Cuba, and the short overwater flight involved was not adequate for training navigators for the much longer flights they would encounter in the Pacific. He also instructed his crews to practice low-altitude night missions and use radar to locate targets. He told Hansell that he would avoid high-altitude daylight missions until the crews were properly trained and the mechanical problems had been eliminated. Hansell was upset. He ordered O'Donnell to cease training for night operations and reminded him that Wolfe had been replaced for doing the same thing.

Hansell did not concur in Arnold's selection of O'Donnell to be commander of the 73d Wing. He had not forgotten O'Donnell's scathing criticism of the plan to bomb Germany without fighter support. Hansell felt that his remarks had been directed toward him personally. Now, like Wolfe, he was trying to avoid high-altitude daylight bombing, whereas LeMay was loyally trying to make it work in the CBI theater. O'Donnell was going to bomb Hansell's way, or he would get a new commander of the 73d Wing.

I knew nothing of these high-level conflicts—or that I would soon be in the middle of the Hansell-O'Donnell controversy. In the last week of August, I had an unexpected meeting with Hansell. He seemed pleased to see me. He told me that by the end of the summer, when the central Pacific island of Saipan was secure, he would be taking command of the new XXI Bomber Command there. O'Donnell would operate out of Saipan as commander of the 73d Wing, and eventually there would be other wings on Tinian and Guam.

"I'd like you to come with me to the Marianas as XXI Bomber Command navigator," he said. "I'm sure you know that LeMay is commander of the B-29s in China. I want some Eighth Air Force veterans in my command. We plan to commence daylight bombing of Japan from Saipan by early November. The 73d Wing has been training for night operations. You can help by training them in high-altitude daylight bombing procedures. I know you flew more combat missions than were required in Europe. This is not an order but a request that you come and help me and the young crews of the 73d Wing. Those of us who survived those first missions over Germany have a duty to prevent a repetition of similar losses over Japan. We know that navigation over the Pacific to Japan from the Marianas is going to be tough. You worked for LeMay in developing lead crew schools and made navigators out of bombardiers. They tell me that you are now a rated radar navigator-bombardier. Will you join me?"

Later, when I was being strafed by kamikazes on Saipan, washing my clothes in a helmet, fighting off flies, and taking cold showers with seawater, I had second thoughts about my decision to go to the Pacific. But at that moment, I didn't know how I could refuse Hansell's request. I was already becoming bored with the training routine at Salina. I liked Hansell personally and was confident that I could work for him. Finally, I thought about that second Schweinfurt mission and the losses of our group that day. I had somehow survived a combat tour over Germany. I had an obligation to my lost friends in the 305th and these new, untrained crews. They would learn about combat soon enough. Perhaps I could help them get through some of the rough times.

I thought about another tour in a combat zone. It had been more than six months since my last combat mission over Germany. I was rested. How could I refuse Hansell? Untrained crews were going to need all the help they could get flying the new and unpredictable B-29s from Saipan to Japan. I told him that I felt honored by his request that I accompany him.

Hansell's headquarters was in Colorado Springs. I had never been there or had the opportunity to spend time in the Rocky Mountains. Perhaps my wife and I would get a chance to climb Pike's Peak. I didn't look forward to spending the remainder of the war as an instructor in Salina. Long overwater missions in the Pacific would be a challenge for navigators. I had used celestial navigation on only three occasions since navigation school: the flight across the North Atlantic, the night mission to Munich, and the trip to Gibraltar with General Eaker. I knew that if a navigator were not proficient in celestial navigation he and his crew would wind up in the Pacific.

I wasn't scheduled to join Hansell until early September. During the first week in August, we were still flying practice missions in B-17s from Salina, encountering serious thunderstorms in eastern Missouri. I was about to report the weather conditions to Tom Bowman, our weather officer, when I saw LeMay studying the local weather map. I had not seen him since the planning meeting for the October 1943 Schweinfurt mission.

He smiled, greeted me warmly, and asked if I was in the 73d Wing.

I told him that I had obtained a radar navigator-bombardier rating and was about to join Hansell's staff at XXI Bomber Command in Colorado Springs.

"Perhaps after a tour in China I'll see you in the Marianas," he replied.

I had learned about the problems that Wolfe and the 58th Wing were encountering in India and China. I felt that if anyone could solve those problems, it would be LeMay.

He remained in Salina for a few more days and I saw him again at the flight line, where he told me he was waiting for repairs and modifications to the engines of his B-29 so he could fly direct to India. A few days later I saw him in the mess hall. He told me that he couldn't wait any longer and that he was going to catch a flight to India with the Air Transport Command.

He arrived at the B-29 base in Kharagpur, India, a short distance from Calcutta on 29 August and was shocked to learn that the 58th Wing crews were unacquainted with the rudiments of formation flying and high-altitude precision daylight bombing.

He flew to Chengtu and led the crews of the 58th Wing in a formation similar to the one he had pioneered with our 305th Group in England. He then had a meeting of his group and squadron commanders. He told them they were going to start flying their missions in formation and that there would be no evasive action on bomb runs. It was on-the-job training similar to the program he had put us through in 1942.

He scheduled a mission to the Anshan Steel Works in Manchuria for 8 September.

A total of 109 planes took off, with LeMay flying as an observer in the lead aircraft. His plane was hit by flak as it started the bomb run. A gunner was wounded and called for assistance. LeMay replied that he would give him first aid later. After the bomb run, LeMay crawled back through the pressurized tunnel over the bomb bay and treated the gunner's wounds. The bomb results were good. The coke ovens of the Japanese steel mills were heavily damaged, cutting production by at least 35 percent. LeMay had made a good start with the B-29s. The crews no longer criticized him as a "hotshot" from the Eighth Air Force. They recognized him as a true combat leader.

During the Anshan mission, LeMay had observed aggressive attacks on the formation by Japanese fighters. He changed the formation to the twelve-plane unit we had used over Germany. On 26 September the 58th Wing returned to Anshan. The entire area was covered with clouds. The crews used radar to drop the bombs through the overcast, but this time the results were unsatisfactory.

The B-29s could not carry a full bomb load on missions. They were required to limit the gross weight of bombs in order to carry extra fuel. LeMay realized that he had to change the maintenance procedures if he were going to get enough bombers over the targets to inflict meaningful damage. He decided to employ the same maintenance procedures he had used in England. The weather remained a substantial problem, however. He was concerned that he had no reliable information on weather conditions to and from Japanese targets when he briefed the crews.

Although the Soviets claimed to be our ally, they refused to provide weather information available on the Asian continent or on the Soviet coastal centers opposite Japan. LeMay was also concerned about the safety of crews forced to land in communist-controlled China on their return from a mission. He didn't expect any assistance from the Nationalists because Chiang Kai-shek and his cronies were both unreliable and corrupt.

Although LeMay was a staunch conservative, he was not unwilling to seek assistance from the Chinese communists. His first duty was to assist and protect his combat crews. Although his staff was pessimistic, he said he would deal with the devil if it would help win the war. He decided to take a chance and ask Mao Tse-tung, the communist commander, for assistance. He sent a C-47 transport loaded with radio equipment to Mao's headquarters in Yenan. In response, Mao agreed to help whenever one of LeMay's crews landed in territory controlled by Mao's forces.

LeMay decided to make a second approach to the communists. He sent another C-47 loaded with medical supplies, including the new sulfa drugs. Medical supplies would assist wounded B-29 crewmembers as well as the communists. Mao and his doctors were astonished. He sent LeMay a captured samurai sword. When LeMay reciprocated with a pair of binoculars, Mao allowed him to set up a radio outpost at Yenan to provide regular weather reports and report to him about rescue possibilities for downed B-29 crews.

On 25 October, LeMay ordered a mission on an aircraft plant in Omura on Kyushu. The crews used incendiary bombs for the first time with a ratio of two high-explosive bombs for every incendiary. They returned on 11 November but encountered extensive cloud cover in the target area. Only twenty-nine aircraft were able to bomb Kyushu. The rest of the group hit Nanking, the designated target of opportunity. On 21 November they again hit the Omura aircraft plant. Six planes out of 109 were lost, and the heavy cloud cover forced most of the bombers to use radar. They achieved only moderate results.

The B-29s hit Mukden on 7 December. There they encountered eighty-five Japanese fighters. The Japanese tried a new tactic: they attempted air-to-air bombing, dropping phosphorous bombs containing time fuses designed to explode in the formation.

On 18 December LeMay conducted what proved to be his most important mission in the CBI. The target was Hankow, on the Yangtze River, one of the largest Japanese military bases in China. Major Generals Claire Chennault and Albert Wedemeyer urged LeMay to bomb Hankow with incendiaries, and lower the bombing altitude to less than twenty thousand feet to ensure accuracy. LeMay was concerned. B-29s were not supposed to bomb from less than twenty-five thousand. He finally agreed to an altitude of nineteen thousand feet and to replace four-fifths of the bomb load with incendiaries. Eighty-four B-29s dropped five hundred tons of incendiaries on Hankow, setting huge fires along the waterfront that burned for three days.

It was the first time U.S. bombers relied almost entirely on incendiaries, and LeMay was impressed with the results. Moreover, the B-29s experienced fewer engine problems at lower altitudes.

LeMay reported that the docks burned brilliantly and sent photos of the devastation to Arnold's staff in Washington and to Hansell on Saipan. Arnold was impressed. The Hankow incendiary mission was a harbinger of the massive firebomb attacks on the Japanese home islands starting in March from the Marianas.

The success of the mission did not change LeMay's opinion that B-29 operations in China were a waste of resources, and he recommended to Arnold that his units in China be transferred to the Marianas. Yet the China operations were not a total loss: LeMay and his crews had learned the positive and negative characteristics of the B-29 as a combat aircraft, and they had learned how to combat Japanese fighters. The lessons were invaluable when he began bombing from the Marianas. He didn't know it, but LeMay was about to be given the most important air force command of World War II.

16: The Battle of Culver City

I n the second week of September 1944 I was ordered to report to General Hansell's headquarters.

"I have an unusual assignment for you, Ralph," he said. "You're going to a movie studio in Hollywood. The army motion picture unit has taken over the Hal Roach studios in Culver City. The air force calls the motion-picture unit Fort Roach, and the personnel there are 'celluloid commandos.' They've been making training films, and General Arnold believes they may be able to assist us in making a film to brief the crews for our first mission to Tokyo."

Hansell suggested that we call the film "Target Tokyo."

He said the maps and photos we had of the Tokyo area were out of date and that we had very little intelligence about Japanese industry and other military targets there. The first mission from Saipan would be to hit an important fighter and aircraft factory at Ota, a few miles from Tokyo. The planes would fly at an altitude of approximately thirty thousand feet and avoid the center of Tokyo, where the antiaircraft defenses were expected to be the heaviest. He added that we would not have any accurate weather data.

The studio special-effects people were building a one-hundred-by-one-hundred-foot mock-up of the terrain in the region. A camera mounted on a motorized shooting platform would be used to film the model from a height proportional to our B-29s flying at thirty thousand feet. Hansell instructed me to plan our route from the Japanese coast, through Tokyo Bay, to the initial point of the bombing run, and on to the target at Ota.

Colonel Jack Warner, the commanding officer of the motion-picture unit, was head of the famous Warner Brothers studio. He had taken directors, actors, writers, and cameramen from Warner and arranged for them to be made officers and enlisted men in the army. Most of them were happy to be playing war in Culver City without any interruption of their Hollywood careers.

Hansell told me to draft the script in the same way we had briefed the crews in England. A Warner scriptwriter would assist me, but I would have final approval of the wording. He emphasized that the project was very important to General Arnold. As soon as the film was finished, I was to deliver it personally to him on Saipan.

What a difference two years had made. Hansell's personal pilot flew me to Los Angeles where a driver from the studio met me. I had never been to a motion-picture studio. Apparently no changes had been made except for a sign in front reading, "1st Motion Picture Unit," and some barbed wire in front of the building. I showed the sergeant at the gate my identification, and he took me to a hangar. A sign outside read: "Project 152. Top Secret. Restricted Entry. All others keep out." Inside I was introduced to Colonel Warner, and he and his office personnel greeted me warmly. Apparently I was the first air force combat veteran they had met. I was astonished by the special attention I received.

He took me to the sound stage containing the mock-up of the Tokyo area. The model makers had done a remarkable job. The foundation was made of plaster and chicken wire. Looking through the camera lens I saw a remarkably realistic view of the Japanese coastline. The ocean was blue, Mount Fuji was snow covered, the buildings were gray, and the fields green. I noticed that a large residential area surrounded the Ota aircraft factory. The bombing would have to be accurate if we were to avoid destroying thousands of homes and killing many civilians.

They assigned me an office in the writer's department. At the entrance I saw a sign reading, "The Flying Typers." As I was about to sit down at a desk, Warner entered with a captain he introduced as Ronald Reagan. He was more than six feet tall, slim, broad shouldered, and had a thick thatch of hair. He flashed a warm, friendly smile as Warner explained that Reagan would narrate the script. Reagan said it would be a pleasure to be working with me and asked when I expected the script to be ready and the cameras ready to roll. I told him I had a strict schedule and needed to leave for Saipan with the film within a week. I said I would have a first draft of the script by seven or eight that evening.

After they left, I sat down at my desk and started planning our route. After roughing it out I went to the sound stage and made a few suggestions to the model makers. I worked through dinner, pausing only to down a Coke and a sandwich a sergeant brought me. At 7:30 I decided to make a dry run and synchronize the camera with the script. I walked around the lot looking for Reagan. The sergeant at the gate told me that he always left at 4:30 for his home in the San Fernando Valley. I suggested that he telephone Reagan and order him to return to Culver City immediately. He showed up an hour later, apologized, and said he hoped he hadn't kept us waiting. He told me he had left early because he was bored sitting around with nothing to do. I told him that I was personally responsible for production of the film and that I had to deliver it to Saipan in ten days.

"I understand now," Reagan replied, smiling sheepishly. "I will report to you before leaving in the future."

After making our first dry run over the completed model with Reagan reading the script, I decided that I needed to amplify the instructions to the crews. I told him that I would make the changes in the morning, and we left the studio at 11:30 P.M. Reagan drove me back to my hotel and again apologized for the delay.

As I reviewed the film the next day I attempted to put myself in the position of the navigator and bombardier in the lead plane. What would happen if the target area were partially covered by cloud? What landmarks on the model would be most prominent? Was it realistic to assume that the landmarks could be sighted visually from an altitude of thirty thousand feet?

I looked for rivers leading from Tokyo Bay to Ota. I had used rivers to lead me to targets while flying over Germany. They were easiest to follow. I had to consider the possibility that the entire area would be covered with 100 percent cloud cover. If so, bombardiers would have to locate the target with radar only, and the film would be of no value.

Radar was a poor substitute for visual observation with the Norden bombsight. I hoped that it would be possible to pick up Ota's large aircraft production facilities on the radar screen. Radar was most effective when there was land-water contrast, such as rivers or along a coastline. But Ota was a crowded urban area. It might not be possible to isolate the aircraft factory.

I spent the next day revising the approach from the Japanese coast to Ota. I wasn't ready to begin shooting the film until seven in the evening. I again toured the sound stage in search of Reagan. The sergeant on duty told me that he had again gone home at 4:30. I found it difficult to believe he could have such an offhand, cavalier attitude toward a top-secret war project. It appeared that the war had not changed his priorities. I telephoned his home and told him to return to Culver City without delay. He arrived an hour later. He again smiled sheepishly and repeated his apologies of the night before. This time I didn't return his "aw shucks" smile.

I glowered at him and said, "If you cause any further delay in shooting this film, I may be required to take disciplinary action and replace you with another narrator."

He didn't reply. It was clear that my threat of disciplinary action didn't bother him. I asked one of the writers if Reagan was working on a civilian movie or had some other reason for his lack of interest in the project. I mentioned that Reagan had never inquired about three other members of the motion-picture unit who had been serving in the Eighth Air Force while I was there.

The writer said Reagan was completely self-centered and that he rarely talked about anything that did not involve him personally. Although he was always outwardly congenial and friendly, Reagan had no interest in anything but his acting career. He made no effort to remember the names of people who worked with him. I asked him about Reagan's habit of leaving by 4:30 every afternoon. He said Reagan often joked that hard work never killed anyone, but he didn't want to take a chance. He felt that Fort Roach was the best place to sit out the war and continue his movie career. Reagan claimed he had eye problems that disqualified him for any other duty.

The following is the text of the script I wrote for the Ota mission:

Ota is located on the Tonegawa River, fifty miles northwest of Tokyo. It is the site of Japan's oldest and largest aircraft manufacturing plant. The city also contains several munitions factories. It manufactures some of Japan's best fighters and almost half of all Japanese aircraft engines.

The last landmass between Saipan and Japan is the island of Iwo Jima. We don't know how many Japanese fighters are based there. You're to fly no closer than seventy-five miles to Iwo. It is possible that some of their fighters may be patrolling in the area. Keep a sharp lookout for fighters. From Iwo, it will be three hours over water to the Japanese coast. You should reach your bombing altitude of twenty-nine thousand feet about a hundred miles south of the Japanese coast.

General LeMay tells us that the Japanese fighters have not been effective at that altitude, but it is possible that they may have more lethal fighters in the Tokyo area than at Kyushu. Don't assume that the fighters are going to be ineffective. Once you attain bombing altitude, navigators should identify your position precisely. Unless there is substantial cloud cover, Mount Fuji should be the first land you see in Japan. It will be covered with snow. If the area is completely obscured by cloud, Mount Fuji will probably be the first landmass you can see on your radarscope.

After seven hours of flying, it is possible that you will be as much as thirty miles off course. As you approach Japan, there will be strong crosswinds at higher altitudes. You must make accurate course corrections to the left. These corrections will be based on your own navigation computations should you leave the formation. You cannot rely on the weather briefing's estimation of wind velocities and direction over Japan. They are, at best, educated guesses.

The bombardiers must have accurate wind direction and velocity before they reach the initial point of the bombing run. If there is cloud cover and you haven't been able to make celestial observations, you may be able to make wind computations from your radar and visual landmark identification. If you are at all uncertain about your exact location, Mount Fuji, Tokyo Bay and its peninsula will be prominent features on the radar screen. Don't assume you can visually sight landmarks in the target area. Radar operators and navigators must work together. The navigator must give wind and target information to the bombardier as quickly as possible.

It will be only a matter of minutes from the time you leave Tokyo Bay until you approach the initial point of the bomb run on this peninsula. You should be able to pick it up on your radar screen in case Ota is covered with clouds. It is possible that you will encounter winds of up to two hundred knots at twenty-nine thousand feet. Do not bomb in a crosswind. We have planned a downwind approach to the target. This is for your protection. The fast downwind speed will give you protection from flak and fighters, but it will make locating the target more difficult with the wind behind you.

Your ground speed may be in excess of five hundred miles per hour. This means that the bombardier must locate the target and make his calibration and computations as much as thirty miles away from the target. You cannot take evasive action on the bomb run. The bomb run must be straight and level to give the bombardier a proper platform for releasing the bombs. After you drop your bombs, the lead aircraft will slow down by at least five miles per hour to allow the wing aircraft to remain in formation. We don't have accurate information on the location of the enemy antiaircraft guns.

You can take mild evasive action after you turn off the target. Try to stay in the center of Tokyo Bay as you head south for Saipan. Remember to stay seventy-five miles away from Iwo Jima on the return trip. Japanese fighters may be waiting for you. They will be on notice that you have bombed Tokyo. Gunners must be alert and watching for enemy fighters at all times.

I made similar plans for missions against other major targets in the Tokyo area.

After he narrated the films, Reagan left without comment. I didn't see him again until shortly after he was elected governor of California in 1966. I was the presiding officer at a judges' conference in Los Angeles. As I introduced Reagan to the judges, I could see that he didn't recognize me. I met him again four years later. We exchanged greetings, but I knew he had no recollection of me or anyone else he had worked with at the Culver City motion-picture unit.

I had to wait two days for the film to be processed. When it was finally delivered to me, I said good-bye to my wife and caught a courier plane to Hamilton Field, an air base north of San Francisco. I slept in a locked room at the officers' quarters with the can of film by my pillow. The next evening we took off in a B-29 for Saipan. I sat with the regular crew's navigator and we took turns taking celestial shots of the moon and stars. The weather was perfect, quite unlike my trip across the North Atlantic in a blizzard two years before.

As we approached the island of Oahu in Hawaii, I looked down on Pearl Harbor and Diamond Head. It was a peaceful and idyllic scene. I thought about the Japanese attack almost three years before and found it hard to believe that this was the scene of that disaster, the starting point of nearly four years of war.

We stayed overnight at Hickam Field, but I had no opportunity to visit any of the tourist sights in Honolulu. We took off early the next morning for Johnston Island and then flew to Kwajalein, a small, isolated coral island in the center of the Pacific. Its vegetation had been obliterated in the bitter battle for its capture from the Japanese. It was the most desolate place I had ever seen. I wondered what the base commander had done to deserve being assigned to such an isolated spot. I also had my first experience with the navy at Kwajalein.

I was having lunch at an open-air navy officers' club. The tables were adjacent to a marine mess hall, but they were separated by barbed wire. While we were eating roast beef, the marines were eating beans. I didn't endear myself to the navy. When I saw no naval officer looking in my direction, I passed some roast beef to the marines. A navy officer spotted me, however, and said I was interfering with discipline and morale.

I was happy to leave such a godforsaken place. As soon as we refueled we headed for the Marianas. As we approached Saipan and Tinian, the islands looked as peaceful and quiet as Hawaii. They didn't seem like an appropriate place for launching what were to be the most massive area bombing attacks of the war.

As we began the final descent of our five-thousand-mile flight, I thought about what Hansell had told me regarding his assignment to command the B-29s at Saipan. I knew he considered it to be the culmination of his military career. The evening I left Colorado Springs for Culver City, he had been in an expansive mood. He told me that the Eighth Air Force had not succeeded in bombing Ger-

many in 1943 because it had been obliged to divert planes and resources to support the North African and Mediterranean campaigns.
Nothing like that would happen in the Pacific. The B-29s were under General Arnold's personal control and would operate independent of the army, the navy, and the theater commanders, Nimitz
and MacArthur. They could not divert Hansell's campaign for tactical purposes. He told me that he would assist them in an emergency,
but his focus would be precision daylight attacks on key military targets. He then compared our operations from Saipan with those of
LeMay from western China. He said that both he and Arnold did not
expect anything to come from LeMay's operations. His B-29s had
been placed there solely to mollify Chiang Kai-shek. The success of
our campaign in the Marianas would at last prove that victory could
be achieved with airpower alone.

B-17 turning off target, Lille, France, December 12, 1942.

Return from mission over Bremen, April 17, 1943—some of the men shown are Major Preston, Captain Breeding, Captains Malec and Nutter (second from right).

Senator Henry Cabot Lodge, Jr. congratulates Lt. Harry Benson and Capt. Ralph Nutter for Kassel mission, July 25, 1943.

Ralph Nutter boarding plane for Munich mission, October 1943.

Generals Hansell and LeMay, January 1943 at 305th bomb group.

General Hansell (second from right) next to Capt. Albert Martini and "the cocktail kids," a crew of the 305th bomb group, after a mission over Germany, May 13, 1943.

Colonel LeMay and Major Preston at Chelveston, 305th bomb group, January 1943.

B-17 combat damage from 20-mm shell at author's navigator's window.

Brigadier General LeMay at his desk at Elvedon, England, September 1943. His tough and steadfast personality is apparent from the picture.

B-17 after crash and fire on landing at Chelveston, England 1943. (William Sault collection)

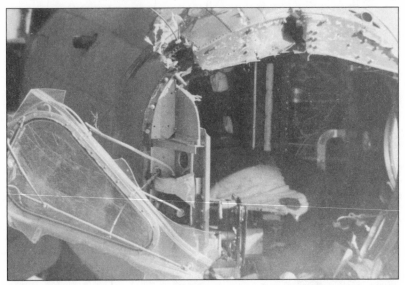

Nose of Whitson-Venable B-17 when Venable was killed May 1943.
(William Sault collection)

B-17 tail shot off by flak.
(William Sault collection)

B-17 forced to make belly landing with wheels up on July 29, 1943. (William Sault collection)

B-17 leaving Berlin, March 6, 1944. (William Sault collection)

On January 20, 1945, Major General LeMay replaced Brigadier General Hansell on Guam. Brigadier General Ramey is at right of picture.

B-17 at Huls, Germany, June 22, 1945. (William Sault collection)

Bombardment of Iwo Jima prior to invasion, February 1945.

Bombing by B-29s on Japanese held island of Rota, north of Guam, January 1945.

B-29 leading P-51s from Iwo Jima to Japan, May 1945.

Operation room, Guam, XXI Bomber Command, April 1945.

North Field Tinian. Home base for B-29 mining operations and the *Enola Gay*, the B-29 atomic bomber.

B-29 (named *Deacon's Disciples*), with bombs in foreground.

B-29 (*The Spearhead*) taxiing at Tinian.

B-29s at Guam-North Field, March 1945.

17: A Different War, A Different Enemy

As we approached the Marianas in a bright, cloudless sky, I moved up from my navigator's table to a position between the pilot and copilot for a better look. I was anxious to see my new home.

The campaign to capture the Marianas in the summer of 1944 featured the largest amphibious assaults of the war in the Pacific up to that time. Organized resistance on Saipan, Tinian, and Guam had ended on all three islands by mid-August. A few scattered Japanese remained to harass us until the end of the war. Only the island of Rota north of Guam was still in Japanese hands; our forces had bypassed it. It became a favorite practice bombing area for our aircrews. On several occasions we threw empty beer cans out of the bomb bay after dropping our bombs, certain that the cans would whistle like real bombs and the Japanese would wait for an explosion that never materialized.

The Marianas are a series of volcanic islands several hundred miles long in the central Pacific, thirty-five hundred miles from Hawaii, fifteen hundred miles east of the Philippines, and fifteen hundred miles south of Japan. Saipan is seventeen miles long and about five-and one half miles across at its widest point. It is the most northerly of the inhabited islands closest to Japan and one hundred and twenty miles from Guam. Guam is the largest island in the Marianas chain.

By July 1945, a thousand B-29s were taking off from Saipan, Tinian, and Guam to bomb Japan. The *Enola Gay*, the B-29 that dropped the A-bomb, took off from Tinian.

As we made our final approach to Saipan, the control tower warned us that there was only one runway. It was only seven thousand feet long, with two thousand feet unpaved. I noticed that it ended on the edge of a cliff above the Pacific. I wondered if the runway would be adequate when our planes were taking off for Tokyo with a full bomb and fuel load. I knew it would be a hairy situation if they lost power on takeoff.

Saipan's barren landscape reminded me of Muroc in 1942. There were only three small Quonset huts and no hangars, hardstands, or revetments for the aircraft, which were parked in a row along the runway. Hansell's staff, the aircrews, and ground personnel all lived in tents.

Heavy bombing, shelling, and artillery fire had decimated almost all of the island's tropical vegetation during the invasion. Sugar cane had been the island's chief crop, but it was all destroyed during the fighting. The dead vegetation was covered with millions of flies. The army sprayed the area with DDT, but it had not made much progress. All of the prewar buildings were destroyed. It was the first time I had observed the devastation inflicted by ground fighting.

I looked to the north and saw a barren mountain called Topatchau. It had been the scene of much bitter fighting. I talked to some marines who had remained to mop up the remnants of the Japanese resistance. They told me they would never forget the mass suicide of most of the surviving Japanese civilians and soldiers. They had retreated to the coral caves and gullies on the north end of the island. There, screaming "banzai," they had jumped off eight-hundred-foot cliffs into the sea. Some of them were mothers holding small children in their arms. They had been told our troops would massacre them all. It was a totally different environment and war than I had encountered in Europe. I would have a lot of adjusting to do.

I asked if there were any surviving natives. They said there were a few Chamorros, the mixed-blood descendants of Spanish and Philippine soldiers and local islanders. The Japanese had treated them harshly and most of them were friendly to our troops.

Hansell had landed on Saipan the previous day. He flew in from Washington after conferring with Marshall and Arnold, and Hansell's successor as chief of staff of the Twentieth Air Force, Brig. Gen. Lauris Norstad. Marshall told him that the president was concerned about the exorbitant casualties that would result if we invaded Japan. He wanted B-29 operations to start from the Marianas by mid-November. Hansell promised Marshall and Arnold he would comply.

Privately, Hansell worried about his promise. He feared that the crews and aircraft would have a hard time achieving readiness that quickly. He was also disturbed by comments Norstad had made about the air force having changed its bombing policy in Europe in 1944. Arnold insisted that the Eighth Air Force fly at least ten missions a month. This meant that at least half would require bombing through cloud cover. It was really area bombing. Norstad told Hansell that Arnold might demand ten missions a month from Saipan and that he should also consider using incendiaries on Japanese cities.

In June 1944, Arnold's committee of operational analysts recommended the firebombing of sixteen major Japanese cities to take advantage of the flimsy wooden construction of their homes and factories. The report concluded that if more than half of these targets could be destroyed it would eliminate one-fifth of all Japanese war production. In essence, the analysts argued that it would be more productive to burn down entire cities than to attempt daylight precision bombing. An earlier national defense research memo stating that ten thousand tons of incendiaries would be enough to burn down Japan's major cities predated the report.

Hansell asked Norstad if the report had considered the effects incendiary attacks would have on innocent civilians. When Norstad replied that the decision was being made at the top levels of government, Hansell retorted that he would not conduct massive incendiary attacks unless he received written orders from General Arnold.

Norstad denied that there was ever any intention to bomb civilians indiscriminately and reminded Hansell that it was official policy to destroy Japanese war industries wherever they were located. Hansell did not reply. He didn't see Norstad again until 7 January 1945, when he was replaced by Curtis LeMay.

After we landed on Saipan I was driven to the Quonset hut that housed General Hansell's headquarters. I gave him the cans of film we had prepared in Culver City. He greeted me warmly and ordered me to report back the next morning for a viewing.

"This is not Brampton, Ralph," he said, smiling. "We're all living in tents. We have a hell of a lot to do before we can call this an air force base. There's hardly room for our B-29s on this runway. I'm worried about concentrating our planes like this without adequate defenses. They tell me the Japs come down from Iwo periodically to bomb and strafe the runway. We have no fighter protection, and our antiaircraft is almost useless against their low-level attacks. I don't know how much support we're going to get from the army and navy. I'll have my aide take you to your tent."

I was driven to a promontory about a mile from the runway overlooking the ocean and Tinian. We pulled up to a four-man tent and I met my new tent mates. I knew two of them. Colonel Jim Seaver was the senior weather officer whose advice had been disregarded by Colonel Travis before the Stuttgart disaster. His assistant was Maj. Tom Bowman, our weather officer in Colorado Springs, who had roomed next to me at the Antlers Hotel. He became my closest friend in the Marianas.

The fourth man in our tent was Capt. Hugh Troy, a statistician from Arnold's headquarters. I learned that Troy was an accomplished artist and practical joker. He had done the murals at the Rockefeller Center. Bowman had been a weather officer in Alaska, based in Nome. He said it looked as if he was trading Alaskan "cabin fever" for "island fever" in the Pacific. Troy asked Seaver and me why we'd left England for this Devil's Island. I told him I thought it was a good question, but I was unable to answer it. Troy told us he was Hansell's statistical officer.

He pointed to the flies that had engulfed the tent and said, "I think my first task will be to keep a record of the number of flies we kill." He made a chart of what he called his daily kill figures. Later, when a general visited us from the Pentagon, Troy showed him his chart. The general was impressed and said he would instruct all air force units to keep similar records.

I asked about the water. Seaver told me the navy brought in the drinking water. "There's no hot water," he added. "You have to wash your clothes in a helmet." I asked about showers and they all laughed. "We hope you'll enjoy seawater in a bucket."

After looking at the desolate landscape, I decided that it was useless to ask them about recreation. They volunteered that the swimming was great. The navy had an officers' club. It was the only source of liquor on the island, but they didn't share it. One of the first things Hansell did when he learned that was to send his aide looking for Japanese sake in the island's caves. Occasionally the Air Transport

Command flew in liquor from the States and sold it to the troops. In England, Doug Venable had sung a ditty that went: "Mother take my star out of your window. I'm in the ATC."

"You can always try rubbing alcohol and grapefruit juice," said Bowman, "but I don't recommend it."

We could also listen to "Tokyo Rose" on "Radio Free Japan." Tokyo Rose was an American-born woman of partial Japanese descent. She was in Japan when war broke out and soon was doing Japanese propaganda broadcasts. I told Jim Seaver she sounded like Lord Haw Haw, who made propaganda broadcasts from Germany.

"Welcome to the Pacific, Yanks," she said. "I'm Tokyo Rose, your only friend on the radio. I tell it to you like it is. I play all your favorite recordings and even keep you up to date on your baseball scores. I have a special greeting for your commanding general, Possum Hansell. Welcome, Possum. I must tell you, we know how you struck out over Germany. You'll have even less luck over Japan.

"Germany was a milk run compared to flying three thousand miles over water in the Pacific with those lousy B-29 engines. We'll have special greetings for you over Japan that will make the Germans look like pikers. You had better not bail out over Japan. The Japanese people will have a special reception for you. If your planes manage to escape our flak and fighters, you will never make it back to Saipan. We will be waiting for you off Iwo Jima. Even if you're short of gas you had better stay away from Iwo. You will never leave the island alive. If you should get back to Saipan, you won't get much sleep at night. We try to visit you regularly. So sorry. We are pleased the way you have those B-29s lined up wingtip to wingtip on the runway. They will be sitting ducks for our planes from Iwo. Now, here is some music."

I made no comment as Bowman turned off the radio. I pondered her comments for a few moments and then asked Seaver, "How do you figure the Japanese found out Hansell's nickname?"

"They have shortwave radios in their hideouts and there are spies everywhere. They're probably paying off the Chamorros who work on our base. Just don't invite any of them into our tent."

I didn't try the alcohol and grapefruit until New Year's Eve. Tom was right. I became deathly sick. I ran to the edge of the jungle and vomited violently. Tom said that if there were any Japanese in the jungle they would think we Americans had a new secret weapon.

I reported to Hansell early the next morning. His aide set up a screen and we reviewed the Culver City films. The general seemed pleased. After we discussed their merits, he told me he had scheduled a meeting of the 73d Wing's aircrews. He suggested that I accompany him and meet them and O'Donnell's staff.

General O'Donnell introduced Hansell, and then offered a short summary of the wing's problems. He congratulated his crews for their conscientious efforts under the most difficult conditions. It was apparent to me that Rosie O'Donnell was well liked and had a strong rapport with his men. He was an extroverted, black-haired Irishman from Brooklyn who usually spoke with a smile on his face. He had been a B-17 squadron commander at Clark Field in the Philippines with Joe Preston. Their planes were destroyed on the ground.

Later, Rosie became a trusted but unorthodox member of Arnold's staff. In sharp contrast to O'Donnell, Hansell made a formal, almost perfunctory, talk to the crews. He welcomed them to the XXI Bomber Command and told them that they should not be discouraged by the living conditions. He was working with both the army and navy to improve the facilities. The important thing, he explained, was that they were beginning a historic effort to achieve victory through airpower. "The B-29 is a new aircraft," he said. "It has been designed to bomb at altitudes of over thirty thousand feet as a defense against enemy fighter attacks. The maintenance and engineering staff are making a maximum effort to solve our mechanical problems. Ours is the closest American combat force to Japan. There have been no air strikes on Honshu, Japan's main island, since the token Doolittle raid in April of 1942. Now your B-29s are going to make meaningful daylight, high-altitude strikes against Japan's war industry.

"Our first priority will be aircraft plants. The Eighth Air Force went through a learning period over Germany. They're now on their way to victory over the Nazis with high-altitude, daylight precision bombing. It may be necessary for us to have a similar learning experience with a new aircraft against a different enemy. I have promised Generals Marshall and Arnold that we will bomb Tokyo by mid-November, and we will keep that promise.

"I realize that you have had only limited experience flying and bombing at high altitude in formation. We will fly practice missions to Truk and Iwo Jima. When we're not flying to Truk and Iwo, the bombardiers can make bomb runs on Rota. LeMay's XX Bomber Command has been making high-altitude daylight strikes on Manchuria and Kyushu, but they're too far away to damage Japan's main war industries on Honshu. It will be up to us to bomb targets there from here in the Marianas. Our operation will be the first real opportunity for the air force to demonstrate that we can achieve victory through strategic bombing."

When Hansell mentioned that the missions would be flown in daylight at thirty thousand feet, I heard a low murmur from the crews in the back of the room. I looked at O'Donnell. He frowned and his face darkened. I wondered what displeased him more: the murmur from the crews or Hansell's remarks. I knew that Hansell had ordered him to stop training his crews for night bombing with radar when we were still at Salina, but I did not learn the extent of their conflicts about bombing tactics until LeMay took over from Hansell in January 1945.

O'Donnell and LeMay were former classmates and close friends. I later learned that they had never been impressed with the theories Hansell had taught at the Air Tactical School. I wondered what O'Donnell thought about Hansell's suggestion that LeMay's China operations were futile.

As I was about to leave the meeting with Hansell, I heard O'Donnell ask if he had time to discuss the training of his crews. Hansell hesitated. I could see he was bothered by the request. Finally he said, "Let's do it right here."

"My crews are not ready for a high-altitude, daylight formation mission to Tokyo," said O'Donnell. "Most of our crews have only been here three weeks. The missions we've flown to Truk and Iwo Jima so far aren't enough to train the crews. Because of mechanical and maintenance problems we have yet to put more than thirty planes over Truk or Iwo. Our pilots, flight engineers, and navigators are just not ready to fly three thousand miles over water.

"The climb to thirty thousand feet in formation is pushing the crews and planes to the limit. It not only puts a strain on the engines, it uses more gas. The pilots and flight engineers still haven't worked out their cruise control problems. The time spent assembling and flying in formation uses more fuel. As crews start their climb to high altitude they will encounter strong cross winds.

"We don't have any accurate weather information. The weather may be our worst enemy. If there is extensive cloud cover we will have a problem picking out targets visually. If it's overcast above us, the navigators won't be able to check their courses with celestial shots. There's serious danger that they won't make appropriate corrections for the crosswinds. If they're blown off course they will not only miss the target and fly more miles, they'll use up the fuel reserves that they'll need to make it back to Saipan.

"If we bomb in daylight, we'll be returning home at night. Any plane suffering even minor damage or mechanical problems will be in trouble. There's no way we can save them if they've been damaged over Japan, have mechanical problems, or run out of fuel and have to ditch in the Pacific at night. Until we work out these problems, I think a high-altitude daylight mission in formation is too great a risk. We risk a disaster that is not justified by the chance of a successful mission."

Hansell scowled. "You seem to be telling me that most of our fuel, weather, engine, and navigation problems are caused by flying in formation at thirty thousand feet. Are you telling me we should lower the altitude in daylight? Have you forgotten about the disastrous low-level daylight mission to Ploesti?"

"I have never suggested that," replied O'Donnell. "I'm asking for a temporary delay until our crews have more daylight, high-altitude formation training and we've eliminated some of the B-29's mechanical problems. Until then we can fly individual night missions. Most Japanese targets are near the coastline. The water contrast with the land will enable our navigators and bombardiers to make reasonably accurate bombs runs at night with radar."

Hansell scowled again. "You know my position about day and night bombing. I've been given a written directive to engage in high-altitude daylight bombing of precise military targets. Those are my orders and they are your orders."

He turned and walked away. I followed at a discreet distance. It was apparent to me that O'Donnell's protests about daylight bombing were becoming a sore point in the relations between the two men. I knew that he was repeating arguments that Wolfe had made concerning his China operations. Hansell had persuaded Arnold to remove Wolfe. I wondered if he would do the same with O'Donnell.

Hansell could tell Arnold that O'Donnell's request for a delay of daylight bombing played into the hands of MacArthur and the navy. Both the army and the navy were requesting a delay of the Tokyo mission because they wanted the B-29s to support an attack on the Philippines. Hansell felt that this was a repeat of the North African diversion of the Eighth Air Force in 1942. He wouldn't let it happen again. He had been surprised that Arnold's staff had not opposed the navy's request to delay the Tokyo mission.

Hansell knew that O'Donnell had close friends on Arnold's staff. He wondered why the staff had told him to use his own discretion. Were they hanging him out to dry? He would stick to his guns. The navy's request violated the entire foundation and premise of an independent Twentieth Air Force. Hansell had suffered through this problem in England. Things were starting out badly before they had flown their first mission. His conflicts with his wing and group commanders in England had been a soul-searching ordeal. He had no intention of giving in this time.

O'Donnell's and the 73d Wing's reluctance to engage in high-altitude daylight bombing was not Hansell's only problem. He had administrative problems quite unlike those in England. His operations were theoretically independent of the army and the navy, but on Saipan they supplied him with most of the materiel necessary for his operations. The navy transported every gallon of fuel and all of his bombs, ammunition, and supplies. He had only a few antiaircraft guns and almost no adequate fighter protection. He had to rely on the army and marines for defense against Japanese fighters and bombers attacking the base. Although he had only one half-completed runway, other air force units were insisting that they had the right to use it for their aircraft.

Hansell decided that he would postpone improving his relations with the army and navy and instead deal directly and immediately with O'Donnell. He again told O'Donnell that area night-bombing missions would not destroy their designated military targets. Moreover, flying night missions would violate his directive from Arnold to destroy aircraft plants in daylight operations.

He sent written orders to O'Donnell to prepare for a mission to the Nakajima-Musashino aircraft plant in Ota, northwest of Tokyo, on 15 November. They would fly in daylight, in formation, and at an altitude of twenty-nine thousand feet. The next morning, Hansell was astonished to receive a handwritten letter from O'Donnell formally repeating his objection to an immediate daylight high-altitude mission. O'Donnell again requested that his crews temporarily be permitted to bomb targets in Japan by flying individually at night at lower altitudes. Hansell, finding it difficult to believe that O'Donnell was still resisting his commanding general, ordered him to report to his headquarters immediately. He reminded him that Wolfe had been replaced because he had also refused to follow official policy. O'Donnell would do so at his peril.

Hansell told him that if he agreed to lead the first daylight mission to Tokyo he would destroy the letter of reprimand he was preparing; otherwise, it would remain in his personnel file. He reminded O'Donnell that the joint chiefs had authorized daylight high-altitude strategic operations. It would be a disaster for the future of an independent air force if they failed. Hansell said he knew there were risks, but he was willing to take them to achieve that objective. If O'Donnell were unwilling or reluctant to do the same, he would have someone else take his place. O'Donnell should consider the consequences and how a refusal would affect his future in the air force. If he refused to lead the mission, it would be on his record.

O'Donnell was furious. He knew that he should control his temper. He didn't know if Hansell was reflecting on his personal courage, but he was certainly threatening his future. He had a lot more combat experience than Hansell. He knew that Hansell had been cool to him at their meetings in Salina when he had first raised the issue of the lack of crew training and had suggested they conduct night missions. A member of Arnold's staff had told O'Donnell that Hansell still held a grudge against him for his 1943 memo to Arnold criticizing the Eighth Air Force's faulty planning.

He finally told Hansell that if his crews had to go in daylight, he should be in the lead plane. He had simply considered it his duty to express his concerns.

Hansell thought that O'Donnell was too much like LeMay. He was overly concerned about his crews and not looking at the big picture. He didn't understand that an independent Twentieth Air Force was the first step in building an independent air force. The army and navy were laughing at the air force's claim that the B-29s could achieve victory with precision bombing. He told O'Donnell that he would tear up the letter of reprimand and issue orders to reschedule the Tokyo mission for 17 November.

Hansell decided that he wanted to brief the crews himself. Before the briefing, I discussed the mission plans with the 73d Wing's operations staff. O'Donnell was concerned that his crews might not be able to locate the IP if it was even partially covered by cloud cover. We agreed that Mount Fuji would be a more appropriate initial point.

At the early morning briefing, I noticed that Hansell and O'Donnell did not speak to each other. Hansell walked into the briefing room without a word, pulled back the curtain covering the route map, and started to brief the crews. He told them that their first mission was to be to the Nakajima-Musashino aircraft plant in Ota, a suburb of Tokyo. The briefing film we had prepared in Culver City was then shown to the crews, after which Hansell made a few final comments. This was the first time I had seen the commanding general of a bomber command brief a mission.

Hansell's comments were not what I considered to be an inspirational talk to the crews on their first combat mission over Japan: "Stick together. Don't let fighter attacks break up formations. And put your bombs on the target. If the bombs don't hit the target, all our efforts, risks, worries, and work will be for nothing. That's what we're here for. If we do our job, this is the beginning of the end for Japan. Put your bombs on the target. You can do it." He walked out of the briefing room with no further comment to anyone.

At dawn, I stood beside Hansell in the control tower. The B-29s were lined up beside the taxiway that led to the takeoff spot at the end of the runway. The planes had a full bomb and fuel load, a gross weight of one hundred thirty-eight thousand pounds, far above the recommended one hundred twenty thousand pounds. It was hoped that the wind would give the overloaded planes a lift on takeoff. Even with this lift, I thought it would be touch and go. The loss of power in one engine on takeoff could be disastrous.

Suddenly the wind shifted and the clouds darkened. O'Donnell called Hansell in the control tower and suggested that the crews shut down their engines and at least delay takeoff until the weather cleared and the winds were at least partially toward them. Hansell agreed. The weather got worse. After waiting another twenty minutes, Hansell canceled the mission without further comment. Luck was with him. Late that afternoon, Saipan was hit by a typhoon. There would have been no way that planes returning from an attack on Tokyo short of fuel could have landed safely in that storm. We could have lost most of the 73d Wing.

The storm lasted for several days, making it impossible fly. The heavily loaded B-29s parked on the edge of the runway would have been an easy target for Japanese bombers and fighters flying down from Iwo Jima had they attempted an attack.

The first mission to Tokyo did not get off until 24 November, when 111 B-29s took off at dawn. I again stood with Hansell in the control tower, watching each takeoff with apprehension. The Saipan runway was on a flat plateau at the southern end of the island, a few feet above the ocean. During takeoff, the pilots kept the wheels down as long as possible. They then pulled back on the control yoke hoping for enough lift to gain flight altitude at the end of the runway. Occasionally, a plane would seem to stagger and drop out of sight below the plateau at the end of the runway. We would hold our breath and wait for it to reappear as it started its climb to cruising altitude. Fortunately that didn't happen too often.

The mission lasted about fourteen hours, and the bombers returned in the dark to Saipan, where a single airstrip with no runway lights awaited them. The first returning aircraft arrived at 8:30 P.M. A few minutes later a tropical storm lashed the island with some of the heaviest rain I have ever seen. The late-arriving planes had great difficulty landing in the torrential downpour. They were short of fuel and had to land in almost blind conditions.

O'Donnell's prediction that a daylight mission was premature had been more than accurate. Seventeen aircraft turned back because their crews feared they would run out of fuel. Six aborted because of mechanical problems. Cloud cover obscured the entire Tokyo area. Only twenty-four planes bombed the primary target area.

Prior to the mission, Hansell had sent a weather reconnaissance plane over Tokyo. The crew reported extremely strong winds at higher altitudes. I was concerned. If the navigators did not make proper corrections they would never hit Japan. I discussed the winds with our weather officers, Seaver and Bowman. They told me that there appeared to be an almost continual jet stream of high winds over Japan at altitudes higher than twenty-five thousand feet.

The winds could also affect bombing accuracy. On a downwind bomb run, the crews could expect a two-hundred-knot tail wind, giving them a ground speed of more than four hundred miles per hour. At such speeds, the navigators and bombardiers would be required to locate a precise target several miles beyond the range of the bombsights. I knew that under such conditions the bombs would be blown away from the target, with bombing accuracy the exception, rather than the rule. There was only one favorable aspect of a downwind bomb run at such speeds: The Japanese fighters were also at a disadvantage. The increased downwind speeds protected our planes on the bomb run, but they also made accurate bombing impossible.

I was equally concerned about the safety of our planes flying the last leg of the return flight to Saipan in the dark. We could not install radio homing devices on the island as long as Japanese bombers were attacking our base. We had not yet installed loran to supplement celestial navigation. Fortunately, we had clear skies until the storm hit after the return of the planes, and none of our aircraft had any difficulty finding the island.

The bombing results were disappointing. The strike photographs indicated that no more than fifty bombs landed in the vicinity of a military target. This first mission made it clear that Japanese fighters and flak were not comparable to the opposition we had encountered in Germany. The main obstacles to accurate bombing and successful missions were the tremendous jet-stream winds, extensive cloud cover, and the undependable Wright engines.

The navigators and bombardiers reported that the winds had the strength of a fire hose, with velocities much greater than our crews had been told to expect at the mission briefing. Each navigator computed them in the target area. After the mission, I computed an average of the winds reported by the navigators and gave the figure to Seaver and Bowman. They were astonished at the discrepancy from what they had given us that morning. I reminded them that conditions were not similar to those in Europe where we had the benefit of daily weather data from the RAF. Still, they were doing the best they could under impossible conditions.

I accompanied Hansell to the mission debriefing. He was in no mood to congratulate O'Donnell for his leadership of the mission. As he turned to leave, Hansell walked over to O'Donnell and said, "This first mission has proven that high-altitude daylight missions are feasible. We can improve our bombing accuracy with more training and experience."

He then made a remark that I knew was intended as a reprimand, "The results of a night mission would have been catastrophic."

I looked at O'Donnell. I could see he was astonished. I wondered about the relevance of Hansell's comment. Catastrophic for whom? He couldn't have been talking about the safety of the crews or the poor bombing results. He must have been referring to his high-altitude, daylight precision bombing program.

As he had done after our Schweinfurt missions, General Arnold issued a glowing press release extolling the bombing results. He stated that the targets had suffered substantial damage and that Tokyo's industries had been severely hit.

In the next weeks the operations staff was aware that unless changes were made in our tactics, high-altitude daylight bombing, if not catastrophic for the crews, could lead to pitiful bombing results. Hansell was not about to change tactics, however.

Missions to the same targets in Tokyo on 27 and 29 November were no more successful than the first mission. Norstad recommended that Hansell attempt a night radar mission to Nagoya at high altitude. Hansell followed his advice. The mission was not successful. Only 20 percent of the planes bombed primary targets. Again acting on a recommendation from Norstad, Hansell attempted a mission on 30 November that employed a mixed load of incendiary and high-explosive bombs. The results were also poor. On 3 December he sent seventy-six B-29s to bomb the Nakajima factories in Tokyo. Six crews were lost, and four planes were forced to ditch in the Pacific. The results were mediocre at best.

O'Donnell and the staff made no further effort to persuade Hansell to schedule night bombing missions. We knew that Hansell for many years had taught that targets could not be destroyed without being seen. He was not about to admit that the weather and jet stream over Japan made high-altitude precision daylight bombing impractical.

After the 29 November mission, I walked back to headquarters with Hansell. He told me that he was not discouraged. "It's my air plan that is defeating Hitler in Europe. It will defeat Japan, too."

I wondered if his devotion to the doctrine he had been teaching and planning for so many years had become a compulsion or an obsession. He had to know that in 1943 we were unable to bomb Germany more than four or five days a month because of the weather. Arnold had consulted him before he had replaced Eaker. He knew Arnold was displeased in part because Eaker did not schedule more missions over Germany. Hansell received bi-weekly summaries of Eighth Air Force operations over Germany, including reports of their massive attacks on German cities on a regular basis. The increased number of missions being flown in Europe could only be accomplished by bombing through cloud cover while using radar to locate targets.

The weather conditions at altitudes above twenty-five thousand feet over Japan were worse than we had encountered over Germany. I wondered if anyone could persuade Hansell to change his tactics? It had become a matter of will and ego. He was determined to prove that his critics were wrong. However, he was about to discover that he had another problem we had not encountered in Europe: kamikazes.

18: The Divine Winds of Heaven

The kamikaze suicide attacks against our facilities and personnel on Saipan brought new dimensions to our preparations to bomb Japan. We were almost never confronted with suicide attacks by German fighter pilots. The Nazis were brutal fanatics, but I had never encountered German fighter pilots who would sacrifice their lives for religious or cultural reasons, or for devotion to an emperor.

The marines told me about the suicides of the Japanese defenders of Saipan and their cries of "Banzai!" as they jumped to their deaths rather than be captured. We were fighting against a foe who gloried in death as "a divine wind of heaven."

Japanese history is culturally different from that of any Western nation. During World War II, Japan's military elite was aided by the nation's ancient samurai tradition. The military aristocracy used Japan's warrior tradition to inspire the Japanese people to fight Americans to the death. The Bushido and samurai codes were used to inspire their soldiers, sailors, and pilots to make reckless suicide attacks on our troops, warships, and air bases. Saipan was relatively close to the Japanese home islands, and Prime Minister Hideki Tojo resigned in disgrace after its capture, which was a crushing defeat for the military elite and warrior class that ruled Japan. Saipan was an ideal target for the samurai tradition. The militarists could send kamikazes there to attack the B-29 bombers and crews threatening their homeland. The young pilots were told their sacrifices had been divinely inspired by the emperor, and they believed they were about to ride the winds of heaven to eternal glory.

The tempo of kamikaze attacks increased as Japan faced the possibility of defeat on Iwo Jima. Reaction to this fanaticism in part fueled the later decisions to use fire raids and atomic bombs. Our planners knew that an invasion would be resisted by millions of fanatical troops and civilians inspired to die for their emperor.

The first kamikaze attack on Saipan came on the night of 3 November 1944. At a little before ten that evening, shortly after I returned to my tent from headquarters, Japanese twin-engine fighter-bombers came roaring down from the north in a bright moonlit sky, strafing the length of our runway. Our few antiaircraft guns opened up on them, but the fighter-bombers were flying so low I doubted that our gunners hit any of the attacking aircraft. They dropped bombs, then peeled off and made three more passes over the air-field, scattering machine-gun fire at anything that moved. At the end of its fourth pass, one of the aircraft dove into an aircraft mainte-nance building, killing a mechanic and damaging three B-29s.

The most serious kamikaze attack occurred early in the morning before takeoff for the second mission to Tokyo. Apparently this at-tack was in retaliation for our first Tokyo mission on 24 November. The surviving Japanese troops concealed in the caves of Saipan prob-ably had given notice to Iwo Jima of our mission preparation by shortwave radio. I was in the bomber command operations Quon-set hut on the flight line a short time before the first planes were to take off for Tokyo. I had been reviewing the bomb route with the lead navigators and bombardiers when I heard the roar of engines and machine-gun fire. We rushed outside and saw several fighter-bombers flash by flying fifty feet above our runway.

They had no trouble locating our B-29s, which were lined up for takeoff on the edge of the airfield. Maintenance crews had set up portable lights by the aircraft, while they made final preparations for the mission. I counted ten fighter-bombers as they made several passes up and down the airstrip. One of them dropped a bomb on a B-29 alongside the runway. It was immediately engulfed in flames and exploded with tremendous force, knocking the three of us to the ground. I shook my head to clear it and saw an unexploded bomb a few feet away. The field telephone inside the Quonset hut began to ring and I rushed to answer it.

It was General Hansell. "Nutter, aren't you the officer of the day?" he asked. "What are you doing to stop this attack on our mission?"

I had no idea how I should answer his question.

"Nutter, are you there?" he asked, his voice rising.

I was about to answer in the affirmative so he would at least know I was at the scene, when there was another tremendous explosion a hundred yards down the runway. The force of the blast knocked me to the ground again. It was either another bomb or a B-29 had blown up. I didn't drop the phone. I lay on my back wondering if the un-exploded bomb would go off.

Without standing up, I yelled to Hansell on the phone, "There's nothing I can do sir!" and hung up.

The Japanese attack lasted for about three-quarters of an hour.

A few minutes later, Hansell roared up in his jeep. My uniform was covered with dirt and mud. "Are you hurt?" he asked. He looked shaken and didn't mention his phone call to me.

"No, I'm not hurt," I replied. "One of the Japanese planes crashed on the runway, and there's debris and a fire from a burning B-29 blocking the runway access. No one can take off until the runway is cleared."

He instructed me to telephone the Seabees and order them to bring over a bulldozer. The Seabees arrived within ten minutes. They put out most of the fires and were using a bulldozer to clear the field of wreckage while enemy fighter-bombers continued to strafe the area. There was a possibility that the burning B-29s might explode. The Seabees risked their lives to make the mission possible.

Our operations phones were ringing off the hook. Group commanders were asking if the mission was still on. Hansell told the group commanders to review their losses and make immediate reports, but to assume that the mission would go as scheduled.

Four of our B-29s were a total loss and six were so seriously damaged that it was doubtful they would ever fly again. The mission went ahead with ten fewer aircraft than we had originally planned.

All but one of the attacking fighter-bombers crashed on our runway. The remaining plane went in behind the base hospital. It was apparent that none of the attackers planned to return to Iwo Jima. I watched the scene with fascination and horror. This type of war was beyond my comprehension, and yet another unforeseen problem for Hansell.

After our planes took off for Tokyo, Hansell requested a meeting with the army, navy, and marine commanders on the island to discuss our air defenses. The naval liaison officer told us that the navy had picket destroyers north of Saipan, but they had only a small number of antiaircraft guns. The attacking planes flew so low that the pickets could not detect them on their radar, so there was no time to give us adequate advance notice of attacks. Within minutes after the pickets spotted the incoming planes they would be approaching our field.

The navy and marine commanders promised to give us fighter support, but they warned that there was no practical way to stop low-flying kamikazes. The army commander offered to put more anti-aircraft guns along the runway. We were learning that there was no realistic defense against the kamikazes; the traditional rules of combat did not apply when dealing with an enemy who was intent on dying in order to complete his mission of destruction.

The next day, Hansell sent two B-29 groups from the 73d Wing to bomb the Japanese airfield on Iwo Jima. He also inquired about basing some B-29s on Guam, but the runways there were not finished and there were no facilities for aircrews or maintenance. We would have to expect the kamikazes as long as the Japanese retained Iwo Jima.

The 27 November attack took a heavy toll, but the attack by twenty-four Japanese planes on Christmas Day proved to be the most devastating on Saipan. We lost eleven B-29s and twenty-four others were damaged. For the next three months the kamikazes were a nuisance, but they no longer posed a serious threat.

On one occasion, while I was escorting a general from Arnold's staff through a B-29 parked on the runway at Saipan, I heard the familiar sound of strafing machine guns. My visitor asked me what we should do. I told him we should get out of the plane as fast as possible and run like hell away from the runway. He was the fastest running general I ever encountered.

My other personal experience with kamikazes was both ludicrous and almost tragic. I had come down with tropical jaundice and been confined to the Quonset hut that served as our base hospital. I was lying on my bunk in pajamas when I heard the roar of an engine overhead and the sound of machine-gun fire coming toward the hospital. I grabbed my .45-caliber pistol and rushed out the door. I had not attached the drawstring of my pajamas, and they dropped to my ankles in midstride, sending me sprawling flat on my face. I lay there for a fraction of a second and then looked up. Fifty feet above, a Japanese fighter was strafing the hospital and me. Apparently the

Red Cross symbol painted on the roof of the hospital had failed to deter him. I futilely emptied my .45 at him, and then watched as he turned toward the runway and crashed his plane into a B-29. A nurse came running out of the Quonset hut.

"Do you have any idea how ridiculous you look, lying there with your pajama bottoms around your ankles?" she shouted. "You're going to give this hospital a bad name!"

I pulled up my pajamas and returned to my bed. Miraculously, none of the patients or nurses had been wounded in the attack.

There were three more kamikaze raids in December and three ineffective raids in January and February. One evening, Tom Bowman and I were sitting on a log in Saipan's open-air movie theater. We were watching *Laura,* a mystery starring Gene Tierney, when we heard the chatter of machine guns. A lone kamikaze must have seen the light from the movie projector. A hail of bullets hit just in front of the screen and we all ran or dove for cover as tracers ripped into the movie projector. I never did find out how the movie ended.

After the invasion of Iwo Jima in February 1945, the surviving Japanese ground troops in the Marianas gave us the most trouble. Many of them lived in numerous caves on Guam until after the war ended. They had never received authorization to surrender from the emperor and they felt that it was their sacred duty to kill as many of us as possible and interfere with our flight operations.

On 24 November, three Japanese soldiers somehow managed to station themselves at the end of the runway, where they tried to shoot down the B-29s with rifle fire as the aircraft left the ground. None of them succeeded, but their presence did not help the morale of our crews, who were taking off in conditions that were already hazardous. The marines estimated there were at least 150 Japanese in the jungle around our base. Occasionally, they would attempt to stab us in our tents or steal food or personal property. Some of our tent mates became so nervous that whenever they heard a noise outside they would rush out, ready to shoot anything that moved. The continuous gunfire made sleep almost impossible. LeMay issued an order decreeing that anyone shooting a weapon without cause would be fined one dollar. The shooting stopped.

After the marines landed on Iwo Jima on 19 February 1945, kamikaze raids on the Marianas ceased altogether. The Japanese were hoarding their aircraft for the defense of Okinawa and a land invasion of their home islands. Occasionally a Japanese soldier would come out of the jungle naked with his hands raised in surrender. We took these men prisoner and turned them over to the marines, who placed them in a stockade in the center of the island.

19: The Beginning of the End for Hansell

I was concerned that Hansell's conflict with O'Donnell was impairing his judgment. He appeared lonely and withdrawn, seemingly engaged in a duel of nerves and will with Rosie. He had to know that he could not make his program succeed if his aircrews were hostile toward him. He also knew that O'Donnell was not alone in opposing high-altitude precision daylight bombing over Japan. MacArthur's favorite air force commander, Lt. Gen. George C. Kenney, and several members of Arnold's staff were pessimistic about Hansell's high-altitude daylight missions.

Arnold's staff would send him memos describing the success of LeMay's operations in China, which angered Hansell, who didn't appreciate the comparison of his bombing accuracy with LeMay's. As the stress and pressures increased, Hansell felt that he had to either get control of the 73d Wing or he would have a breakdown. He wondered how LeMay got such good results. It was obvious that LeMay made no attempt to be liked by his men. Some feared him, but they all respected him. He knew that LeMay would not permit smug or disloyal people to disrupt his command, so he decided to call a meeting of the 73d Wing's aircrews and give them the toughest talking to a commanding officer could give a combat unit. He telephoned O'Donnell and told him to assemble his crews for an immediate meeting. He didn't tell him its purpose.

O'Donnell spoke first. He congratulated his crews for making a valiant effort under adverse conditions and told them he was not going to blame them for the less-than-satisfactory bombing results because of adverse weather conditions and the strong winds they encountered at high altitude. He then introduced Hansell, who glowered at him before turning to face the assembled crewmembers.

His face was dark and clouded. "I don't agree with General O'-Donnell at all," he began. "I disagree with him strongly. I don't think you people are making a maximum effort. You have not been earning your pay. You whine and complain about the wind, cloud cover, and the B-29's mechanical problems. The combat conditions and weather here are no worse than our Eighth Air Force crews faced over Germany.

"In fact, the flak, fighters, and the losses we experienced were much worse over Germany. You navigators and bombardiers are complaining that you don't have sufficient time to pick up a target on a downwind bomb run. All right, I will accept that. From now on, you will make your bomb runs from upwind. You will have more time to locate the target. You can use radar to assist you if you think you need it. The extra time on an upwind run will give you an opportunity to show me that radar is as accurate as you claim. This meeting is dismissed."

The meeting had lasted less than five minutes. Hansell stalked out of the briefing room. I followed him outside trying to look as unobtrusive as possible. I avoided looking at O'Donnell or his combat crews. Hansell had to know that an upwind run at reduced ground speed would make the crews sitting ducks for Japanese antiaircraft and fighters. The jet stream's winds would slow down their approach to the targets by half. I wondered what had motivated Hansell to order upwind bomb runs. A lower and slower bomb run might improve results, but would the crews believe he was risking their lives as a form of punishment or sanctions?

This was not the Hansell I had known and worked for in England. I had always admired him as a sincere, idealistic, and dedicated leader. He had worked well with LeMay when LeMay was his subordinate. I knew that some of our 1st Wing meetings had been difficult for Hansell. This conflict with the 73d Wing had to be resolved before it led to a disaster.

I wanted to tell Hansell about the combat crews' sincerity, dedication, and hard work; of how, with a little more training, the navigators, bombardiers, and radar operators could improve their bombing results by using radar as an adjunct to visual bombing. Would it be presumptuous for me, a twenty-four-year-old major, to make recommendations to a general with Hansell's experience and background?

That evening I had dinner at the mess hall with Tom Bowman, who had been present at the meeting. Neither of us had much to say. The atmosphere was strained and somber. I told Tom I was worried, that Hansell's comments earlier were completely out of character. He had overcome several tense and difficult situations in England. I told him I had been at staff meetings when Hansell had been upset with LeMay, but he had always been courteous, his comments never personal. He was always objective; he never seemed out of control. Now he appeared to be unable to make an objective analysis of the problems confronting him.

I asked Tom if he considered it inappropriate for me to talk with Hansell personally and attempt to reassure him that the crews were putting out maximum effort.

"You can't be serious, Ralph," Tom replied. "Keep out of this situation. I've been studying the weather over Japan for two months. The cloud cover, jet stream winds, and visibility will be worse in the next few months. If our crews couldn't see their targets in the last two months, they sure as hell won't be able to see and hit them this winter. Who is going to be blamed for that?"

I knew that Tom was probably correct, but I wasn't ready to give up. As we left the mess hall, I suggested that we walk over to the promontory overlooking Tinian.

"Why do you want to go there?" Tom asked. "That's close to Hansell's tent. I hope you're not thinking of going to his tent to talk to him about his problems with Rosie and the 73d Wing. Hansell is unhappy enough with them now. If you try to explain things to him, it not only won't help, it will make life more difficult for us on the staff. He's not about to listen to a young major with barely three years of service. You can't do anything about the problems between Hansell and Rosie. There's a lot more involved than the jet stream or cloud cover over Japan."

I told Tom that I was going to walk by Hansell's tent. If he was alone and the tent flap was open and he didn't seem busy, I would ask if I could talk to him for a few minutes.

"You're a fool," said Tom. "I'm not about to get involved. I'll see you later."

I walked alone over the promontory behind Hansell's tent. I stood looking toward Tinian, and then back toward his tent. The flap was open and I could see he was reading. I turned and walked over to the entrance to his tent and looked inside.

I hesitated a moment, then said, "Sir, are you busy? Do you have time to talk about our bombing over Japan? I'd like to discuss some of the problems the crews are having."

Hansell scowled at me and said, "Can't you see I'm reading?"

I knew that Tom Bowman had been correct. I looked at the cover of the book he was holding. It was *Lee's Lieutenants,* the story of how Robert E. Lee dealt with his Civil War generals. I had read a review of it just before we left the States. I wondered if Hansell was hoping to learn how Lee had dealt with his problem generals. Did he perhaps see a similarity between the problems Lee had with Longstreet at Gettysburg and those he was encountering with O'Donnell?

"Yes sir," I replied. "Have a pleasant evening." He didn't look up. I turned and walked back toward our tent.

As I approached, Tom said, "You're back early. Was he there? Did you talk to him? It must have been a short conversation."

"Yes," I said. "You were right, Tom. Hansell was quick to let me know that his problems with the 73d Wing are none of my business. I guess I'll find out tomorrow if I'm going to have any prop wash from this."

The next morning, Hansell gave me his usual friendly greeting. We discussed the plans for our next mission as if nothing had happened. I wondered about the future, though. The problems between Hansell and O'Donnell had not been solved, and it was common knowledge that Arnold was always impatient for immediate results. I was convinced that the 73d's crews were doing everything possible to make Hansell's precision bombing tactics work. Even if the weather did clear up, it would be impossible to do any serious damage to Japanese military targets until we had a larger bomber fleet.

Although our poor bombing results were Hansell's greatest problem, he seemed overwhelmed with administration and other unique problems and obstacles that no one had anticipated when we arrived on Saipan. In England, the British took care of the administrative details at our air bases. Hansell not only had what seemed like impossible combat problems, he was confronted with many others he had never considered when making his plans for B-29 operations from isolated islands in the central Pacific.

He was not about to change course, though. True to his threat to the crews, on 13 December Hansell had seventy-three bombers make an upwind bomb run on the Mitsubishi aircraft factory in Nagoya. The ground speed of the attacking aircraft was reduced to less than two hundred miles per hour. At that speed our crews were extremely vulnerable to antiaircraft fire and fighter attacks. It was also the first occasion on which the crews carried a substantial amount of incendiary bombs. General Norstad had sent Hansell a memo informing him that Arnold's committee of operational analysts had concluded that Japanese urban target areas were susceptible to incendiary attacks because of the flimsy, mostly wooden construction of their industrial buildings. Hansell protested that the lighter incendiaries would be less accurate. He told Norstad that the jet stream would blow the incendiaries into civilian residential areas.

Ironically, the 13 December mission was Hansell's first partially successful mission. In spite of heavy cloud cover, the radar assisted the crews in locating the target area. For the first time, a majority of the bombs hit the target. Hansell agreed that radar had been an aid to the crews. However, on 18 December sixty-three B-29s bombed Nagoya's Mitsubishi facilities in heavy cloud cover with only partially favorable results. We again lost four B-29s.

On 22 December, Hansell reluctantly agreed to Norstad's request for a small-scale incendiary mission. Although seventy-three planes took off for Tokyo, only thirty-nine reached the target. There was heavy cloud cover, and incendiaries were scattered all over the city. On 3 January, Hansell sent another partial incendiary mission to Nagoya. Clouds again obscured the target, and again the results were unsatisfactory. No military targets were hit and all of the bombs dropped landed in the general urban and dock areas. This time we lost five aircraft. On 9 January, Hansell sent seventy-two bombers to Tokyo. The strike achieved only mediocre results.

Hansell's last mission, on 19 January, was his only success. It was directed at the Kawasaki aircraft plant in Akashi, west of Kobe. Sixty-two of eighty aircraft bombed the target on the clearest day that winter. More than 20 percent of their bombs landed within a thousand feet of the aiming point. This was the first mission on which more than 40 percent of the planes that took off from Saipan reached the target area.

Although Hansell had two hundred B-29s based on Saipan, he was never able to schedule more than a hundred of them for a mission due to the plane's inherent mechanical problems. It was unusual if seventy planes bombed the primary target.

Arnold and his staff reviewed Hansell's performance. Since his arrival on Saipan in October, Hansell's XXI Bomber Command had flown five small missions to the islands of Truk and Iwo Jima and nine to Honshu. Except for the last mission to Akashi, the bombing results ranged from disastrous to mediocre. His command bombed Tokyo five times and Nagoya four times, and his crews carried incendiaries on three missions. In all, thirty-nine B-29s were lost, a much lower percentage than his bomb wing had suffered in England in 1943. However, the Japanese defenses were nowhere near as good as the Germans' had been. In all, only five planes were lost as a result of enemy action. Twenty-four were known to have been lost because of engine failure, fuel exhaustion, or various operational causes.

There were five basic reasons Hansell's bombing program was unsuccessful. The first was his inflexible belief in the merits of high-altitude daylight precision bombing. He should have learned in our missions from England in 1943 that overwhelming weather problems made visual bombing especially difficult and mostly inaccurate. The second was his compulsion to demonstrate that accurate precision bombing could be achieved in daylight without serious losses, and without causing excessive Japanese civilian casualties. The third was his rash promise to Arnold that he would commence bombing Japan by 15 November 1944. He made that promise in August, when he was fully aware that the crews were not ready to cope with the mechanical and operational problems of the B-29s at high altitude in combat conditions. The high altitude magnified and increased both the weather and engine problems. The fourth was his unwillingness to accept O'Donnell's suggestion that they fly night missions until the crews became more familiar with the problems caused by weather, long overwater flights, and the B-29's balky engines. Finally, he refused to recognize the unique character of Japanese military production facilities. Unlike German targets, Japanese factories were scattered all over urban areas. It would have taken months or years to search out and destroy these targets using traditional precision bombing methods.

When Hansell assumed command of the XXI Bomber Command, the B-29 was not as reliable as the Boeing B-17s we had flown in Europe. He did not need to concern himself with maintenance problems in England; he was overwhelmed trying to cope with them on Saipan.

Moreover, he had not kept up with the changing opinions and environment in the United States regarding the conduct of the air war. By the winter of 1944–45, the American people were becoming tired of the war and the number of casualties. He had always counted on Arnold's continuing friendship and support, and therefore resisted advice from the Air Corps chief's staff. Generals Kuter and Norstad, Arnold's most trusted staff assistants, had worked closely with Hansell in the early days of the war. Until the fall of 1944, they supported the air force policy of high-altitude daylight precision bombing. Unlike him, however, they were flexible enough to change tactics and strategy to meet the demands of the new mood of the country to end the war.

Hansell had another source of stress. His high-altitude precision bombing program was competing with a successful naval air campaign in the Pacific. Admirals Chester Nimitz and William "Bull" Halsey had discarded the old navy dogma that battleships controlled the sea. By December 1944, carrier-based aircraft were gaining air supremacy over the Japanese, and Nimitz and Halsey began planning to bomb Japanese targets on Honshu. If they were successful, questions were sure to be asked about the value of the B-29 missions.

Hansell had patterned his B-29 tactics on the same high-altitude daylight precision bombing tactics that failed over Germany in 1943. By early 1944, Generals Eisenhower and Spaatz understood that unless they modified their tactics, weather and cloud cover would limit the number of bombing missions against Germany to no more than four or five per month. Arnold did not object when they told him the time had come to overwhelm Germany with massive bombing attacks. Flying more missions would require de facto area bombing on at least ten missions a month.

Hansell was determined that his command would not employ similar tactics over Japan. It is impossible to know if his enmity toward O'Donnell influenced his opposition to experimenting with night bombing. When he said in November 1944 that a night mission to Tokyo would be catastrophic, he was probably worried about more than crew losses. He may have been thinking about the impact it would have on validating his theories that victory could be achieved by daylight precision bombing of military targets.

Yet he had to know that Arnold was not interested in theories or even the unique problems he encountered in bombing Japan. Arnold wanted results, and he had supported Arnold's decision to replace both Eaker and Wolfe when they failed to meet Arnold's expectations. Now it was Hansell who was being accused of failing to produce.

In late December, after XXI Bomber Command had only one month of bombing operations against Japan under its belt, Arnold began growing impatient. He bombarded Hansell with memos and strike photographs describing the results of LeMay's B-29 operations out of China. He reminded Hansell that he had more than two hundred bombers in his command, yet he was averaging no more than seventy planes a mission. LeMay's groups were making maximum use of all of his aircraft despite seemingly impossible logistical restraints. Arnold noted that LeMay, unlike Hansell, did not send him almost daily excuses and apologies explaining his operational problems. Arnold wrote Hansell that he was not fighting a paper war. He didn't need daily written reports. He wanted results—not explanations for poor results. Hansell would be better off if he wrote fewer memos and spent more time riding herd on his bomber groups.

Arnold had no cause to criticize Hansell's loss rate. His losses were not as high as they had been in the Eighth Air Force. However, Arnold was upset about the number of bombs—or lack thereof—that XXI Bomber Command was putting on targets. He wasn't willing to wait any longer for Hansell to attempt to match LeMay's record. Hansell had been an excellent and loyal staff and planning officer.

He wondered, however, if he was an effective combat commander. Perhaps Eaker had been correct in replacing him as a wing commander in the spring of 1943. Nor were reports from his staff about Rosie O'Donnell's relations with Hansell encouraging. Rosie had never criticized Hansell. He didn't mention him—or even damn him with faint praise. Arnold knew both men well enough to understand that there was no love lost between them. Rosie was usually a gung-ho, take-no-prisoners guy. It was not like him to be subdued. Yet he appeared to be just going through the motions as commander of the 73d Wing.

The last straw for Arnold was the following press release, issued by Hansell from Saipan on 27 December 1944:

> Summing up our accomplishments in the thirty days since we first bombed Tokyo, these first accomplishments have been encouraging but that they are far from the standards we are seeking. . . . The primary target is always a rather small section of enemy territory and it looks particularly small when seen from an altitude of something over five miles. Frequently you cannot see it because of clouds or overcast and must depend upon your instruments. We have not put all our bombs exactly where we wanted to put them, and therefore we are not by any means satisfied with what we have done so far. We are still in our early experimental stages. We have much to learn and many operational and other technical problems to solve.

Arnold shuddered to think how the president and the joint chiefs would react when they read that.

LeMay never talked about experimental stages of his bombing, whereas Hansell seemed to imply that precision bombing wasn't successful because of the high altitude and cloud cover. Then he talked about the necessity of depending on instruments and technical problems. He must have been talking about radar. Arnold knew that Hansell was reluctant to use radar. His suggestion that the B-29 had technical problems was implying that it was not ready for combat. The army and navy had been saying that for some time and telling people it was a waste of money.

Generals Chennault and Wedemeyer were telling everyone that LeMay had whipped the 58th Wing into an effective, well-disciplined fighting force. Arnold had replaced Wolfe with LeMay in part because of Hansell's advice. Hansell had been right: LeMay was a superb professional, and Wolfe was an amateur. Now Arnold had reservations about Hansell. Combat command and planning required different talents. Arnold knew Hansell wanted to fight a civilized war, but it was too late for that. He needed someone like LeMay. Maybe he was an iron ass, but at least he had the support of his people and was getting bombs on the target. Moreover, he knew how to take advice. LeMay had listened when Chennault and Wedemeyer recommended that he use incendiaries on Hankow on 18 December.

Arnold decided it was time to make an immediate change. He couldn't wait for Hansell to defeat the Japanese with his theories of civilized precision bombing. They stood in the way of ending the war in a hurry. Bombing their cities and mining their major harbors was the only way to defeat the Japanese. Norstad had told Arnold about his last conversation with Hansell in October as he was leaving for Saipan. He had reminded Hansell that Eisenhower and Spaatz had ordered Doolittle to implement the air war plans of 1941 and 1942—plans that Hansell had drafted. They gave the air force authority to attack important German industrial areas and use whatever bombing techniques were necessary to win the war.

It was clear that Hansell was reluctant to do whatever was necessary against the Japanese. He was reluctant to use radar as an aid to visual bombing. While his press release admitted that high altitude, strong winds, and cloud cover had made it difficult to locate and hit targets, he appeared to be blaming O'Donnell and his 73d Wing for the pitiful results. Arnold concluded that it was doubtful that Hansell would admit it was time to change tactics or that incendiary bombing was permissible or appropriate. LeMay was not that inflexible. He was willing to do whatever it took to defeat the Japanese.

Arnold recalled that Hansell had been shocked and disturbed when LeMay had praised the RAF's successful firebombing of Hamburg. LeMay had been correct in pointing out that the RAF had destroyed military targets at Hamburg. It was not a coincidence that

Doolittle had selected LeMay's air division to lead the first area bombing of Berlin in March 1944.

Although LeMay didn't like to deal with the press or engage in public relations campaigns, he did give Arnold strike photos and tonnage figures that impressed the American people and even Admiral King. Arnold didn't have the time or the energy to micromanage B-29 operations in the Pacific. Arnold decided to give LeMay complete discretion in developing tactics that would destroy Japanese military production and the people's will to continue the war.

Hansell seemed oblivious to the changed tempo of the war in both Europe and the Pacific. President Roosevelt's thinking had changed. He was getting tired and didn't look well. He was becoming impatient about ending the war. At the last meeting with the joint chiefs, the president had pointedly asked Arnold when the B-29s in Saipan were going to begin bombing Japan in earnest.

Now came the difficult part. Firing old friends was the toughest part of Arnold's job. Ira Eaker was still bitter and angry about losing his command in England. It was ironic that Eaker had replaced Hansell because he thought Hansell was nervous, couldn't handle stress, and was not tough enough to be a combat commander. Hansell had joined Vandenberg and Kuter in recommending Eaker's replacement. Now it was Hansell's turn. Oh well, what goes around comes around.

Arnold considered how and in what manner to tell Hansell he was being relieved. He would be heartbroken. It would be too stressful to fly to Guam and confront Hansell personally. He decided to have Norstad deliver a personal letter extending him his heartfelt thanks for his splendid past work and loyalty. He had laid the groundwork for the future success of the B-29 program. But what should Hansell's next assignment be? He had worked well with LeMay in England. If they both agreed, he could be LeMay's second in command and advise him on the selection of strategic targets. Hansell was a proud man. In the past, he had suggested that LeMay was lacking in social amenities, that he was too abrupt. No, it probably wouldn't be a good fit. He decided to leave the decision up to them. If Hansell were unwilling to serve as LeMay's second in command Arnold would find a place for him in the training command—a momentous comedown for him because it would destroy his hopes of achieving a higher command. Arnold hoped that he was not about to lose another friend and loyal supporter, but he feared it was inevitable.

Before making his final decision, Arnold decided to meet again with Generals Kuter and Norstad. He told them that Hansell's Marianas operations weren't working. He asked Norstad if LeMay should replace Hansell. Norstad replied that they had no choice since they were phasing out B-29 operations in China. LeMay was the only commander who understood the aircraft and knew how to get bombs on target. He was a major general. Hansell still had only one star. Although LeMay had worked for Hansell when he was a colonel, it was unlikely Hansell could handle working for an iron ass like LeMay. It wouldn't do to have Hansell sulking in his tent because LeMay had hurt his feelings.

Perhaps LeMay was ruthless and had a one-track mind. It didn't matter to his combat people; they were his strongest supporters. If he was all substance and no form—well, that was just what was needed. He was the best heavy bomber commander in the air force. He would do whatever it took to get the job done.

Arnold asked Kuter if he agreed.

Kuter said that if they had more time, Hansell might come around. But under the circumstances, Hansell had to go. LeMay was the right man at the right time.

Arnold turned to Norstad and said he couldn't face Hansell. His heart was acting up. He would draft a personal letter for him to give to Hansell.

20: The Eagle Stretches His Wings

When LeMay received Norstad's memo ordering him to fly to Guam, he was not told the meeting's purpose. For more than two months, LeMay had been telling Arnold and Norstad that B-29 operations from China were a waste of resources. The logistical situation in China was impossible. The bases in the Chengtu area were too far from Japan. Kyushu, Japan's most southerly island, was the only home-island target within range of the B-29s. Norstad did not tell LeMay he was replacing Hansell, only that his 58th Wing would be transferred to the Marianas during the winter of 1945. The meeting was a planning session for that move.

Norstad arrived without notice at Hansell's new Guam headquarters on 6 January. As was usual among old friends, Hansell gave him a warm welcome. It was an awkward and embarrassing situation. He and Hansell were close personal friends and for a year had been the most important planners on Arnold's staff. He had recommended that Norstad succeed him as chief of staff of the Twentieth Air Force, and he assumed that Norstad had traveled to Guam to work out the details of the transfer of LeMay's units to the Marianas. After their initial greeting, he asked Norstad if he wished to make a tour of his new headquarters and the operations facilities on Guam.

Norstad replied that he had something more personal to discuss. He told Hansell that LeMay was flying in to take over as commanding general of the XXI Bomber Command. Hansell was shocked and dismayed. He couldn't believe he was receiving this message from a man he believed to be one of his oldest and closest friends. This was déjà vu: they were following the same script he had experienced with the Eighth Air Force in England. Norstad didn't wait for a response. Subject to Hansell's consent, he continued, Arnold was prepared to appoint him vice commander, second in command to LeMay.

Hansell hesitated. He finally replied that he couldn't believe Arnold was serious. Arnold was not being fair to him. He had been working to build up the Twentieth Air Force for almost a year to engage in strategic daylight bombing of Japan. When he had left Washington in October, Arnold gave him specific instructions to conduct a high-altitude precision daylight bombing campaign. Arnold had replaced Wolfe because he wasn't making a real effort to make daylight visual bombing work. When Hansell took over in August, he had faced a similar refusal by O'Donnell and his 73d Wing group commanders. He put them back on daylight operations.

In November, a few days before the first scheduled mission to Tokyo, O'Donnell had sent him a letter repeating his request that they conduct night operations. Dealing with O'Donnell and his wing had been a nightmare. It was only after he had threatened to replace O'Donnell that he relented. Five weeks was not enough time to prove that high-altitude daylight operations could not succeed. Rosie O'Donnell and others believed that it was impossible to do so from the Marianas. O'Donnell and his entire wing had sold themselves on radar bombing at night. He should have gotten rid of O'Donnell and his group commanders in August before they'd left for Saipan. Hansell looked directly at his old friend and told him that he knew Norstad was dissatisfied with him because he wasn't enthusiastic about firebombing the Japanese cities. Well, he was wrong if he believed LeMay was ready to give up on daylight precision bombing because he had flown one successful incendiary mission. Hansell's voice trailed off.

Norstad knew that Hansell's account was basically correct. He didn't know how to reply.

He began by reviewing the history of their long friendship. Yes, they had worked successfully together. He also agreed that five weeks of combat operations would not usually be a fair test for any air combat campaign. But Hansell needed to understand that the pressures on Arnold were greater than ever. Norstad then reviewed the problems of the war in Europe, the tremendous casualties they had suffered in the Battle of the Bulge, and the potential casualties involved in an invasion of Japan. Invading Japan would be much tougher, with many more casualties than in Europe. The United States wouldn't have a readymade base of operations in the Pacific, as they did in England. Moreover, unlike the Germans, the Japanese would rather die than surrender their homeland.

Nordstad paused and, looking directly at Hansell, told him that his 27 December press release had triggered Arnold's decision. A few days before, Arnold had received Hansell's personal memo objecting to Norstad's request that he experiment with an incendiary mission on Nagoya. Norstad emphasized that he was not objecting to Hansell's attempt to go over his head to Arnold. What Hansell probably didn't know was that a week earlier, LeMay's headquarters in China sent out a press release that directly contradicted his own. Unlike Hansell, LeMay stated that the experimental phase of B-29 operations was over. He was ready to launch a smashing attack on Japan's war potential.

Hansell didn't seem to understand that high-level thinking about bombing policy had changed. The committee of operational analysts recommended firebombing to take advantage of the flimsy wooden buildings that housed Japanese war industries. They had learned in Germany and Japan that military targets were hard to locate in cloud cover from high altitudes. If military targets couldn't be pinpointed, then the only alternative was to destroy the entire area where they were located. Norstad pointed out that the war was in a critical stage in both the European and Pacific theaters. Eisenhower and Spaatz had authorized de facto area bombing through cloud cover in Germany. LeMay himself had done it to Berlin and, if necessary, Norstad was sure he would do it to Tokyo. Norstad then said something he later came to regret. He told Hansell that perhaps he was too civilized to fight a war the way it had to be fought. They had to finish off Japan from the air or there was going to be an invasion with hundreds of thousands if not millions of casualties.

Hansell felt his face flush. He knew he had to remain in control. He thought back to his conversation with LeMay after the Hamburg fire missions in July 1943. LeMay had approved of the RAF's area bombing because it could destroy military targets. He decided that there was no point in defending his strategy and tactics with Norstad. Some of what he said was true. Norstad was probably correct in saying that he didn't have the killer instinct. Hansell knew he was not aggressive by nature. He had always tried to avoid confrontations with his subordinates. It was different when he had been a staff officer for General Arnold. He could anticipate what Arnold expected.

As a combat commander he had to be accepted by the combat crews and their leaders. He knew that he did not have the confidence or even the respect of the crews in the 73d Wing. Hansell was confident that at last the Allies were winning the war against both Germany and Japan. Now was the time for patience: it was not absolutely necessary to engage in area bombing. Hansell realized that he had made a mistake in not keeping up with the change in thinking about area bombing at air force headquarters. Arnold's heart problems had almost made him a figurehead. Kyter and Norstad were running the show now, and they would do anything to end the war as quickly as possible. They believed the end justified the means. He was another casualty of the impatience to end the war in a hurry.

Hansell would not be a hypocrite and deny that area bombing killed innocent civilians. He felt that even if the Japanese acted like beasts, Americans shouldn't do the same. Killing innocent civilians was a matter of moral and ethical consideration. The Hague International Convention made it clear that international law prohibited terror attacks on innocent civilians.

Norstad decided there was no point in continuing the meeting. He ended by telling Hansell that LeMay was scheduled to arrive in Guam the next day.

After landing at North Field on Guam, on 7 January, LeMay went directly to Hansell's office. Hansell, Norstad, and LeMay were three of the youngest generals in the air force. LeMay, a major general, was the youngest at thirty-eight. He had been a colonel when Norstad and Hansell were brigadier generals. He was now senior to both. Norstad was forty, and Hansell, the oldest, was forty-one.

After the initial pleasantries, Norstad turned to LeMay and told him that they were phasing out his China operations. Hansell had moved his headquarters to Guam from Saipan. Guam didn't have the facilities for LeMay's 58th Wing. It had only one runway and no facilities for his groups.

Arnold had decided to consolidate LeMay's XX Bomber Command with Hansell's XXI Bomber Command in the Marianas. Norstad told LeMay that he would be commander of all of the Twentieth Air Force's B-29 operations. LeMay's expression didn't change.

Norstad then said that Arnold had recommended Hansell remain as LeMay's second in command. He concluded by saying that Arnold wanted him to take over as quickly as he could break away from the CBI.

LeMay looked at Hansell. He wondered if Hansell thought he was in some way behind the change in command. Hansell and LeMay had never been close friends, but they respected each other and had worked well together in England. LeMay knew that Hansell had joined in recommending his promotions to brigadier general in September 1943 and major general in March 1944. The situation was awkward for both of them. He knew that Hansell had never wavered in his support for high-altitude precision daylight bombing. Hansell had left England in the fall of 1943 before Spaatz and Doolittle had increased the Eighth Air Force's tempo of operations and engaged in de facto area bombing when weather conditions precluded visual bombing.

LeMay told Hansell that the change of command was news to him. When he told Arnold that he thought B-29 operations from China were a waste of resources, Arnold didn't mention a possible change of command. They both knew that he was impatient for immediate results. They had experienced that when he replaced Eaker in Europe and Wolfe in China. Moreover, they had endured some rough times together in the winter and spring of 1943 in England. They had flown missions together and worked out of some tough situations in B-17s.

In some ways, the combat conditions over Germany were probably worse than they had encountered with the B-29s. He knew that Hansell had always supported him. Hansell's problems had been different from his in the CBI. He said he hoped to have the benefit of his contributions and input as soon as he took command. He concluded by telling Hansell that the country and the air force owed him a lot.

Hansell smiled nervously. He told LeMay that he was not blaming him for the change. He knew that LeMay was not the type who would go behind his back. Ever the gentleman, he said that if he was going to be replaced by anyone, he was glad it was LeMay. He was the best heavy bomber commander in the air force. When things were rough in the Marianas, he often asked himself what LeMay would do in the same situation. He then asked LeMay if he had discussed his problems with Rosie O'Donnell.

LeMay replied that the last time he had talked to O'Donnell was at Salina in August when they discussed the B-29's mechanical problems and the fact that the crews weren't ready for combat. Hansell's name had not been mentioned.

Hansell told LeMay that he was sure he would do his best to make daylight precision bombing work. He hoped he would be able to satisfy Arnold. Arnold would put pressure on him to fly a mission every day and send back glowing reports of lots of bomb tonnage on targets.

Hansell asked LeMay if he intended to engage in area bombing. LeMay replied that he would try to make high-altitude daylight precision bombing work. He intended to continue Hansell's policies, but he would not rule out the use of incendiaries, which he had used effectively at Hankow. He saw no reason not to use incendiaries on Japanese cities if it would destroy military targets more effectively.

Norstad interrupted and announced it was time to wrap up the meeting. He told LeMay that Arnold had assigned Roger Ramey to replace him in the CBI. LeMay should take Ramey back with him to Kharagpur and brief him on CBI operations during the long flight to India. Ramey in turn could brief LeMay on the XXI Bomber Command. LeMay and Hansell would change commands on 20 January.

As LeMay turned to leave, Hansell stopped him and thanked him for offering to make him his vice commander. He then politely declined the job. The past six months had been a nightmare for him, he explained, and he thought he could use a change of pace. He hadn't been in the training command since before the war. He enjoyed teaching. It would give him a chance to recuperate. He said he hoped LeMay would continue precision bombing. When the war was over, they would be judged by the way they had won it.

General Arnold had his fourth serious heart attack on 17 January. LeMay arrived on Guam two days later. Hansell had not confided in any of his staff members about his replacement. One of his closest friends on Guam was St. Clair McKellway, a sophisticated writer for the *New Yorker* magazine before the war who was in charge of our public relations. Hansell became acquainted with McKellway in Washington and was responsible for his appointment as the XXI Bomber Command press officer. McKellway had assisted Hansell in preparing the 27 December press release that had so irritated Arnold.

Like most *New Yorker* writers, he was not willing to fudge a story. McKellway had heard about LeMay, but had never met him. He first saw LeMay when he walked into the operations room after his plane arrived from India on 19 January. He knew of his reputation as a tough combat commander and was not surprised when LeMay passed by him, making no effort to greet him. Press officers in Washington had told him that LeMay was less than hospitable to the press on his November 1943 bond tour. As a well-known combat commander, LeMay's presence on Guam was news, which merited an explanation.

McKellway visited Hansell in his tent before dinner as he was packing his footlocker. He asked him why LeMay was on Guam. It had to be more than a social call. Hansell told him that LeMay was there to take command of all B-29 operations in the Pacific. His command in China was being phased out and moved to the Marianas. McKellway replied that the change sounded like a raw deal to him. Hansell had been bombing Japan for less than two months. He hoped that the press release they had prepared didn't hurt him.

Hansell replied that the press release probably didn't help, but that it was not the real problem. Arnold had been comparing his bombing results with LeMay's. LeMay had been getting more planes and bombs on the targets. Arnold had been showing his bomb strike photos in Washington and talking about the results, such as LeMay's successful firebombing of Hankow. Also, he probably should not have gone over Norstad's head to Arnold, protesting his plan for incendiary area bombing.

There was a big story for McKellway about a change in bombing policy; he should look into it but be careful. No one at the top would admit that the air force had given up on high-altitude precision daylight bombing. Hansell said that he guessed that he was not tough enough for them. They wanted a quick fix; it was a classic case of "the end justifying the means." He asked McKellway if he knew that LeMay had worked under him as a colonel in England and supported him for both of his promotions. Now he outranked him. It was the ultimate irony.

McKellway asked him about his future plans. Hansell replied that he was going to return to the States and see his family. He didn't want to go back and serve on Arnold's staff because it would be awkward working with Norstad and Kuter. Although he thought they were his friends, he suspected that they had told Arnold that LeMay was a doer, whereas he was an intellectual best used as a planner. He suspected that Rosie O'Donnell might have had a part in his replacement. He was close to Arnold and had been on his staff. He then said he would rather not talk about the situation anymore.

Hansell invited McKellway to sit with him at dinner. No one mentioned the impending change of command. McKellway looked across the dining area at LeMay sitting at another table and noticed that he was not conversing with the other men at his table. McKellway did not look forward to preparing press releases with or for LeMay as he didn't seem gracious or friendly to the new men he would be working with. LeMay didn't appear to be gloomy, but he definitely appeared to be unsociable, if not rude. He wished he were flying back to the States with Hansell.

I returned from Saipan the next day. I had been there working with the 73d Wing's navigators and so knew nothing about the change of command. There was no formal parade area for military ceremonies, but as I left our plane I observed several squads of men in formation out on the tarmac. I saw Hansell facing Norstad, and I was surprised to see LeMay standing behind them with McKellway, holding his pipe in his hand. I walked up to the fringe of a group of onlookers and heard Norstad commend Hansell for his outstanding leadership and service to the B-29 program as he pinned a Distinguished Service Medal on his tunic. When the ceremony was over, LeMay walked over and greeted me warmly. One of the 305th's former squadron commanders, Joe Preston, was a few yards away. He was now a full colonel. Joe walked up and we shook hands.

"Well Ralph, here we are, together again," said Joe. "We finally did get to the Pacific. We thought we avoided that at Syracuse." Joe filled me in on the change of command and we arranged to meet for dinner.

I walked over to Hansell. Several members of his staff surrounded him. I didn't know what to say. I stepped forward to say good-bye and we shook hands.

Hansell wished me luck and said, "I'm sure you'll enjoy working with LeMay and Joe Preston again. Look me up when you get back to the States and let's talk about something besides the war."

I was learning that war could ruin careers as well as lives.

Hansell's refusal to remain in the Marianas as LeMay's second in command and his request for a training command assignment ensured his isolation from his old associates at Arnold's headquarters. He had expected a more important and prestigious assignment, but he was too hurt to ask for it. On 21 January 1945, he flew back to the United States in an Air Transport Command plane. He didn't report to the Pentagon in Washington, but instead took a commercial airline flight to his home in Atlanta. He commenced his new duties in Arizona on 1 March.

Hansell spent his first week getting to know the officers of his training command. They were courteous and respectful. He wondered if there were any rumors about why he'd been sent back to the States after such a short tenure in a combat command. He decided that at this point in his career it didn't make any difference. He planned to relax and do some serious reading. Later, he would write his memoirs and describe his experiences with world leaders. He had enjoyed the prerogatives power, but he would also enjoy the opportunity to engage in true intellectual pursuits.

He wondered why he had not been offered a more important assignment. He compared his status with Wolfe and Eaker. Wolfe had been given a second star and command of the air materiel command at Wright Field. Eaker had been given command of all Allied air forces in the Mediterranean.

Hansell felt that he might as well have been in Siberia. It wasn't his style to pout or sulk. He appreciated the opportunity to rest.

Hansell suspected that his command of the B-29s in the Pacific would be the high point of his career. Now, he had nowhere to go but down. It was going to be difficult to adjust to being commander of a remote, unimportant training facility in Arizona, but he would have plenty of time to make it.

He had spent four years working at the elbows of the top leaders of the Allied powers. The president had commended him for his 1941 and 1942 air war plans. Churchill had been enthusiastic about his plans to put B-29s in China. He had worked well with General Marshall and Admiral King. Now, he was responsible for training aircrews to drop bombs in a chalked circle in the desert. Ironically, he would probably get directives from LeMay about bombing procedures. He had one consolation: he had been true to his beliefs and stood firm against area bombing, even if it had cost him his career.

He spent several weeks reviewing his command in the Marianas and decided that it was appropriate to spell out his problems in writing. He decided not to write to Arnold, choosing instead to send a letter to Arnold's chief of staff, Lt. Gen. Barney Giles. The letter was remarkable for what it did and didn't say about his problems with O'Donnell and the 73d Wing. (See Appendix C.)

LeMay was impressed with the results of Hansell's last daylight mission to Akashi on 19 January. On the twentieth they attended mission debriefings together. LeMay called a meeting of his operations staff at 8 A.M. on the twenty-first. Present were Cols. J. B. Montgomery, Del Wilson, and Joe Preston, other operations staff officers, and me.

"Three of you men here were with me in England," LeMay began. "You know the importance of training and discipline. I understand that some of the people in the 73d Wing have not had confidence in this bomber command and its headquarters staff. I have been told that they have ignored bomber command directives. I don't know the extent of this or the reason, but I will not tolerate this kind of conduct in my command. Training and discipline save lives. We are going to practice, practice, and then practice some more.

"I've also been told that some of the crews are complaining about combat conditions over Japan. From what I hear, and what I learned in our operations out of China, the flak and fighters over Japanese targets are not nearly as bad as we had over Germany. The bottom line is that, except for the Akashi mission two days ago, this outfit has not been getting enough planes over the target or enough bombs on the target. The B-29s have been getting a hell of a lot of publicity without any real bombing results. I am not interested in publicity. I want results.

"Some of you may conclude that I'm a tough SOB. I'll accept that. I am not a Boy Scout leader, but you will find that I will be tougher on myself than any of you. Monty, I want you to be my deputy chief of operations. Joe, I want you to set up a lead crew school like we had in England and China. Nutter will be in charge of the navigation and radar training. Our next mission to Japan will be on the twenty-third.

"I want to lower the altitude by at least five thousand feet. We'll fly some missions at twenty thousand feet. I've been working on the B-29's mechanical problems in China. We haven't worked them all out yet, but the lower altitude will result in less strain on the engines and less fuel consumption. It should also improve bombing accuracy. Tomorrow I'll lead the 73d Wing in a formation practice mission at an altitude of twenty-five thousand feet. Joe, I want you and Nutter to meet with Monty and get his recommendations on the best lead crews in the 73d Wing. They'll be your first students in the lead crew school."

We would be employing the same training programs LeMay had used with us in the 305th Group in England. I flew on the formation-training mission the next day with LeMay and Montgomery. LeMay was in the pilot's seat and he spent much of the time on the radio ordering the planes to tighten up the formation. He spent many hours each day inspecting and supervising maintenance procedures. He supervised the construction of a new runway at North Field on Guam. When it was completed, the senior leaders asked for permission to make the first landing on the new runway. LeMay refused. He piloted the first plane to land there. His passengers were Seabees who had built the runway out of crushed coral.

If Arnold and his staff expected a dramatic change in bombing tactics or results when LeMay took over command from Hansell, they must have been disappointed by his first six weeks of operations. In the week following the change of command, LeMay ordered two high-altitude missions with no change in the tactics used by Hansell. His first mission was an attack on the Mitsubishi aircraft and engine plant on the outskirts of Nagoya on 23 January. The usual cloud cover was present and the bombing results were poor. We lost two B-29s. Four days later, he lowered the bombing altitude to twenty-seven thousand feet. Almost total cloud cover again frustrated the crews. Hundreds of fighters hit the formation while the planes were over Japan. The fighters and the cloud cover impeded bomb accuracy. Only fifty-six bombers hit the general area of the target with radar. Nine bombers were lost. Several fighters made kamikaze attacks, attempting to break up the formation by ramming the lead plane.

LeMay was concerned about the loss of almost 10 percent of the attack force and the meager bomb results on the Nagoya mission. Norstad repeated a suggestion he had made to Hansell. He recommended that LeMay try an incendiary attack on Kobe, one of Japan's largest industrial cities and ports. The command sent 129 aircraft to Kobe, but only sixty-nine hit the target area at the center of the city. However, the incendiary attack was successful: more than a thousand industrial buildings were either destroyed or badly damaged.

On 4 February the new 313th Wing flew its first mission. On the tenth, LeMay sent 120 bombers to hit the Nakajima aircraft plant at Ota. The training film we had prepared at Culver City was used to brief the crews for this mission. The planes carried two-thirds high-explosive bombs and one-third incendiaries. Eighty-four aircraft hit the target destroying a third of the factory area. The mission knocked out Japanese fighter production there for two months. LeMay attempted two more high-altitude precision daylight missions the following week. Both were unsuccessful.

On 25 February, LeMay launched a daylight incendiary mission that bombed Tokyo from thirty-one thousand feet. This was the first mission for the 314th Wing flying from Guam. A total of 231 aircraft took off with each plane carrying three tons of incendiaries and a single five-hundred-pound high-explosive bomb; 171 planes reached the target. The strike photos showed that the mission had eliminated an entire square mile of Tokyo.

After bombing Japan from the Marianas for about the same period of time as Hansell, the only missions on which LeMay's command inflicted major damage on Japanese targets were those employing a mixed load of incendiary and high-explosive bombs. From 24 November 1944 to 8 March 1945, the XXI Bomber Command had flown twenty missions. Only two had been successful, and losses were close to 6 percent. It was time to reassess high-altitude daylight bombing tactics.

It was futile to wait for clear skies or a change in the jet stream over the targets. There had been only one cloud-free day in six weeks. There were almost always more clouds, high winds, and unpredictable weather above twenty-five thousand feet. Hansell and Arnold's staff had planned for the B-29s to bomb at thirty thousand feet or higher because they did not expect to have fighter support for B-29 missions. The high altitude, coupled with the B-29's speed, was expected to be a defense against Japanese fighters. Unfortunately, they had not considered the effect the weather would have on bombing accuracy.

LeMay decided that flying above twenty-five thousand feet was unnecessary. Flying at lower altitudes would improve bombing accuracy and put less strain on the engines. Japanese antiaircraft and fighters were not nearly as lethal as the defenses the Eighth Air Force had encountered over Germany. Although both LeMay and Hansell had experienced loss rates of 6 percent with B-29s, the bombing results did not justify such losses. LeMay knew that he would have to start producing or he would suffer the same fate as Eaker, Wolfe, and Hansell.

Unlike Hansell, LeMay was willing to change tactics. The RAF had been forced to give up daylight bombing without fighter support in Europe because it was too costly. The British had then made effective use of incendiaries at night. LeMay had always admired Air Marshal Harris. He would follow Harris's bombing strategy.

21: LeMay Firebombs Japan

Norstad arrived at our Guam headquarters on 1 March. He told LeMay that Arnold had sent him to review LeMay's B-29 operations from the Marianas since he had assumed command on 20 January. LeMay was aware that although he had put more planes and bombs over the targets, his bombing results were not dramatically superior to Hansell's. He reviewed the strike photographs of the B-29 missions since November 1944. Although seventy-eight bombers had been lost, no high-priority military targets had been destroyed.

Except for Hansell's Akashi mission, the most damage had been inflicted with a mixed load of incendiary and high-explosive bombs. Norstad suggested that the percentage of incendiaries carried on the missions be increased. LeMay agreed, but expressed doubt that high-altitude incendiary missions achieve the desired results. To obtain accuracy with incendiaries, he said, the planes would have to fly at lower altitudes, preferably below ten thousand feet.

He told Norstad that only twenty-five of the seventy-eight planes they had lost were shot down. The majority of losses were caused by the strain of climbing to and flying at high altitudes. However, B-29s could not fly low-altitude incendiary missions in daylight without fighter support. During the previous two weeks he had given thought to flying such missions at night. He asked Norstad if Arnold was willing to permit him to take a calculated risk. He wasn't asking Norstad to clear night missions with him. Arnold didn't need the heat and stress if they were a failure. If they failed, the monkey would be on LeMay's back.

He planned to meet with his operations people to discuss and evaluate his plans in detail. Norstad replied that the ball was in LeMay's court, the change in tactics was at his discretion and his alone.

Later that day, LeMay told me, "I've been discussing our bombing results with General Norstad. Only three missions since B-29s began bombing from the Marianas have done any substantial damage to Japanese military targets. There are several reasons for this. The weather was bad over Germany, but it's much worse here—particularly at high altitude. At least when we were bombing Germany we had some weather information. Out here we don't get any. As a result, I've been considering low-level night incendiary attacks on the major Japanese cities.

"You trained the 305th's navigators for experimental night missions over Germany in the fall of 1943. Rosie O'Donnell has been anxious to try night operations since last summer. Montgomery has also recommended them. I'm scheduling an operations staff meeting to discuss night incendiary missions to be flown at altitudes of from five thousand to seven thousand feet. I want you to be prepared to discuss the radar and navigation problems we can expect to encounter. Be ready to tell us the pros and cons of day and night missions from the viewpoint of navigators, bombardiers, and radar operators. There will be no formation flying on night missions. Each navigator will be on his own." He paused and then asked me if I thought our navigators were up to the task. I told him that I thought they could do it if we conducted an accelerated training program. I figured I could have them ready for a night mission within a week.

The staff meeting took place the next morning. Present were General LeMay; his chief of staff, Brig. Gen. August Kissner; General Norstad; Brig. Gen. Thomas S. Power, commander of the 314th Wing; Brig. Gen. John H. Davies, commander of the 313th Wing; General O'Donnell; Colonels Montgomery, Preston, Wilson, and Seaver; and the command intelligence, ordnance, and bombing staff officers. I was present as the command navigator.

LeMay opened the meeting by informing us that what we were about to discuss was top secret. We were not to talk about what we heard with anyone, including the aircrews. He summarized the history of XXI Bomber Command operations from November through February. He paused briefly before continuing. "I'm recommending a night incendiary attack on Tokyo at an altitude of from five thousand to seven thousand feet. It's a critical decision for our future operations. It could have an important effect on the course of this war, specifically the need for a land invasion. My analysis and recommendations are not grounded in concrete, but I think it's clear that we can't continue flying high-altitude daylight missions. They won't do the job we were sent here for. We have to face the fact that those tactics have been a failure over Japan."

He looked around the room and his gaze settled on Colonel Montgomery. "Do you have any comments or suggestions, Monty?" he asked. "I understand that you recommended night missions to General Hansell."

"I concur with what you just stated, sir," Montgomery replied. "If we don't start hitting targets soon, we'll be the targets. We haven't been hurting the Japanese. Navy carrier aircraft made a successful attack on Yokohama on 16 February. We have to hit the Japanese with a punch that really hurts if we're going to persuade them that they're defeated. If we fly low-altitude night missions our radar will be more effective and we will be more independent of the weather."

LeMay turned to General Norstad and said, "I know that such a change will not result in precision bombing. We'll be using the same tactics the RAF has been employing against Germany. Do you think General Arnold will approve?"

"General Arnold didn't go to the Malta and Yalta conferences in mid-February," replied Norstad. "General Kuter represented the air force. Before they went to Yalta, the British and American military leaders met at Malta. They agreed that major German cities should be bombed in an effort to impede the German evacuation from the eastern front and hamper German efforts to shift reinforcements to other fronts. Kuter told me that at Yalta, under pressure from Churchill and Stalin, President Roosevelt agreed to increased area attacks on German cities. He is now willing to use whatever bombing tactics will speed up victory in Europe. I assume he will adopt a similar policy in the Pacific.

"The Eighth Air Force is now engaging in area bombing of German communication and transportation centers to assist the Allies in their drive toward Berlin. The Dresden missions two weeks ago were part of this campaign. Our top operational analysts have recommended that we engage in incendiary bombing to take advantage of the vulnerability of the flimsy wooden construction of the buildings in Japanese urban areas. Arnold's staff thinks it would be a mistake to delay the end of the war by searching for specific military targets hidden in Japanese cities. His staff is not going to microman-age the war from Washington. The tactics you employ are your re-sponsibility."

LeMay looked around the room, letting his gaze fall briefly on each of us. "I haven't heard anyone say that a low-altitude night mis-sion is an unreasonable risk to our crews. On a recent daylight mis-sion we lost 10 percent. I wouldn't be recommending this change in tactics if I thought our losses would be that high on night missions. If we keep up these daylight raids we will lose more crews than in a much shorter night incendiary campaign.

"Incendiary bombing is not intended to be terror bombing. It is the only way we can wipe out their war production capacity. We don't look upon Japanese civilians as our targets. Civilians have been killed in assaults on cities and in sieges throughout recorded history. The Japanese have dispersed their war industries all over Tokyo and other urban areas. Their factories are close to or in residential areas.

"A general conflagration in their major cites will make it unnec-essary for us to attempt to locate individual military targets. It will take too long to knock them out one at a time. The president and General Arnold want results now. I was sent here to win the war in the air without an invasion.

"Until we secure Iwo Jima, we'll have no fighter support over Japan. This means that we can't lower our altitude in daylight suffi-ciently to engage in even partially accurate incendiary bombing. The weather is not going to improve. We can't wait for clear weather dur-ing the day or for the jet-stream winds to diminish at high altitude. The weather is better at night.

"The Japanese appear to have no effective night fighters, and their flak doesn't compare with the Germans. I don't believe they have ef-ficient antiaircraft guns at low altitude. If the planes fly individually to targets at night at low altitude, we'll put less strain on the engines and use less fuel. Long formation flights contribute to crew fatigue and shorten the life of our engines. We can fly almost the entire mis-sion at a low cruising altitude. With the savings in fuel, we can in-crease our bomb loads. At night, the gunners won't be much help; by the time they see an enemy fighter it'll be too late. If we take out the gunners, guns, and ammunition, we'll save more weight. We might be able to double our bomb capacity.

"Let's talk about navigation and bombing accuracy. There is more accurate Loran and radar reception for navigation at lower altitudes. Japan is an ideal area for night radar bombing. Most of their major cities and military targets are close to harbor areas with coastlines and peninsulas that stand out on the radar screen. This land-water contrast will enable our least experienced radar operators to get to within a mile of the target area. Then the bombardiers can set their sights on the area lit up by the pathfinders.

"I expect that some of you are thinking about the losses in the low-level mission to Ploesti and other low-level efforts we made in Europe. Those missions were in daylight. The Germans killed us with flak and fighters. We tried night bombing from England in late 1943. We had a low percentage of losses. Nutter bombed Munich at night. He trained the navigators in his group for those night operations. The 73d Wing did some training in night radar bombing last summer."

He paused a moment to let all he'd just said sink in. "At the present time we have no choice," he concluded. "I'm not giving up on visual daylight bombing. If the weather is clear, we'll still fly daylight precision missions, but at a lower altitude."

"Aren't firebomb attacks on cities the type of terror bombing used by the RAF that our air force has been trying to avoid?" asked the intelligence officer.

"I know there may be some who will call it uncivilized warfare," replied LeMay. "But you simply can't fight a war without some civilian casualties. General Norstad tells me that the press has been howling about the civilian casualties caused in Dresden. We didn't start this war, but the quicker we finish it, the more lives we will save—and not just American. We want to avoid killing civilians if possible, but keep in mind that the Japanese workers who manufacture weapons are part and parcel of their military machine. My first duty is to protect and save as many of our crews as possible."

He looked at Norstad, and added, "I'm sure General Arnold will permit us to burn all of Tokyo if that's what it takes to win the war. The reality is that the only way we can destroy Japan's military targets is to burn down every city that has military targets." Norstad nodded his head in approval.

"You've convinced me," said one of the wing commanders. "But I don't know if we can convince our crews that this isn't a suicide mission."

"I wouldn't be recommending this if I thought it were a suicide mission," LeMay replied. "It's your job to convince your crews. Go back to your groups and commence training for night missions. Your navigators will need intensive celestial practice." He glanced at me and said, "Nutter, I want you to go up to Saipan and Tinian and meet with the group navigators and set up an intensive training program for the navigators and radar operators. If there are no more questions the meeting is dismissed."

I couldn't sleep that night. I had been involved in planning the bombing of German targets during the "Big Week" bombings in February 1944. But at those briefings, combat crews were given specific primary military targets and were told that if clouds obscured the targets they should attempt to hit the primary target using radar or bomb targets of opportunity.

Radar had improved significantly in the past year, but there was no way that it could be as precise as visual bombing.

The staff made a tentative plan for the first Tokyo mission. The command bombardier mapped out a fifteen-square-mile area of Tokyo in grids with napalm incendiaries dropped at spaced intervals. When the fires joined up, the city would be engulfed in a "blanket of fire." No mission in history had ever been planned to create such mass devastation.

I was also concerned about the Japanese flak at low altitude. If it were effective, we would see a repeat of the Ploesti disaster. A member of the staff suggested that we should fly an experimental mission to determine the extent and capability of Japanese antiaircraft. LeMay disagreed. He said that surprise was absolutely necessary. If the first mission worked, he would plan five missions against Japan's other major cities over the next ten days, before they had an opportunity to position antiaircraft guns or organize fire defense procedures.

I reviewed the details of the mission plans. I remembered when LeMay had first explained his "no evasive action" policy for bomb runs to us in England. Was this a greater risk? How many of the three hundred planes would return?

I noticed that General Norstad had said nothing negative about LeMay's audacious plan. If the mission were a failure, Arnold wouldn't blame Norstad. If thousands of civilians died it would not be Arnold's fault. He hadn't authorized a policy change. If LeMay were willing to start fires that burned Tokyo to the ground he would have to take the heat if the mission failed.

I was pleased that no one had questioned me about potential navigation problems. The staff was subdued as we left the meeting. I had been with LeMay in Europe when he made tactical changes that had seemed radical at the time, but he never failed the crews. I had to persuade the navigators and radar operators that the change was in their best interest.

The next morning I flew to Saipan and met with the navigators and radar operators of the 73d Wing. I then flew to Tinian and met with the 313th Wing. I felt guilty about not telling them the altitude they would be flying at on the night mission. I knew that some navigators would be flying other missions before the 9 March mission to Tokyo. We could not afford to risk a breach of security.

LeMay had been in the Marianas for almost six weeks. His rigid and demanding training program and direct involvement in solving the B-29's engine and mechanical problems had improved the morale of both the combat and maintenance crews. They had confidence in his leadership and judgment.

I attended the mission briefing for the 314th Wing on Guam the afternoon of 9 March with General LeMay and Colonels Montgomery and Preston. Norstad had issued orders that LeMay and staff members involved in mission planning not go on the mission. LeMay selected General Power, the 314th Wing commander, to lead the mission. The crews had spent the previous week training for a night mission to Tokyo, so no one was surprised when General Power unveiled the map and said that was where they were going on this trip.

The wing commander looked around the briefing room and then unloaded the bombshell: "We're making some tactical changes on this mission, gentlemen. Our three wings from Saipan, Tinian, and Guam are going to put three hundred planes over Tokyo at night. This will be the largest B-29 mission of the war. Four-fifths of your bomb load will be incendiaries. You will drop on the flares and fires started by our pathfinders. I am going to lead the mission. We will take off forty minutes before the 73d and 313th Wings so that we can arrive together over Tokyo about midnight. By arriving together we should saturate the enemy flak and fighter defenses. Our wing has certain specific aiming points on this grid map. We will attack targets individually at an altitude of seven thousand feet; the 73d will bomb at five thousand feet, and the 313th at six thousand. I will circle Tokyo until the last plane drops its bombs."

At the mention of the low altitude there was a loud murmur of protest from the crews.

"I know this comes as a surprise to you, but it's going to be more of a surprise to the Japanese. They don't have antiaircraft guns with radar capable of tracking aircraft at altitudes below seven thousand feet. Nor do they have any effective night fighters. Because of this, the gunners, machine guns, and ammunition are being removed from each aircraft to save weight."

There was another murmur of protest from the crews and someone yelled, "You can't split up our crews!"

Power ignored the outburst. "We've given this a lot of thought," he continued. "If we remove the guns and ammunition we'll be lighter, we'll use less fuel, and there will be less strain on the engines."

I could feel the tension in the room. I looked at the faces of the crewmembers. They had the same forlorn expression as the men of the 305th in October 1943, when they were told they had to return to Schweinfurt a second time.

"Five thousand feet," a voice called out from the back of the room. "You have to be kidding!"

Another voice spoke up, "This is stupid. It's suicide. Surprise may help us with the fighters. It won't help us with the flak. We could lose 75 percent of our force."

I looked at LeMay. He made no reply. He sat puffing on his pipe with no change in his facial expression. General Power felt he was obliged to reply to the acid comments.

"I would not lead this mission and we would not be sending you if we thought it was an unreasonable risk," he said. "General LeMay has had more combat experience in heavy bombers against both the Germans and the Japanese than anyone in the air force. His losses on missions are the lowest of any combat commander. We've lost more crews from engine and mechanical failure than from the Japanese opposition.

"Many of our losses have been caused by the strain of the climb to high altitude. With the lighter loads and in the cover of darkness, you can fly over Tokyo and get the hell out of there with the least strain on the engines. I know you hate the idea of breaking up your crews and losing your gunners, but we have to face reality. There's no advantage to be gained by continuing to bomb at high altitude and keep returning to the same targets again and again. More missions mean more losses. This is a plan to quickly defeat the Japanese. We have studied every potential problem in detail.

"You will fly the last leg of the approach to Japan at thirty-five hundred feet. If there's no cloud cover the navigators can use celestial navigation for almost the entire mission. Loran will be an additional navigational aid for the first thousand miles. If there is cloud cover, the navigator may have to use dead reckoning for the last five hundred miles. The radar operators should be able to pick up the Japanese coast approximately seventy miles before landfall. The irregular coastline should enable the navigators and radar operators to determine their positions precisely.

"You will encounter crosswinds as you approach Japan. I know many of you navigators have been relying on the lead navigator when flying in formation. This time you will be on your own. You should check your position every few minutes. If you don't keep correcting to the left, you will never hit Japan. If you have mechanical problems or you run short of fuel on your return flight, you can make an emergency landing on Iwo Jima. The runway is short, but it's better than ditching, and it'll be much safer landing in daylight. Be sure to turn on your IFF as you approach Iwo. Some of those navy and marine gunners are flak happy.

"This is the most important mission of the war. Success will mean that our troops may not have to invade Japan. I know you all have the guts to make this mission a success."

He turned to LeMay and asked, "Would you like to make any comments, sir?"

LeMay shook his head. "No, you said it all much better than I could."

I walked out of the briefing room with some of the navigators. Most of them seemed to be reassured by General Power's remarks, but others seemed to be truly frightened or incredulous.

"If this isn't a gamble or suicide, why aren't you going on the mission?" one of them asked me.

I didn't mention that I had served more than a full combat tour over Germany. I simply said that because I was a planning officer, LeMay had ordered me not to fly any missions over Japan.

I stood in the control tower with LeMay as Power's plane took off first late that afternoon. His plane and the pathfinder aircraft carried M-47 napalm incendiaries, fragmentation bombs, and flares. The flares were intended to light up the target area. The planes that followed him carried a load of M-69 napalm clusters. Napalm is a form of jellied gasoline that bursts into flame on impact and spreads flames over a wide area. Once the fires started, it would be difficult, if not impossible, to put them out. The crews following Power were to drop their bombs on the flames started by his flares and bombs. It was planned that each bomb load would spread fire over an area of up to two thousand feet.

It was a seven-hour flight to Japan, and the first aircraft would arrive about midnight. The weather was clear and the navigators were able to determine wind drift and velocity precisely. Almost all planes approached the IP on course. The weather was unusually dry with low humidity and strong winds. By the time the main bomber force reached Tokyo, the pathfinders had already started tremendous fires with burning gasoline. The light from the fires permitted the bombardiers to make visual sightings of their assigned targets. The first bombs fell shortly after midnight, and the attack continued until nearly 3 A.M.

Within minutes after the first incendiaries hit the ground, the fires merged and a mammoth firestorm engulfed Tokyo. It was the worst conflagration in history. Tokyo was lit up as if it were daylight and dense clouds of smoke blanketed the sky.

The crews were faced with a danger that we had not anticipated: The tremendous heat created turbulence that rocked the bombers as they flew over the fires. The updrafts caused some pilots to lose control of their aircraft. A few planes were flipped over on their backs. Most of the planes made miraculous recoveries and avoided crashing into the raging inferno below. Some crewmembers reported that they could smell smoke and the odor of burning bodies. Gale-force winds, high explosives, and incendiaries made fire fighting almost impossible. The fires jumped across canals and blanketed the city. The flames also consumed oxygen, causing many people to suffocate.

Throughout history cities have been destroyed by enemy ground action. But never before had an attack caused such a holocaust in a heavily populated area in so short a time. More than sixteen square miles of Tokyo were gutted, leaving only a few concrete shafts and chimneys standing. At least a hundred thousand people were killed—more than died in the atomic-bomb attacks on Hiroshima and Nagasaki. Only the German siege of Leningrad, which lasted several years, caused more civilian casualties. Reconnaissance photos showed that at least twenty-two military targets had been destroyed.

The Japanese press and radio condemned LeMay for the slaughter of innocent civilians, including women and children, and denounced the Americans as barbarians. Only 5 percent of the crewmembers who crash-landed or parachuted over Japan survived. Local civilians decapitated most of them.

Starting at 1:30 A.M., Power began sending cryptic radio messages to LeMay reporting the mission's progress. After he dropped his bombs, he circled the area above the incoming bombers. We learned more details about the inferno at the crew debriefings. We lost fourteen B-29s, less than 5 percent of the attacking force. Forty-nine planes were damaged. The losses were much less than those on our missions over Germany in the summer of 1943.

The staff cheered when we received the first optimistic radio reports from Power. LeMay told us to be quiet. He wanted to know the extent of our losses before we did any celebrating. We couldn't conceal our relief when it was over. For almost a week, most of us wondered if we were planning the greatest disaster in aviation history. On two occasions we had lost nearly 20 percent of our crews over Germany. We were worried that this mission could be a greater disaster than either Schweinfurt or Ploesti. I thought about my assurances to the navigators that the mission was not a gamble. Once again, LeMay's careful planning and analysis were correct. Ultimately his audacious change of tactics saved both American and Japanese lives.

LeMay's predictions about the flak and fighters over Tokyo were remarkably accurate. Our crews encountered much less enemy action than they did on daylight missions. Surprise was our greatest defense. Only one B-29 was lost to antiaircraft fire. The other thirteen aircraft lost went down for a variety of reasons not involving enemy action. The relatively low loss percentage and the mission's success inspired the crews. LeMay, who had always been economical with praise, issued a most unusual statement of congratulations: "You have established that you can not only withstand every stress in battle, but you can strike with the power to defeat the enemy."

General Arnold received the news of the Tokyo firebombing while he was still in Florida recuperating from his latest heart attack. Almost ecstatic about the results, he wrote LeMay a personal letter and for the first time addressed him as "Curt." He commended him for a superb and impressive operation, saying that he had proven that he could destroy all of Japan's industrial cities, should that be required. Norstad also congratulated LeMay. He pointed out that he had solved an acute operational problem by using B-29s at low altitude while unloading more bombs on the enemy than on any mission of the Pacific war.

Three weeks earlier, the American press had criticized what correspondents called "the brutal terror bombing of Dresden and other German cities." The first comments about a change of U.S. Army Air Forces bombing policy arose from a background press conference concerning the incendiary attacks on Dresden on 14 February 1945 by the Eighth Air Force and the RAF. An official air force spokesman denied that the attack on Dresden was terror bombing and defended it as an attempt to disrupt German transportation and communication on the eastern front. He said bombing attacks such as those on Dresden would affect Germany's internal economic system and destroy the morale of the German people.

The Associated Press stated that the Dresden mission was the result of "a long awaited decision to adopt terror bombing of German population centers as a ruthless expedient to hasten Hitler's doom."

General Kuter was upset. He called the Associated Press story a setback to precision bombing policy. It was never our policy to attack civilian populations. It was unfortunate, but attacks against targets in populous centers always would endanger civilian lives.

Norstad sent a memo to LeMay telling him that the news media were questioning incendiary attacks upon cities. He suggested that LeMay emphasize that the destruction caused by firebombs was a necessary part of a strategic bombing campaign to eliminate dispersed industries. He said LeMay should guard against stating that firebomb missions involved area bombing.

Colonel McKellway responded with a press release stating that the XXI Bomber Command's object in the firebomb attacks was to destroy industrial and military targets in urban areas.

LeMay instructed the staff to plan similar missions against other major Japanese cities immediately. We planned a mission to Nagoya for the following night. The crews were exhausted, however, and Colonel Montgomery suggested a twenty-four-hour delay before the crews flew another mission. LeMay reluctantly agreed.

Late in the afternoon on 11 March, 312 B-29s took off for Nagoya with more incendiaries than had been used on Tokyo. We didn't expect to have the benefit of surprise the second time around. If the Japanese reacted in the logical manner of the Germans, we expected that they would defend their cities with more antiaircraft and night fighters. LeMay decided to restore some of the guns and gunners, and increase the altitude a little in order to avoid the thermal updrafts created by the conflagration.

A total of 285 bombers reached the target area. To our surprise, the Japanese did not beef up their antiaircraft or fighter defenses. We lost only one B-29, probably to flak. Another twenty-four were damaged by flak but were able to return to base. There was no holocaust as there had been in Tokyo. The weather and winds did not fan the fires. Nevertheless, at least two square miles in the heart of the city were burned to the ground.

LeMay scheduled a mission to Osaka two days later. Now the maintenance crews were getting tired. They had been making a maximum effort for nearly a week preparing for the three-hundred-plane missions. Osaka was Japan's second largest city and nearly rivaled Tokyo in industrial war production. LeMay told us that he was not pleased with the Nagoya results. He ordered the crews to drop their incendiaries at closer intervals. The result was more successful than at Nagoya. This time eight square miles were leveled. There was still no extensive night fighter defense or basic change in the pattern of antiaircraft fire. Only two planes were lost and thirteen damaged. Again, civilian losses were heavy. There were thirteen thousand civilian dead and half a million people were left homeless. Strike photos showed that as many as 120 factories may have been destroyed.

Next came a mission to Kobe on the night of 16 March. The planning staff continued to experiment with the placement of incendiaries in target areas. The crews were directed to drop their bombs in tighter patterns to ensure that the fires merged.

The last mission in this series of incendiary missions involved a return to Nagoya on 19 March. Aside from the first mission to Tokyo, which had been fortuitously aided by unusual weather conditions, the second Nagoya mission was the most successful. In all, 85 percent of the bombers arrived over the city in the first two hours, and the crews layed a closer pattern of bombs. This time they leveled more than three square miles in the city.

Our success resulted in an unexpected problem: We were about to run out of bombs. Five concentrated missions in ten days had exhausted our supply. LeMay depended on the navy to supply us with incendiaries, and after the 2 March planning meeting he had informed Admiral Nimitz that he planned to launch five incendiary missions over a period of ten days. He told Nimitz the number of bombs required. Nimitz, refusing to believe that LeMay would schedule five missions in ten days or use the amount of bombs he had requested, made no effort to schedule the delivery of the needed bombs.

With no more incendiaries available, LeMay resumed daylight bombing with high explosives, but at lower altitudes. We received no incendiaries until the middle of April. On 20 March we had a staff meeting to plan operations until we received more incendiaries. LeMay gave me a list of potential targets. I noted that several well-known, middle-sized Japanese cities were not on the list. Our intelligence officer told me that Hiroshima was an army base and military supply port on the Japanese Inland Sea, which we had targeted for mining. It was rumored to be the location of an American prisoner of war camp.

Nagasaki had extensive war production facilities and was the center of the Mitsubishi steel and iron works. Kokura was considered to be a military arsenal. There were two other cities not on the list of planned targets, Kyoto and Niigata. I knew Kyoto had been the ancient capital of Japan and that it was a well-known Buddhist cultural center. I asked LeMay why none of these cities were on the list of potential targets.

LeMay looked at me sternly and said, "Nutter, we are not going to consider these cities until further notice. They are now off limits."

General Norstad summed up the incendiary missions for the American press. He said the five missions in ten days had inflicted the greatest damage ever suffered by any enemy in such a short period. Thirty-two square miles in four of Japan's largest cities had been destroyed.

Two shiploads of incendiaries arrived on the Marianas on 9 April. LeMay made plans to resume the firebombing of Japanese cities. The public outcry about the civilian casualties resulting from the fire raids on Dresden and Tokyo had diminished.

President Roosevelt and General Arnold were in no condition to oversee the air force bombing campaigns against Germany and Japan. Arnold's heart condition had slowed him considerably, and the president had returned from the Yalta conference in late February physically and mentally worn out. He had remained seated while reporting the results of the conference to a joint session of Congress, for the first time making no attempt to conceal his crippled condition. He was confined to the White House for the remainder of March. Finally, late in the month, he agreed to follow his doctor's instructions and go to Warm Springs, Georgia, to rest. He left the White House on 29 March, never to return.

By the end of the war in August 1945, sixty-six Japanese cities had been almost totally devastated. LeMay's bombing campaign had destroyed Japan's capacity to produce war materiels. He accomplished this while reducing our casualty rate to 1 percent. The devastation of their cities convinced the Japanese people that they could not win the war. Whether the devastation would convince their leaders to surrender was another matter.

The B-29s made another contribution to victory that no one in the air force had planned or anticipated: aerial mining. Although planned by the navy, that service did not have the long-range bombers needed for the mission. Instead, the job fell to LeMay's B-29s.

22: The Aerial Mining of Japan

The aerial mining of Japanese harbors, straits, and the Inland Sea may have been LeMay's greatest strategic contribution to the defeat of Japan. Military historians may have overlooked this because it lacked the drama of the firebombing of major Japanese cities or the atomic attacks on Hiroshima and Nagasaki. The navy was behind the mining of Japanese waters. Its submarine campaign against the Imperial Fleet and Japan's merchant shipping had been a tremendous but overlooked success. The navy inflicted more damage on Japanese shipping than the Germans did on the Allies in the Battle of the Atlantic. Ocean shipping was Japan's lifeblood. Its war industries required vast amounts of iron and steel, aluminum, and chemicals—nearly all of which had to be imported.

In the fall of 1944, Arnold's civilian committee of operational analysts joined with the navy in recommending a joint submarine and aerial mining blockade of Japan. It was given the code name Operation Starvation.

Japan's three main islands are Honshu, Kyushu, and Shikoku. The Inland Sea, which divides these islands, handled at least 70 percent of Japan's commerce. Japan had to import 75 percent of its oil, 85 percent of its iron ore, and more than one-fifth of its food. The narrow Shimonoseki Strait at the northwestern ends of Honshu and Kyushu was the only outlet from the Inland Sea to Japan's occupied territories in China and Korea.

Arnold's staff officers were opposed to the navy's plan because it meant diverting B-29s involved in the strategic bombing campaign. In November 1944, Generals Kuter and Norstad cautioned Hansell not to give in to the navy's request. Hansell wholeheartedly agreed; he considered mining to be a misuse of airpower.

Admiral King eventually submitted his requests for B-29 assistance to the joint chiefs with the support of General Marshall. Arnold in turn directed Hansell to begin smaller mining operations than those requested by the navy by April 1945. Nimitz, unwilling to be deterred by the delay, suggested to Hansell in early January that he try low-altitude night mining missions, at least in the Shimonoseki Strait. Hansell again refused. He told me that he was trying to avoid night operations and that he was not about to repeat the mistake the Eighth Air Force had made in 1942 and 1943 by bombing the German submarine pens. "Mining is a tactical naval operation," he explained. "I am opposed to sending B-29s singly on low-altitude night missions. I have always been opposed to night operations."

In his first meeting with LeMay shortly after he arrived on Guam, Nimitz tried again for support. At first, LeMay demurred. Nimitz asked him if he would give him time to explain the importance and strategic implications of aerial mining. LeMay was impressed. He agreed to set up a joint task force of naval officers and XXI Bomber Command staff officers for mining operations.

LeMay appointed me a member of the joint committee. We met on Tinian in early February. The naval officers informed us that the mines would have to be dropped by parachute at an altitude of less than ten thousand feet, preferably below eight thousand feet. We replied that there was no way we could do that in daylight because of our aircrafts' vulnerability to antiaircraft fire and fighter attacks, and offered an alternative suggestion. The 313th Wing's radar bombing accuracy was improving, and the land/water contrast in the area of the mine drops would be ideal for night radar operations by single aircraft. We agreed to schedule six experimental missions, and I delivered the plans to LeMay. He ordered us to fly a night practice mission to Japanese-held Rota, a few miles north of Guam, on 27 January.

I flew as navigator and radar operator on that first mission and had no difficulty picking out the aiming point on my radar screen at an altitude of five thousand feet. The 313th then flew four training missions from Tinian against Rota and the Pagan Islands. They flew the first missions with high explosive or water bombs, the last with actual mines. I informed LeMay that I was concerned that these practice missions would be a signal to the Japanese that we were about to commence night mining missions in the Japanese home islands. He said we would have to take that chance.

The navy requested the mining of the Shimonoseki Strait to support the upcoming invasion of Okinawa, and on 27 March LeMay ordered the 313th to make a maximum effort. The mission was a great success. Ninety-two B-29s dropped several thousand magnetic and acoustical mines into the strait. Three planes were lost to anti-aircraft fire. A second mission on 30 March was equally successful. Our reconnaissance aircraft reported that the Japanese had halted all shipments through the straits. These two missions cut Japanese imports in half. As a result, Japanese naval units avoided the strait and took a southerly, more hazardous route to Okinawa, where waiting submarines and other U.S. naval units could pick them off.

The joint mining and submarine campaign was living up to its code name, Starvation. LeMay decided to increase the pressure. In April he ordered the 313th Wing to drop two thousand mines at the entrances of Kure and Hiroshima harbors. In May the 313th mined Kobe and Osaka harbors. In June they mined the Tokyo, Kure, and Nagoya harbors.

During the mining campaign, the 313th flew forty-six missions and dropped thirteen thousand mines, stopping the delivery of all essential oil, fuel, and raw materials. They dropped more mines in five months than were dropped by all other aircraft in the Pacific in two years. Mining, which resulted in the sinking of 170,000 tons of Japanese shipping, may have had a strategic value that exceeded the damage inflicted by the bombing of Japanese cities. It was a remarkable strategic victory that cost few civilian or military lives.

Admiral Nimitz sent LeMay a congratulatory message stating, "The planning, operational and technical operation of aircraft mining, on a scale never before attained has accomplished phenomenal results and is a credit to all concerned."

Hansell's opposition to this mission was a product of his own dogma. After the war, he changed his opinion, stating: "The aerial mining campaign, as pushed by General LeMay, succeeded beyond anyone's expectation. His decision to launch a massive mining campaign was sound."

He may have been considering his own view that mining was not strategic bombing when he said: "I think General LeMay did not view mining at night as abandonment of selective targeting. It is quite clear I could have endorsed mining as an aspect of strategic bombing against the Japanese transportation system rather than as an auxiliary aspect of the sea blockade. The night mining, like night urban bombing, could be carried out regardless of cloud cover at the target."

He even conceded the need for a change in strategy and tactics. In reference to LeMay's operation, he wrote in his memoir: "In retrospect, the actual evolution of events was probably about right."

While praising LeMay, he made no effort to conceal his sensitivity about the navy: "It [XXI Bomber Command] did preserve its identity and structure as a separate command even though operating in an area under 'navy jurisdiction.'"

LeMay did not agree that a joint effort with the navy was a concession to navy jurisdiction. He had no problem cooperating and working with the navy when he believed it was part of a joint war effort.

The army and Marine Corps invaded Okinawa on 1 April. I was confident that there was now light at the end of what had seemed to be an endless tunnel. For the first time I began to think about the future and what I would do at the end of the war. Both LeMay and Preston had asked me if I would consider a career in the air force. I expressed an interest but avoided answering them directly. I thought about returning to law school. My personal hero was Supreme Court Justice Oliver Wendell Holmes, who enlisted in the Union Army in the Civil War before he had graduated from Harvard. He was wounded on three occasions and became a lieutenant colonel. I wrote my parents to send me a biography of Holmes. It arrived on 10 April. Perhaps the story of his return from military service would give me some direction. After reading it, I thought I might like civilian life after all.

LeMay's success in mining operations improved his relations with the navy. He complimented Nimitz on the accuracy of the bombing attacks on Japanese aircraft plants by naval carrier aircraft. Although Nimitz and his staff on Guam respected LeMay as a tough and competent combat leader, they did not accept him as a social equal.

Nimitz and his staff were not pleased when Arnold insisted that XXI Bomber Command headquarters and a wing of B-29s should operate out of Guam in January 1945.

When we arrived on Guam in January, there was one uncompleted coral runway through the jungle at the northern end of the island and no permanent buildings for our operations or personnel. We all slept in tents, and LeMay ordered that the construction of housing for the enlisted men be given top priority. There was no mess hall. We all ate outdoors and officers waited to go through the chow line until after the men had been fed. LeMay also ordered that the enlisted men wash their mess kits ahead of the officers. By the time it was the senior officers' turn to wash their mess kits, the water in the fifty-gallon drums was cold and usually half-filled with garbage.

Except for powdered eggs at breakfast, it seemed like every meal featured beans and Spam. My weight dropped to 125 pounds. I supplemented my diet with emergency flight rations from our aircraft.

Field-grade officers also dug latrines and helped clear jungle for the enlisted men's tents. All personnel had to do their own laundry without hot water. I grew tired of washing my pants in a helmet. I decided to emulate the British and wear shorts. I cut my pants off above the knee, and the first time the chief of staff saw me in shorts at a briefing he told me I was out of uniform and ordered me to return to my tent and replace them with long pants. I told him that the British had been wearing short pants for generations in the tropics. He was not dissuaded and he said he would take disciplinary action if I didn't change my uniform. He was shocked by my response. I told him that General Hansell had promised me that my tour in the Pacific was voluntary because of my combat service in the Eighth Air Force in England and that he would honor my request to return home at any time. I continued to wear short pants. Although LeMay never wore shorts, he never again commented on my appearance.

I wore the same unpressed short pants when my brother-in-law, Harry Race, a navy lieutenant, invited me to lunch aboard his ship. I walked into the wardroom wearing my tattered uniform and a baseball hat with major's insignia pinned on it. Harry and his fellow officers were immaculate. Filipino mess boys in white uniforms served us. It was not a friendly occasion. At best it was corridor courtesy. As I left, I went through the motions of inviting the naval officers for lunch at North Field. Of course, I knew that they would not accept.

I told LeMay of my luncheon experience with the navy and their rejection of my "gracious" luncheon invitation.

"Forget it," he replied. "The web feet don't approve of the way we fight. If you wanted to fight the war as a gentleman you should have joined the navy."

Admiral Nimitz followed protocol. After LeMay arrived on Guam, Nimitz invited him for lunch at his headquarters on a hill overlooking the harbor. LeMay had no pressed uniform for social occasions. He wore a rumpled GI uniform like the rest of us. He stored his personal belongings in a government-issued B4 bag.

He grinned as he told me of his visit to Nimitz's headquarters. It was the first time I had seen him smile in a long time. He described the starched and pressed uniforms of the officers and mess boys, and the five-course dinner with salad and dessert. He conceded that he had enjoyed the brandy and fine cigars: "Nutter, those cigars were a hell of a lot better than the two-for-a-nickel 'King Edwards' we've been smoking."

When he first arrived on Guam, I went with him to inspect the B-24 that Hansell had furnished for his personal use. It had a refrigerator, a lounge, and a luxury chair. Syndicated columnist Drew Pearson had written a column suggesting that LeMay was living in luxury on Guam and accused LeMay of outfitting Hansell's plane. We thought it ironic that Pearson said nothing about the navy, but made a personal attack on LeMay. When I mentioned it to LeMay, he told me to forget it. "That Pearson is a no good," he said. "He doesn't know who I am. The important thing is, I know who I am. You have to live your life without being upset by people like him."

I had one other social experience with the navy. They had the only movie theater on Guam, and the seating was segregated, with officers and enlisted men in separate sections. Company-grade officers were in different sections from field-grade officers. I made the mistake of inviting an enlisted man to sit with me in the field officer's section. When my protest that he be seated was ignored, I left and did not return. Our own movie theater was an open field with logs for seating.

• • •

I had many opportunities to work with the navy on Saipan, Tinian, and Guam. Although we were treated as poor relations in social situations, my contacts and work with them as military professionals was more than satisfactory. We had a senior naval officer attached to our command as liaison officer, Lt. Comdr. George McGee. I first met him when we set up a procedure for the air-sea rescue of our crews who had to ditch in the Pacific. The navy had an average of two destroyers, six submarines, and a dozen amphibian aircraft at locations along our bombing routes to Japan. On occasion, the submarines surfaced within sight of the Japanese mainland.

We often had three or four B-29s ditch on return trips from bombing Japan. When a B-29 crew was in serious trouble, the navigators were instructed to locate their position as precisely as possible and then break radio silence and send their latitude and longitude to our headquarters along with their planned course and ground speed to Saipan. I would then plot their position and attempt to estimate their courses within the next half-hour. Commander McGee would relay their position to navy headquarters, which would then radio the information to submarines, ships, and aircraft in the area. I always was concerned about the accuracy of the information I gave to the navy. I knew that even a minor error could result in a crew being lost.

The problems encountered by aircrews that were obliged to ditch at sea were not new. The threat of dehydration, starvation, and exposure was very real for aviators downed in both the Pacific and Atlantic. The big difference was that our crews did not have to cope with the cold weather and icy water in the North Sea and the English Channel. Most crews that ditched in the Pacific could avoid hypothermia; they did, however, have to worry about the presence of sharks.

Our recovery rate for ditched B-29 crews was never more than 25 percent in the daytime, and it was much lower at night. However, our success rate improved after we secured Iwo Jima in March 1945. The navy had a two-engine amphibious plane called a "Dumbo." We outfitted special rescue B-29s with radio and survival equipment. They were called "Superdumbos" and were on call from Iwo Jima during every mission. During the return flight, the chances of a B-29 not sinking immediately on impact with the water was improved because the fuel tanks were at least half-filled with air. Unless the aircraft broke up, the crews had an opportunity to get out and climb aboard life rafts. On some occasions the aircraft would float for ten to fifteen minutes.

Landing was always dangerous, even in the best of circumstances, because hitting water is like hitting cement. It was not practical for either the pilot or crew to prepare for the tremendous impact. Even when the crewmembers were not seriously hurt, however, escape hatches were often crushed and the men trapped inside the sinking aircraft.

Marines from the Marianas invaded Iwo Jima on 19 February 1945, and the fighting continued until late March. Prior to the invasion, LeMay promised Nimitz that our B-29s would attempt to neutralize Japanese fighters on Iwo's airfields and destroy Japanese defenses and fortifications. The 73d Wing made several missions to Iwo Jima from Saipan, filling the airfields with bomb craters. Many Kamikaze fighters were destroyed on the ground, but the bombing of the island fortifications was another story.

The Japanese had built miles of tunnels in the island's volcanic rock. As was so often the case in World War I, a successful advance was measured in feet rather than yards. It was one of the bloodiest battles of the Pacific war and casualties were the worst, per capita, in U.S. history: twenty-five thousand marines were wounded and more than six thousand were killed.

I learned of the buildup for the Iwo invasion from the Marianas in early February. I had become friendly with several marines on Guam, and the night before the invasion I was walking alone about a mile from the navy's officers' club around 11 P.M. when a sergeant I knew pulled up in a jeep. Marines were not permitted to drive or use navy vehicles.

"I'm going to the navy officers' club, get in Major," he said.

"What are you doing driving a navy jeep to the officers' club?" I asked.

"I borrowed it," he said, grinning broadly. "I'm leaving tomorrow morning for Iwo, and I have to stock up for a tough battle. The navy has all the liquor. I need some scotch. They don't supply marines with liquor."

"Thanks, but no thanks," I replied. "You'll be off for Iwo before dawn, but I'll be here in the brig. The navy would have me court-martialed for burglary."

He laughed and drove off in a cloud of dust. I never saw him again. I later learned he was killed in the first landing.

Lieutenant Commander McGee told us that Admiral Nimitz's staff expected the marines would take the island in four days. It was not to be. Mount Suribachi, on the southern end of the island, was captured on 24 February, but fierce fighting continued for almost a month. During the first week of March we were told that Seabee construction teams had built an airstrip on the south end of the island. The first B-29 made an emergency landing there on 4 March.

While I was in Europe I had never observed the casualties or horror of land warfare. On Guam I saw the suffering of wounded marines firsthand. Commander McGee told me that no one had anticipated such a high casualty rate. Wounded marines landed at Guam's harbor and were placed in tents set up at the edge of the beach. I sometimes helped medical personnel carry the wounded on stretchers from the landing barges to the tents.

On an earlier visit to naval headquarters I had noticed some empty barracks adjacent to the officers' club, so I suggested that the wounded marines be placed in the empty barracks and the club be used as a medical headquarters. McGee informed me that it was not navy policy to house enlisted men in officers' quarters.

On 11 March, LeMay's staff briefed him on a proposed route for the firebombing of Nagoya. I stood up in the briefing room in front of the map and said, "We have planned the route for the flight to Nagoya and return, seventy-five miles away from Iwo Jima."

"Why are you still routing our planes seventy-five miles from Iwo?" asked LeMay. "We had one of our planes make an emergency landing there on the fourth and another one on the tenth. They tell me the airfield is secure and suitable for emergency landings. Iwo is an important checkpoint for our planes going and coming. When we detour around Iwo we use too much gas."

"Admiral Nimitz's staff wants our B-29s to steer clear of Iwo until the island is fully secure," I replied.

LeMay's eyes flashed as he said, "Get McGee over here immediately."

He arrived thirty minutes later and LeMay said: "Nutter tells me that the navy is still demanding that our planes stay seventy-five miles from Iwo. Is that correct?"

McGee flushed and said, "Yes, sir."

"McGee," LeMay replied in measured tones, "you tell the navy our planes will fly right over Iwo and make emergency landings whenever they are required."

This didn't help LeMay's relations with the navy. They were still smarting over his criticism about their failure to supply his bomber command with incendiaries. McGee did not reply. He saluted and left the room. From that day on, Iwo became a haven for B-29s returning from Japan, saving the lives of many crews. It also simplified the work of our navigators, as it was a checkpoint halfway to and from Japan. As we left the planning meeting, LeMay turned to me and said, "Those web feet think Iwo is their personal preserve."

In mid-April, two P-51 fighter groups arrived at Iwo Jima to provide fighter escort for our bombers to and from Japan. The P-51s had saved many B-17s over Germany, so we hoped they would do the same for B-29s over Japan. However, the P-51s ran into an obstacle in the Pacific they had not encountered over Germany: the 750 miles of ocean between Iwo and Japan. The round trip took seven hours and was one of the longest missions of the war for fighter aircraft.

There was no long-range navigation equipment in the small cockpit of the P-51s. We selected our best navigators to lead them in a B-29. After the shepherd B-29 arrived over Japan, it circled in a designated assembly area until the fighters were ready to return to Iwo. The program worked well except on the one occasion when the fighters attempted to land on Iwo in a tropical storm. Twenty-seven fighters were lost on that mission, their worst disaster of the Pacific war.

The support provided by the P-51s was a great morale booster for our crews. By the middle of May, Japanese leaders had decided to conserve their fighter resources and save them to resist an invasion. As a result, fighter support was usually not necessary. The P-51s then flew on low-level strafing missions, hitting targets of opportunity.

After the war, Lt. Gen. Holland M. "Howlin' Mad" Smith questioned the high price his marines paid to capture Iwo. He compared the number of B-29 crews saved to the marines lost and wounded and said the loss of life was unnecessary. LeMay and Hansell disagreed. The island's capture eliminated a Japanese fighter and bomber base and provided the only landing field for disabled bombers. It also served as a navigation aid and checkpoint for crews flying to and from Japan.

The situation in the Pacific was vastly different in 1945 than in late 1943, when the decision to take Iwo Jima was made. No one anticipated the success of our night missions or Japan's rapid disintegration by the late spring of 1945.

LeMay's firebombing and mining campaigns, together with the navy's blockade and successful naval campaigns, shortened the war by at least a year.

My last encounter with the navy was in June 1945 while we were training the lead crews at Muroc. We were practicing a radar bomb run with our new Eagle APQ-7 radar equipment with my close friend, Lt. Col. Henry Covington. Hank was a descendant of the aristocratic Covington family of Virginia. He was a graduate of Virginia Military Institute: a daring and superior pilot in the tradition of the Old South. Like LeMay, he couldn't stand stupidity or meaningless military policy. But unlike LeMay, he lost his temper on occasion.

As we began a practice bomb run over Los Angeles, adjacent to the San Pedro harbor area at an altitude of twenty-five thousand feet, we suddenly saw black clouds in front of our aircraft. I had no difficulty recognizing the black smoke. It was antiaircraft fire. I had seen it many times in Europe and the Pacific. I looked down in the harbor and couldn't believe it. Navy ships were shooting at us. Suddenly, the plane shook from a severe jolt.

"They're shooting at us," yelled the copilot. "They hit us in the wing!"

Hank banked our plane sharply and headed for Muroc. When we landed Hank grabbed me by the arm and said, "Ralph, would you like to be my copilot? I'm going to fly to San Diego and see the admiral about this attack on our plane."

I suggested that he report the incident to Joe Preston and LeMay, and let them handle it through proper military channels.

"Channels, hell!" shouted Hank. "We can't wait. We're here to train our crews on urban targets. We have crews flying over this harbor every day. Come on, we'll take our B-25."

I flew as Hank's copilot to San Diego and we landed at Lindbergh Field, where I had never been before. I noticed that the harbor was crowded with aircraft carriers, a battleship, and several cruisers. We obtained an air force jeep and drove to the naval headquarters there. Hank demanded to see the admiral in charge. He told the admiral's aide that he wished to discuss a matter of immediate urgency. We were ushered into the admiral's sumptuous office. We stood at attention in front of his desk and saluted.

"What do you gentlemen want to see me about?" the admiral asked. "This must be a matter of extreme importance. There are appropriate channels for handling matters between the navy and the air force. What is your problem?"

Hank described the incident and then informed the admiral: "We took a picture of the hole in our wing. I will forward it to you tomorrow."

"I don't need your picture," said the admiral. "The ships in Los Angeles harbor were following SOP. All our ships are instructed to fire at any bomber flying above them."

"I can understand such a policy in the central and western Pacific," Hank replied. "But not here in the States. The Japanese have never had any four-engine bombers, and there hasn't been a Japanese aircraft within four thousand miles of Los Angeles since Pearl Harbor."

"Navy policy is out of my hands," replied the admiral. "I doubt if we are going to change it for the air force."

Hank's face reddened. "Is that your answer, sir?"

"This meeting is over, gentlemen," the admiral said curtly.

"Thank you, sir," I responded immediately. "I will report this incident and this meeting to General LeMay." I saluted and turned to leave. I grabbed Hank by the arm and ushered him out of the room.

"I wasn't finished, Ralph," he said angrily when we were outside the admiral's office.

"I know that," I replied. "That's why I wanted to leave. We're in enough trouble already."

"All right," said Hank. "I have a way of getting the attention of these navy types."

"What are you planning to do?" I asked.

"You'll see. Let's go to our plane."

We took off from Lindbergh Field, but instead of turning north toward Muroc, Hank turned south toward the ships in Coronado Bay. He made no attempt to gain altitude.

"Hank, where the hell are you going?" I yelled.

"You'll see."

He continued toward Coronado flying just above the deck. I saw a battleship and several aircraft carriers directly in front of us. Hank headed toward them and pushed the throttles to full power. The B-25 was always a noisy aircraft. It was obvious to me that Hank was planning to buzz the navy ships. I could see the headlines: "Navy shoots down B-25 in Coronado Harbor." Hank made a second run over the ships in the harbor and then turned north to Muroc. Apparently the gunners were so surprised that they didn't shoot at us.

"I wasn't planning on getting shot down over San Diego," I said. "Wait until Colonel Maxwell hears about this."

"I'm not worried about him," Hank replied. "I know LeMay will back us up. We're just protecting the most valuable crews in the Twentieth Air Force." Hank was correct. We had no more trouble with the navy over Los Angeles, and no one ever mentioned the incident to us again.

23: Tinian and Muroc

I made several trips to Tinian from Guam to work with the naval mining experts and the 313th Wing operations personnel to plan mining missions. After Iwo Jima was secured, Joe Preston and I met with wing personnel to discuss the possibility of installing navigation aids at Iwo for our crews on their flights to Japan. Although we had bombed Iwo prior to the invasion in February, it was my first trip to the island. The devastation was much worse than I had seen on Saipan, Tinian, or Guam. Joe and I concluded it would be some time before the Loran navigation equipment could be installed and be available for our navigators on their flights to Japan.

We took off before noon for our return flight to Tinian. The engines were running smoothly, and Joe told me he believed that the recent modifications to them were a substantial improvement. Apparently it wasn't enough of one, as we experienced an engine failure during our final approach to Tinian that would cause me problems with my back for the rest of my life.

It was a clear, sunny day, perfect flying weather. We were still over the water as Joe leveled off on the last leg of the final approach to the runway. I looked up and noticed that we were slightly below the cliff at the edge of the island. As Joe nudged the throttles forward to give the engines some extra power there was a sharp backfire and the number-three engine started to falter and then stopped. I looked up. The top of the cliff at the beginning of the runway was still above us. Joe slammed the throttles forward, giving full power to the other three engines and pulled back on the controls. Our nose shot up and we avoided a direct impact, but the center of the fuselage hit the edge of the cliff. There was a tremendous crash. I was thrown back from my navigation table against the gun turret and knocked unconscious.

When I came to I saw Joe kneeling over me. We were on the ground outside the aircraft. He asked me how I felt. I wasn't sure. I tried to get up, but the pain in my back was excruciating. He helped me to my feet. No one else from the crew appeared to be seriously hurt. Joe told me that the force of the impact had cracked the fuselage. He had a meeting with LeMay scheduled on Guam at 5:30 P.M. We would have to borrow a plane to fly there. I knew that he wasn't looking forward to telling LeMay that his personal B-29 had been totaled.

The tower officer assigned us another B-29 parked away from the 313th Wing's other aircraft. I noticed there was some unusual construction going on behind the hardstands and revetments.

"What's going on here?" I asked Joe.

He told me that a special group, the 509th, would be arriving soon. "It's a top secret project," he added. "We're not supposed to talk about it. The group is assigned to the 313th, but it won't be flying any missions with them. They have special facilities and support squadrons. They operate independently, with their own engineering and materials squadron. LeMay won't tell us anything about their operations. Colonel Del Wilson from our 305th Group in England has just been assigned as liaison officer for the project."

I learned later that this was to be the headquarters for the atomic bomb group. It was the best-kept secret of our operations.

We flew back to Guam and prepared to report to LeMay about conditions on Iwo. As we approached his office, Joe asked me if my back was still bothering me. He could see that I had difficulty standing up straight.

"I'm worried about you Ralph," he said. "It'll be bad enough telling LeMay we cracked up his plane, but he'll really be upset if you are injured and will be out of action for a while."

I told him not to worry. I wouldn't mention the problem about my back to LeMay. We told LeMay about the conditions on Iwo and said that it would be a while before we could get Loran in place for the navigators.

When we finished, he turned to me and said, "Nutter, you don't look too good. Are you sick?"

Before I could reply, Preston spoke up. "Sir, perhaps Nutter was a little shook up. We lost an engine coming into Tinian on the final approach and we pancaked as we landed. It looks as if we have a crack in the fuselage. Maintenance on Tinian is checking the damage now."

LeMay frowned. I could see he wasn't pleased, but I knew he had complete trust in Preston's abilities as a pilot. LeMay and Preston had been through many tough combat missions together. He was silent for a moment, and then told Preston to file a report describing the incident.

"You guys seem to be okay," he concluded. "You go finish your report. I have something to talk to Nutter about." As Joe walked away, LeMay turned to me and said, "Nutter, the WPPA is complaining about you."

He was referring to what is jokingly known throughout the army as the West Point Protective Association.

"It's those two West Point captains who came to work for us in March after spending most of the war fighting the Battle of the Pentagon," he continued. "I guess they came out here to get some combat credits for their careers after the war. Anyway, they say that you're dominating the mission planning meetings. What about it? Is that true?"

"I won't claim to be bashful about expressing my opinions," I replied. "They have some interesting combat theories. I don't have the benefit of their West Point education, but I hope I learned a bit about combat while I was in the 305th. I try to plan the navigation and bombing routes the way I believe you want them. What do you want me to do about their complaints?"

He chomped on his cigar and his lips curled up in a slight smile. "Keep it up! Now go see if you can find some hot water for a shower and get some rest."

I didn't find a shower, but I was able to take a sponge bath with hot water I obtained from the mess hall. When I returned to my tent to rest I found Jim Seaver reading a letter from his wife.

As I settled onto my cot he yelled: "Goddamn, didn't she know I was kidding? Ralph, listen to this. About a month ago my wife wrote to me and said that she wanted to buy a fur coat. I wrote her back and sarcastically suggested that she should buy two coats, one for herself, and another one for her mother. She did it! That's all I need. She's really fighting a tough war in Connecticut."

After the 19 March Tokyo mission, the navy informed us that no further incendiaries were to be delivered to the Marianas until mid-April. For a week, our combat and maintenance crews had a well-deserved rest. Meanwhile, I worked with the 313th's navigators and radar operators, planning the aerial mining missions. The army and marines were all over Guam. They were preparing for the invasion of Okinawa, and their commanders were concerned that the battle for Okinawa might be even bloodier than Iwo Jima. Okinawa is only three hundred miles from Japan's most southerly island. The navy and marine commanders expected the defenders to launch a wave of kamikaze attacks on the ships, landing craft, and troops wading ashore. Nimitz asked LeMay to bomb the kamikaze airfields on Kyushu. I spent many hours planning the routes and bombing runs. Although we filled the runways with bomb craters, the Japanese were not to be deterred. It seemed that as fast as we made them they filled them in and continued their attacks on the invasion fleet. It was impossible to bomb their airfields around the clock. LeMay informed Nimitz that it was a waste of our B-29s and that we should go back to attacking strategic targets.

By the end of March, LeMay was receiving a hundred new bombers and crews a month. Without incendiaries, he decided to fly daylight missions at altitudes of sixteen thousand feet. There was no fighter defense. The Japanese were saving their pilots, fuel, and remaining planes to defend against the anticipated invasion. The lower bombing altitudes improved visual and radar bombing accuracy. There was less cloud cover in the spring and summer months, so the results were excellent, with a quarter of the bombs hitting precise military targets. But that wasn't good enough for LeMay.

The new crews arriving from the training command in the States were not ready for combat operations. The navigators and bombardiers could locate a city, but they had difficulty picking out specific targets. The lead crew school we had set up on Guam was unable to teach them how to pick out precise targets in crowded urban areas. A change was required.

On 11 April, LeMay told Joe Preston and me that it was impossible to practice radar bombing anywhere in the central Pacific. We had no place where radar operators and navigators could practice bombing runs on precision targets in cities. The only available urban areas for training were in the United States.

A slight smile curled his lips as he said, "I'm about to give you both an assignment, which I'm quite sure you won't refuse. How would you like to go on temporary duty to our old base at Muroc, California? It's no longer the primitive place we lived in during the summer of 1942; it now has buildings and facilities like any other air force base in the States.

"I want you to set up a lead crew school for our best crews and do for us what you did in England. The crews will be on temporary duty at Muroc for two weeks. You will train them on the new radar equipment that's being installed. It's called the Eagle APQ-7. It's designed for precision bombing at night and in bad daylight weather. They tell me it's a big improvement over our current APQ-13, but it has some drawbacks. It's more difficult to operate and install on the aircraft.

"You both know that many of our current radar operators are converted gunners. Only our most skillful and experienced navigators have been using radar with real accuracy. I want you to make them effective radar operators. When the crews are not flying at Muroc, the radar operators and navigators must spend several hours a day learning to operate the equipment. I'm told that it has a range of sixty-five miles and an accuracy of one thousand feet in target area.

"I know you both knew Frank Armstrong in England. I'm sure you remember that he led our first mission to Germany in January of 1943. He will command the 315th Wing with the new APQ-7 equipment. It will probably be mid-June before we can send any of Armstrong's crews over Japan.

"Arnold's committee of operational analysts has recommended that this new radar equipment be used on missions against Japanese oil facilities and refineries. When we cut off Hitler's oil, we knew it was just a matter of time before the war in Europe would be over. The colonel in charge of recommending targets is a Colonel Leach. He was one of those so-called experts who recommended the Schweinfurt missions.

"Nutter told me Leach was his professor at Law School. You should report to him at the Pentagon. He's been critical of our use of the APQ-13. I guess he doesn't know that the gunners we've been using as radar operators aren't exactly Harvard types. He and Nutter should have an interesting meeting. I wish I could be there with you. Maybe their role of teacher and student will be reversed.

"I haven't heard either of you object. Joe, you should prepare to take off tomorrow. I would like you to fly nonstop from here to Hickam Field in Hawaii. I don't know if anyone else has made that flight nonstop. It should be a good test for both of you."

We left immediately to plan the flight. I conferred with Jim Seaver and Tom Bowman about the weather. Joe selected a plane that had a good maintenance record. We were to remain under LeMay's command while at Muroc. He had not told us the length of our assignment. I left most of my personal belongings with Seaver and Bowman. We expected to return to Guam by early summer.

The first two thousand miles of the flight were uneventful. The weather was clear and I had a good opportunity to make several celestial navigation sightings. After we leveled off, Joe put the plane on automatic pilot. I had a remote control at my navigation station, so I was able to make course adjustments without his assistance. Most of the crew dozed while I kept track of our route. My assistant navigator kept asking me about our position. I asked him why he was so impatient, and he told me he hadn't been with a girl in more than six months.

The last thousand miles were *not* routine. We lost our number-two engine. Joe feathered the propeller and changed the cruise control. Fortunately, it was not a repeat of my hairy flight across the North Atlantic. We were able to maintain our altitude, but we arrived at Hickam Field an hour late.

It was 13 April. As we pulled up to the revetment, we were met by a jeep that had been sent out to take us to operations. We were groggy after nineteen hours in the air. The driver asked us if we knew that President Roosevelt had died. I found it almost impossible to believe. He had been president for more than twelve years; the only president I could really remember and appreciate. I had difficulty sleeping that evening at Hickam. I wondered how his death would affect the outcome of the war. We appeared headed for victory in Europe, but what would happen in the war against Japan?

We arrived in Washington the next evening and were taken immediately to the Pentagon. Most personnel at the Pentagon were subdued. There was an air of uncertainty. How would President Truman conduct the war? No one had any answers.

The next day we reported to Colonel Leach. I had not seen him since my last class on real property law in Cambridge on 5 December 1941. After a formal and perfunctory introduction, I mentioned this to Leach.

"I'm not interested in talking to you about law school," he snapped. "You're here to report about your radar operations in the

B-29 bombing program. We have not been receiving good reports about the accuracy of your radar bombing."

I didn't disagree with him. "Your reports are correct, sir. But there are several reasons for the poor results. Most radar operators are untrained gunners, and our current APQ-13 equipment can't pick out precise military targets. Radar sightings simply can't compare with the accuracy we get when observing targets with the Norden bombsight."

"Then your training must be deficient," Leach replied.

I told him that I did not disagree. "That's the reason General LeMay is setting up the lead crew school at Muroc." Joe Preston didn't speak. Instead he gave a slight nod of his head toward the door, suggesting that it was time for us to leave. I saluted and followed Joe out. He did not salute. As we left Leach's office, I told Joe that I thought he had given our bomber command a failing grade.

"He's a classic intellectual with no understanding of the reality of combat," said Joe. "I'm sure he never heard a shot fired in anger. Ralph, if you return to law school, I think that you should stay away from Leach."

Then, changing the subject, Joe observed: "Now I know why the Schweinfurt missions were so badly planned. LeMay was correct. Armchair strategists like Leach should have no part in planning bombing missions. Let's go over and talk to General Norstad. He's a realist."

Norstad greeted us warmly. He told us that our bomber command was on the way to winning the war with Japan. Our visit was brief, however, and after our first meal in a restaurant in many months, we took off for Muroc.

We couldn't believe the changes that had been made since we left in 1942. It was no longer a little airfield with one runway and two shacks. Our first duty was a courtesy call on the base commander. We were ushered into a plush air-conditioned office. Colonel Maxwell was cold and formal with Preston. Although they were of equal rank, their backgrounds could not have been more different. Maxwell looked like he must have been the oldest colonel in the Air Corps. Joe had been a combat flying officer since the Japanese strafed him at Clark Air Base on 10 December 1941 in the Philippines. During the same period, Maxwell had never been promoted or been overseas. He was older and outranked both LeMay and Preston in the regular army.

I soon learned that he believed in form over substance. Although LeMay believed in tough discipline, he considered it a necessary training method for the teamwork required in combat, not an end in itself. In contrast, Maxwell made it obvious that it flattered his ego to give orders and to have troops pass in review before him on the parade ground.

His only remarks were directed to Preston at our first meeting. He asked no questions about our combat operations in the Pacific or the purpose of our training mission. It was clear he was not pleased that we were there to operate on what he considered his personal territory.

"I understand that you're in charge of all B-29 flying operations," he said, starring sharply at Joe. "I hope *you* are aware that *I* am the commander of this base. Your personnel may be here on temporary duty from the Twentieth Air Force, but they are under my command anytime they are on the ground."

Joe did not reply. I started to speak up, but he motioned for me to keep quiet, saluted, and turned to leave. I followed.

"Ralph," he said as soon as we were outside, "Leach taught you a lesson about intellectuals, and today you learned a lesson about some of the relics from the peacetime army. Now I understand why that SOB was never sent overseas. I'm afraid we may have some problems with him."

Our first crews arrived from the Marianas by the end of the week, and we began flying practice bomb runs on targets in the Los Angeles, San Diego, and San Francisco metropolitan areas. Preston refused to cancel any training flights for Maxwell's daily parades and drills. My primary responsibility was scheduling the crews for the training missions. After our first week of operations, Maxwell ordered me to report to his office.

"Nutter," he said, "you don't seem to understand that my daily drill and parades have priority over your flight operations. No crewmember is to miss any parades or drills. There will be no exceptions."

I told him that we had only a limited number of B-29s with the new radar equipment and that we tried to schedule training flights to avoid B-29 takeoffs during the hot desert heat in the middle of the day. Temperatures higher than a hundred degrees could cause vapor locks and loss of power on takeoff.

"I said there will be *no* exceptions, Nutter," he replied. "This is a military base, not a flying school. If any of your flyboys miss a parade or drill, I will be obliged to take disciplinary action. If a crewmember has a legitimate excuse he can send me a written letter of explanation."

I called a meeting of our crews and told them of my meeting with Maxwell. I then drafted the following for crewmen who missed a parade or drill because of a training mission:

I am a member of a lead crew in the Twentieth Air Force under the command of Major General Curtis LeMay. Our crew is on temporary duty for two weeks in accordance with orders from General Lemay to engage in lead crew training for the bombing of Japan. This training must be completed in two weeks before I return to combat operations in the Pacific. I was absent from drill to engage in flight training requirements as required by General LeMay.

After the colonel received several of these letters from crewmembers who had missed drill, I was again directed to report to his office. He asked me if I had written the letters he had received from absent crewmen. After I replied in the affirmative, he told me he was going to give me an unsatisfactory efficiency rating and insert an appropriate reprimand in my personnel file. In response, I sent a written report of the situation to General LeMay. He informed me that he was requesting that the Air Corps inspector general investigate and make a formal report to Arnold. He also informed me that on his next trip to Washington he would stop at Muroc on his return flight.

The inspector general arrived on an inspection tour the following Monday. The timing was most inappropriate for Maxwell. He had scheduled drill and a parade for four in the afternoon the previous week. Our ground crews were repairing B-29 engines on the flight line. Maxwell showed up while they were working on the engines and ordered them to stop and report for drill immediately. They told him they needed to stay and cover the exposed engines to protect them from a sandstorm that was approaching. He refused their request. As a result, the exposed engines were sidelined for several days while sand was removed from them. The inspector general mentioned this incident in his report to LeMay.

I thought it was time to give Maxwell a reality check. I asked Preston if Maxwell had ever piloted a B-29. Perhaps he would enjoy the experience in the bumpy desert air.

Joe smiled and looked at me. "You know, Ralph, I think you're right. It's only appropriate that the colonel should have a chance to pilot a B-29. I'll schedule a training mission for him tomorrow morning."

The next morning we took off in a B-29 with Maxwell in the copilot's seat. In the summertime, a flight over the desert can be extremely bumpy. When the hot desert air comes in contact with colder air above, it often creates extreme turbulence. This was a particularly hot summer day. Joe headed straight for Death Valley, the area of greatest turbulence.

He called me on the interphone and said, "Ralph, the colonel is going to take over. Would you like to stand between the seats?"

I moved into position behind them just as Joe said, "It's your airplane, Colonel."

I saw Maxwell's knuckles turn white as he clutched the controls. The plane was bouncing around wildly and he had trouble holding onto the wheel. Sweat was dripping from his brow.

He looked worriedly at Joe and said, "Preston, I think you'd better take over."

Maxwell turned in his seat and looked back at me. I wondered briefly if I would receive another entry in my personnel file.

LeMay arrived at Muroc on the evening of 19 June. Preston and I were surprised when he walked into the bachelors' quarters on the base. As a major general and commanding officer of a bomber command, protocol dictated that he should have been invited to spend the night at Maxwell's home on the base. However, the colonel had recently received a copy of the inspector general's report supporting our contention that the radar navigation training for combat operations would take precedence over routine drill. It was apparent that he had concluded there was no point in attempting to gain LeMay's support. He was correct. The next morning, LeMay called a hearing to review the inspector general's report. After sitting down next to Maxwell, he turned and asked him if he had anything to add to the inspector general's report.

"I think discipline is important," he replied. "Drill instills discipline."

LeMay arched his eyebrows and said, "Are you suggesting that Colonel Preston, Major Nutter, and my lead crews are undisciplined? These are the most disciplined men in the Twentieth Air Force. They have demonstrated discipline where it counts: in combat against the enemy. I want to commend Preston and Nutter for making an important contribution to our bombing operations over Japan. This hearing is concluded."

Maxwell left without any further comment. Joe and I walked with LeMay to the flight line. He told us of Arnold's visit to Guam and of his meeting with the joint chiefs.

He said the 315th Wing on Guam should be ready to use the new Eagle radar by the last week in June. They would be bombing Japanese oil refineries. He hoped that with it they would get most of their bombs within a thousand feet of the targets. The wings on Tinian and Saipan would receive the Eagle equipment by the first of July.

General Arnold's health had improved considerably by the first week of June. The war in Europe was over, and the joint chiefs were no longer criticizing the B-29's contribution to the war effort in the Pacific. Admiral King told General Marshall that the navy's submarine campaign and LeMay's mining and bombing campaigns had almost totally isolated Japan. Naval aircraft and P-51s were flying at will over Japan, and the country was on the verge of starvation. There was a strong possibility that Japan would be defeated without an invasion of the home islands. Arnold informed the joint chiefs that B-29s had leveled fifty-five square miles in Tokyo, twelve miles in Nagoya, fifteen miles in Osaka, and nine miles in Yokahama. There was no doubt Japan was defeated. The only question was when they would surrender.

On 14 June, Adm. William Leahy, President Truman's chief of staff, was directed by the president to inform the joint chiefs that the president wished to meet with them on the afternoon of the eighteenth to discuss the campaign against Japan. He asked them to determine the number of men, aircraft, and ships they would need to defeat Japan. He wanted an estimate of how many personnel would be killed or wounded in an invasion of Japan. The president also requested a projection of how long it would take and the potential losses if they tried to defeat Japan with a close blockade and bombardment by the sea and air forces. He wanted to know which course of action would save the most American lives. Arnold decided it was time for him to discuss the situation personally with LeMay and ask him when he believed the war would be over. Arnold considered a trip to Guam and the Marianas as rest and recreation. His blood pressure always went down when he was away from the infighting in Washington.

He arrived in Guam on 16 June and told LeMay that Admiral King and the navy had joined him in questioning the need for a land invasion because they believed Japan was already defeated. He asked LeMay if he agreed with that assessment and, if so, when he thought the Japanese would surrender. LeMay replied that he hadn't given much thought to when the war would end. However, there were almost no major targets left. He said he would give Arnold his best estimate at dinner.

That evening he told Arnold that he didn't expect there would be any military targets or Japanese war production facilities standing in Japan after the first week in September. The naval blockade and mining had cut off at least 90 percent of their imports of food and supplies. They still had some ground transportation operating on the main islands, but the air force and navy planned a campaign aimed at disrupting Japanese transportation with P-51s and carrier aircraft. They could bomb and strafe railroad lines and marshalling yards the same way the Eighth Air Force had done against Germany. If their ground transportation network in urban areas could be destroyed, the people should be ready to surrender by 1 October. It might take longer to persuade the ruling military clique, so no one could really predict if they would surrender before the projected November invasion.

Arnold was impressed. For the first time the navy and air force
seemed to be on the same wavelength. He wondered if they could
convince Marshall and the army that an invasion wasn't necessary.
He decided that the joint chiefs should have the benefit of LeMay's
analysis before their meeting with the president on the eighteenth.
He told LeMay about Admiral Leahy's 14 June directive to the joint
chiefs and the planned meeting. Arnold had not recovered from the
flight to Guam, and he was too tired to make the long flight to Washington in time for the meeting.

Besides, Arnold told LeMay, he knew more about the facts and
contingencies of the air war in the Pacific than anyone in the Air
Force, so he should leave immediately for Washington. LeMay could
meet with General Eaker, who was now Arnold's chief deputy, before
the meeting and bring him up to date. Eaker would introduce him
to the joint chiefs.

LeMay left for Washington at 4 A.M. and flew the eighty-five hundred miles in thirty-six hours, a new record. He arrived late on the
evening of the seventeenth and spent most of the night preparing
a statistical analysis of the effects of the heavy bombing on Japanese
cities and the ability of the Japanese to continue the war. He made
charts and graphs summarizing the effects of the bombing and blockade on Japanese war production and military facilities.

General Eaker introduced LeMay to the joint chiefs the next
morning and he summarized his experience in Europe, China, and
the Marianas. LeMay felt nervous and ill at ease as he spoke to the
men who had been determining the course of the war since Pearl
Harbor. He had never enjoyed making speeches or verbal presentations. Without any preliminary remarks he pointed to his graphs
and intelligence statistics on a blackboard. He felt like an engineering graduate student presenting his doctoral thesis to a reviewing faculty committee. He spoke for thirty minutes and then paused
and looked around the room. No one spoke. He offered to explain
his reasoning or answer questions. He ended his presentation by suggesting that it was premature to plan a land invasion until August.

Admiral King finally broke the silence. He congratulated LeMay
for the success of the aerial mining campaign and said he appreci-

ated his complimentary remarks about the contribution of naval carrier aircraft and the submarine campaign to the defeat of Japan. He said that the enemy navy and air force no longer existed as a practical fighting force. LeMay thanked him and looked at General Marshall, who appeared to be dozing during his presentation. There was an awkward silence before Marshall finally said that although LeMay might be correct in his conclusion that Japan was on the verge of defeat, it was not enough to ensure the Japanese would surrender. Only the military dictatorship that ruled Japan could make that decision, and it did not appear ready to accept our surrender terms. The Japanese people would have no say in the decision. The military leaders ruling Japan would fight on without regard for civilian casualties. That had been Hitler's policy in Germany in the last weeks of the war in April and May. Marshall reminded LeMay that it took many months, if not years, to prepare for an amphibious invasion. If the Japanese were prepared to surrender, the invasion could always be called off, even if the ships were at sea.

He raised his voice and said that it would be foolhardy to not prepare for any contingency when dealing with a fanatical enemy. If Japan didn't surrender by the end of summer, the United States would have no choice but to invade. We didn't have sufficient intelligence to anticipate the full extent of Japanese defenses. They expected that Japan would have at least two million troops who would fight to the death rather than surrender. In addition, they would probably equip millions of civilians for a guerrilla force with every weapon imaginable, even bamboo spears.

LeMay had to know what the kamikazes did to the air force and navy in the Marianas, Iwo, and on Okinawa. Kamikazes would be more effective when flying from their home bases. The Japanese probably stopped their fighter attacks on the bombers because they were hoarding them for an invasion. The United States had to prepare for a ground war. The terrain in Japan would be much tougher than the Allies had faced in France. Except for the coastal areas, Japan is a mountainous country. They could expect to encounter suicidal defenders in the caves and gullies on all the home islands. Our troops would be faced with Iwo and Okinawa in spades. The southern island of Kyushu would be just the first phase. The invasion of Honshu would be even more difficult.

Marshall then decided to give some credit. He told LeMay he had been impressed by the damage the mining and bombing had inflicted on Japan. A blockade probably would work, but no one could predict how long it would take or what would happen to American prisoners of war in Japan during that time. It was doubtful they would survive.

Marshall emphasized that they would do everything possible to avoid an invasion. He noted that LeMay hadn't mentioned the possibility of using the atomic bombs being built in New Mexico. Atomic bombs were not just bigger bombs; they were an entirely new kind of weapon that hadn't been tested. He did not know when they would be ready or what they would do. He concluded by observing that an invasion would be the worst scenario. Admiral Leahy had predicted the United States might lose a third of the invasion force. They could not assume that Japan was defeated. They had to assume that the Japanese would fight to the death rather than surrender. He then thanked LeMay for making the long trip from Guam.

LeMay left the meeting with Eaker. When they were safely out of earshot he turned to Arnold's deputy and told him that he knew he had bombed. The joint chiefs were not impressed with a thirty-nine-year-old major general from Ohio State. He said Eaker would have done a better job.

On the flight back to Guam, LeMay landed at Muroc as promised. He planned to conduct a hearing with Colonel Maxwell concerning our flight operations. The next morning he told us that General Eaker had telephoned him. Eaker said he had attended the meeting at the White House and informed the president of LeMay's opinion about the status of the air war in the Pacific.

On 16 July, a tremendous explosion in the New Mexico desert left President Truman another option. The United States could end the war without an invasion and at the same time keep Stalin from dominating the world.

24: LeMay's Role in the Dropping of the Atomic Bombs

After his return from Muroc in June, LeMay increased the tempo of the bombing attacks. Almost daily, the people looked up and saw B-29s flying without interference all over their homeland. By the end of July, LeMay found it difficult to select meaningful targets. In August, his bombers hit Akita, a remote Japanese city in northeast Honshu.

He had leaflets prepared stating, "Attention Japanese people. Read this carefully as it may save your life or the life of a friend. In the next few days eleven cities named on the reverse side of this leaflet will be destroyed by American bombs. We intend to destroy military installations and factories but unfortunately bombs have no eyes. We do not wish to harm innocent people. You should leave these cities. You can restore peace by demanding new leaders who will end the war."

More than fifty thousand of these leaflets were dropped on 27 July. Six of the named cities were bombed on the twenty-eighth and twenty-ninth. Japanese radio responded by stating that the leaflets were a feeble attempt to justify indiscriminate bombing intended to destroy the Japanese people. Their radio response appeared to be almost a concession that the war was lost. But that was not enough. Marshall was correct: It appeared that Japan's leaders would fight to the death rather than surrender unconditionally.

The joint chiefs, while preparing for the final assault on Japan, decided that the senior officers who had directed air operations against Germany during the last months of the war should take command of the aerial campaign in the Pacific. LeMay thus was to suffer the same fate as Generals Eaker, Wolfe, and Hansell. It was decided that he did not have the rank or seniority to command the bomber force in a coordinated assault on the Japanese home islands. Again, like the others, Arnold gave him no advance notice that he would be replaced.

Two unexpected guests arrived at LeMay's headquarters on Guam on 20 July. He was sitting at his desk studying a map of Japan when his executive officer rushed into his office and told him that Generals Carl Spaatz and Nathan Twining were waiting to meet with him. LeMay stood up as they approached his desk and asked them what they were doing in Guam. Twining replied that if LeMay didn't know it was too late. He explained that Arnold's staff had decided to deactivate LeMay's bomber command. Spaatz was going to command all air force operations in the Pacific, and Twining had been sent out to command the Twentieth Air Force. LeMay would remain in the theater as Spaatz's chief of staff.

LeMay replied that he couldn't expect to get any more notice of his replacement than Eaker, Wolfe, and Hansell. He then asked if the WPPA was taking over now that they had defeated the Japanese. They would run out of targets by the end of September, and aerial mining and the navy's blockade had isolated the home islands. The Japanese wouldn't have enough fuel or food to continue beyond 1 October. The end of the war was just a matter of time. A land invasion wasn't necessary.

Spaatz reassured LeMay that he would still be running the show as his chief of staff. He had no intention of looking over his shoulder. Jimmy Doolittle and the Eighth Air Force were going to be based on Okinawa. He had received oral orders to drop a nuclear bomb after 3 August. If it worked, the Japanese would have no choice but to surrender. He said he had requested that the orders to drop the A-bombs be in writing.

LeMay replied that they didn't need that firecracker to make the enemy surrender; they were already licked.

Spaatz said that he didn't disagree, but the decision to drop atomic bombs was not just a military decision. The president had been in the infantry in World War I. He was very concerned about the horrendous casualties that a land invasion would surely generate. There were also political considerations. The Russians were planning to declare war against the Japanese on 8 August. They had promised President Roosevelt at Yalta that they would invade Manchuria three months after Germany's surrender on 7 May. Now, it was clear that Russian assistance was no longer needed. Moreover, said Spaatz, the president was having a tough time with the Russians over the division of Germany and Soviet control of eastern Europe. They were already breaking the Yalta agreements. The president didn't want the Russians to be involved in the occupation of Japan or Japanese-held regions of Asia. They would probably repeat the trouble they were causing elsewhere. It didn't make any difference if the air force and navy believed atomic weapons were unnecessary. They had to follow orders, and he expected a written one to drop the bombs by the end of the week. Two of them were being ferried to Tinian aboard the cruiser *Indianapolis* for delivery to the 509th Group.

Spaatz said he knew that LeMay was upset, and he was sending him a copy of a memo he was planning to send to Arnold saying that his XXI Bomber Command was the best-organized and most proficient military organization the world had ever seen. Then Twining joined in. He told LeMay that the change wasn't his idea. Taking over LeMay's outfit was like taking over Notre Dame from Knute Rockne. He agreed that use of the atomic bomb was unnecessary, but the politicians had something else in mind.

LeMay's face softened. He thanked them and asked them to not misunderstand his position about using the A-bomb. He emphasized that he was willing to use any weapon that would save lives, but he didn't think it wise or appropriate. He had been working with Col. Paul Tibbets and his group on Tinian, and he expected that he was ready to go on the mission. He hadn't told anyone, including his crews, about the nature of the A-bomb. All they knew was that it was a new type of weapon.

He looked at Spaatz and said that if he were going to be chief of staff of operations involving A-bomb missions, they should at least tell him more about what the bombs were supposed to do. He asked how much damage it would do and if the crews were in any danger.

Spaatz replied that nobody really knew. The scientists weren't even sure if it would go off. LeMay should tell Tibbets's crew to get the hell out of the area as soon as the bomb dropped from the bomb bay. He should plan on making a visual drop after 3 August in clear weather. He should pick the date with the weather officer, but not tell him it was going to be an atomic mission. They must be sure the weather was clear.

LeMay directed his executive officer to find housing for Spaatz and Twining, and he moved out of his office and took over the operations officer's. Later, he sat alone pondering the change in his status. He was not a West Point graduate, and he wondered if there were other reasons why he lost his command, such as his less than cordial relations with the navy. It was abundantly clear to LeMay that he no longer had the discretion to determine strategy. Spaatz told him the A-bomb was a military weapon, but political matters were involved. It was not his responsibility to question the decision; he was a professional who followed orders. He felt he was in the same position he had been in as a group commander in England.

The next day he took Spaatz and Twining to inspect the bomber facilities on Guam, Tinian, and Saipan. While at Tinian, he met with Tibbets to finalize preparation for the dropping of the atomic bombs. He asked Spaatz if he thought a second bomb would be necessary and, if so, where it was to be dropped. Spaatz said he had recommended that a second bomb be dropped in an uninhabited area or possibly Tokyo Bay. The final decision would come from Washington. They would have to wait for the Japanese reaction to the first bomb.

Tibbets and the naval weapons officer who would ride with him would make the final decision on when and how the bomb would be dropped. LeMay's responsibility was limited to ensuring the accuracy of the weather predictions and keeping other B-29s at least fifty miles away from the target areas.

The cores of the bombs arrived on Tinian on 21 July. It was time for LeMay to work out the operational details with Tibbets. He had known Tibbets in the Eighth Air Force as a superb combat flyer. He had checked out LeMay as pilot of a B-29. LeMay had no intention of interfering with Tibbets's tactical plans. He informed Spaatz that the crew should be ready to drop the first atomic bomb on 4 August. Spaatz told LeMay that Secretary of War Henry Stimson and his staff had selected Hiroshima as the primary target because it had military importance and no prisoner of war camps.

LeMay and my tent mate, Jim Seaver, our bomber command weather officer, flew up to Tinian on the night of 3 August. There they examined reports from B-29 weather reconnaissance planes that had flown over the Hiroshima area. It appeared that a cold front was coming in from the Russian coast. It was possible that there would not be clear weather there, so Seaver recommended that the mission be delayed until the sixth.

Tibbets met with his navigator, radar operator, and bombardier on the evening of the fifth. They had flown practice missions with dummy A-bombs but they were never told that the bomb they would drop over Japan was nuclear and contained hazardous radiation. Tibbets told them that the bomb was called "Little Boy," and that it was not to be armed until the plane, named after Tibbets's mother, Enola Gay, was airborne. Tibbets explained that arming the bomb in the air was necessary to avoid possible detonation if they crashed on takeoff. If the bomb exploded on takeoff, it could destroy the entire island of Tinian. The crew was astonished. They didn't get much sleep that night. They had been speculating about the nature of their mission for several months. They always knew that they were training for a special, most unusual, and possibly extremely dangerous mission. A bomb containing radiation was beyond their comprehension.

General Spaatz received his written orders from Gen. Thomas Handy, General Marshall's acting chief of staff on 26 July. The orders stated: "The 509 Composite Group, Twentieth Air Force, will deliver its first special bomb as soon as weather will permit visual bombing after about 3 August 1945 on one of the targets: Hiroshima, Kokura, Niigata and Nagasaki. To carry military and scientific personnel from the War Department to observe and record the effects of the explosion of the bomb, additional aircraft will accompany the airplane carrying the bomb. The observing planes will stay several miles distant from the point of impact of the bomb. Additional bombs will be delivered on the above targets as soon as made ready by the project staff. Further instructions will be issued concerning targets other than those listed."

After reading the orders, LeMay sent Tibbets a field order for the first mission to Hiroshima and designated Kokura and Nagasaki as alternate targets. The *Enola Gay*'s takeoff would be the most important since the Wright brothers' first flight. It was the beginning of a new era of warfare. The bomb carried aboard the *Enola Gay* was six feet long and two feet, four inches in diameter. It weighed nine thousand pounds. Its implications for the future of mankind have yet to be determined.

The 1:30 A.M. takeoff on 6 August was routine. It might have been just another weather reconnaissance flight headed for Japan. Two surveillance planes followed the *Enola Gay* at a safe distance. LeMay, waiting at headquarters with Spaatz, and Twining, thought about his earlier opposition to the use of atomic bombs. If an atomic bomb shortened the war by even one day, the saving of American and Japanese lives would be worth it. More than a hundred thousand civilians had been killed on the first firebomb mission on 10 March. Those who had been burned alive in that blanket of fire over Tokyo endured a more prolonged horror than those who would be vaporized by a single bomb.

The *Enola Gay* arrived above Hiroshima shortly after 9 A.M. Residents had seen lone B-29 reconnaissance planes fly over the city many times before. The inhabitants went about their daily routines. No one suspected a bombing attack of any kind. When the bomb exploded, a tremendous fireball engulfed the entire center of the city. A gigantic mushroom-shaped cloud climbed to an altitude of thirty thousand feet. Eighty thousand people were killed instantly. The casualties included American prisoners of war and American civilians in concentration camps.

As the bomb left the bomb bay, Tibbets turned the aircraft sharply and began climbing to avoid any further effects from the blast. The crew watched the cloud mushrooming upward in awe.

As they crossed the Japanese coast for the return flight to Tinian, Tibbets spoke on the interphone. He assured everyone that they should not be upset about what they had done. They should remember that they may have ended the war and saved many lives. They were soldiers. They didn't make policy.

Spaatz radioed word of the mission's success to President Truman, who was returning from the Allied conference in Potsdam. The president issued a press statement and again demanded that Japan accept the terms of the Potsdam Declaration, which called for unconditional surrender.

Japanese leaders in Tokyo were astonished when they were told that a single bomb had destroyed the entire city of Hiroshima. The lethal capacity and the enormity of the destruction impressed most of the die-hard militarists surrounding the emperor. Some argued that Japan should never surrender. They planned to capture the emperor and fight a guerrilla war, as they had ordered on Okinawa.

On 8 August, Emperor Hirohito was advised that if they did not accept the Potsdam Declaration, Japan was faced with mass destruction and national suicide. There was still dissension in Japan's war council.

The first atomic bomb had not persuaded the fanatics. The president instructed General Handy to order Spaatz to drop a second atomic bomb. The second mission was to be commanded by Maj. Charles Sweeney of the 509th Group. He was to deliver the bomb, called "Fat Man," in an aircraft named *Bock's Car.* The bomb was six and three-quarters feet long, and had a diameter of five feet. Unlike the Hiroshima bomb, it was plutonium-based. The primary target was to be Kokura, a city on the northern tip of the island of Kyushu. When *Bock's Car* arrived over Kokura on 9 August, it was covered with clouds. After three aborted bomb runs, Sweeney decided to go to his secondary target, Nagasaki, approximately one hundred miles to the south.

The aiming point was east of the harbor in the commercial center of the city. Nagasaki was at least 75 percent covered by clouds, and Sweeney had been ordered to drop using a visual sighting only. He decided to make a combined visual and radar run on the city. At the last minute, the clouds opened up, allowing the bombardier to visually identify the aiming point.

Nagasaki, like Hiroshima, was devastated. Fifty thousand civilians were killed. Incredibly, this second catastrophe still did not convince the Japanese war cabinet to surrender. It took a day to persuade the emperor to intervene. The two atomic bombs gave him a face-saving device to surrender. He informed the Japanese people that Japan must accept the unbearable. Fanatical diehards attempted a last minute coup d'etat, but it failed. The war council agreed to surrender on 15 August.

LeMay attended the formal surrender ceremonies on the battleship *Missouri* in Tokyo Bay on 2 September. He looked up and saw more than 460 B-29s roaring overhead. He thought about the losses of 414 B-29s and more than three thousand dead, wounded, and missing crewmembers. They had been vindicated.

Hansell had mixed emotions as he read about the surrender ceremonies at his training base in Arizona. He might have been standing on the *Missouri* instead of LeMay. He was pleased that he had no part in dropping the atomic bombs.

LeMay returned to Guam and held a press conference at which he stated that the war would have been over in two weeks without Russia entering the war and without the atomic bombs. The pressures of the Cold War later caused him to modify his view about the use of atomic weapons. His statements that he would use nuclear weapons again if it was necessary caused many people to forget his contributions to winning the war against Germany and Japan. His tough leadership was commended during the war, but it was criticized in peacetime.

Hansell continued to believe that the use of atomic weapons was just another form of area bombing. He wrote that selective precision bombing could have been just as decisive and effective against Japan. He believed the atomic bomb was not used to defeat Japan, but rather to save the army from its obsession with invasion. Moreover, its demonstrated power would be needed after the war to deter Russian domination of Europe.

Joe Preston and I were still at Muroc when the war ended. When we received word of the Japanese surrender, I didn't join in the raucous victory celebrations on the base. I was feeling exhausted and burned out. I had the feeling a deep-sea diver gets when he surfaces too quickly. We terminated our training program and suddenly I had nothing to do.

Colonel Maxwell attempted to make amends with me. He invited me to his office and offered me some black-market steak. I declined and told him that I would not take it unless it was available to all base personnel.

He had a victory party at his home. In accordance with my usual unfortunate habit, I arrived exactly on time. My wife and I were the first guests to arrive. The colonel offered us drinks and we talked about the weather until other guests began to arrive. The next day, we had a formal victory parade. As our flight personnel from the Twentieth Air Force passed in review before Maxwell, I thought what an ironic way it was for us to end the war: We were paying respect to a commanding officer who had never heard a shot fired in anger. To add to the indignity, he required Joe Preston to stand behind him on the reviewing stand. I stood facing them at the head of the flight crews from the Twentieth Air Force.

When Maxwell gave the order for the troop movements in the formation, I garbled a few. I was in no mood for his formalities. The troops behind me knew of my difficulties with the base commander and enjoyed my garbled response. My cadence and inflection were correct, but I changed some of the words. The troops behind me made the appropriate movements and then began to laugh. The colonel glared. Suddenly, a strong wind came along and blew sand toward the reviewing stand. He dismissed the formation. I thought a sandstorm in his face was most appropriate.

My wife and I returned to our quarters and started packing. I had more than enough points to be released to inactive duty in the air force reserve. I was eligible to be on terminal leave until the end of November. I decided to return to law school. We loaded our Plymouth for the trip east to Cambridge. Joe Preston and Hank Covington wished us a warm farewell. It was a difficult moment for each of us. I knew I would never have another friend like Joe Preston.

We started across the country. Our first stop was at Tioga Pass in Yosemite National Park. I thought that the high Sierra Nevada Mountains would be an ideal place for me to begin the long process of adjusting to civilian life. I knew it would be difficult to slow down. I didn't know how or when I would begin to feel like a civilian again. I questioned if sitting in a classroom in law school was the appropriate place to start a new and different life after three years of combat as a flying officer.

Joe Preston remained in the air force and became one of LeMay's key officers in the Strategic Air Command. He retired as a major general in command of Vandenberg Air Force Base. Just before he died, he telephoned me in Los Angeles and asked me to visit him at his new home. As I had done with Hank Wodyalla, I delayed making the trip. Joe died in 1983 before I could say good-bye.

25: A Postmortem

No history of the Army Air Forces in World War II would be complete without a discussion of the strains on Gen. "Hap" Arnold, the leader and driving force of the Air Force in World War II. He sacrificed his health to achieve victory. For the first time in its history, the Air Force had an important role in the conduct of a war. In World War I it was little more than an observation unit and adjunct artillery for the army. Fighter pilots engaged in exciting aerial battles over the front lines, but they contributed little to the Allied victory.

In the late 1930s, the Air Corps's equipment was obsolete. President Roosevelt foresaw that we would eventually become involved in a war against Hitler. Before the war, he selected General Arnold to build up an air force. The president became one of Arnold's strongest supporters during World War II. Arnold attended meetings of the Joint Chiefs of Staff as a subordinate of Gen. George Marshall. Both he and the president believed in the important role airpower would play in achieving victory in Europe and the Pacific.

As commanding general of the U.S. Army Air Forces, Arnold had to make or approve all basic decisions concerning strategy and tactics. He also supervised the conversion of civilian industry to manufacture new and untried aircraft and supporting equipment. Raw civilian recruits were trained to become aircrew members and were rushed into combat in 1942 against battle-hardened German and Japanese fliers.

The army and navy opposed the massive expansion of the Air Corps. Proponents of strategic bombing suffered a defeat in the mid-1920s when army leaders engineered the court-martial of Brig. Gen. Billy Mitchell as punishment for his strong views about the importance of airpower. Arnold, Spaatz, and Eaker supported Mitchell at his court-martial. The scars of that battle had not healed by 1941, and they continued to fester throughout the war.

The army and navy saw no need for heavy bombers or long-range fighters. The concept of victory through airpower was foreign to them, a pie-in-the-sky concept, a waste of money and resources. The battle in Washington for a share of the armed forces budget was fierce. Arnold fought a continual procurement battle with the army and the navy. He was forced to make compromises and adjustments unknown and not understood by combat commanders in the field.

Arnold did not have the technical skills to select new aircraft or supporting equipment. He was obliged to rely on engineers and alleged experts at the Wright Field Materiel Command. Manufacturers had a strong lobby and many congressmen supported aircraft plants in their districts. Inevitably, the strains of command had a serious effect on his health.

Arnold suffered four serious heart attacks during the war, each of which occurred during critical times for both the Eighth and Twentieth Air Forces. I was unaware of Arnold's serious health problems while I was working for Hansell and LeMay. Neither of them mentioned or discussed the subject in their postwar memoirs. I first learned about Arnold's problems while doing research for this book. Each time he had a heart attack, he had to leave Washington for long periods of rest and rehabilitation. His deputy, Lt. Gen. Barney Giles, and other members of his staff were reluctant to make decisions or consult him about important matters while he was ill. They deferred decisions until he returned.

It was suggested to General Marshall that Arnold's precarious health might be a reason for his early retirement. The president and Marshall would not hear of it. They both had faith in Arnold's judgment and ability to understand the complex problems of managing an air war in five separate theaters of operations. They recognized his superb public relations skills. They knew he was a master of military politics. They were not about to disturb a smooth and effective team. Roosevelt was sensitive about health problems and went to great lengths to conceal his own from the American people. In spite of his disability from polio, he was a strong war leader and effective president. He felt that only Arnold had the skills to lead and guide the air force.

Undoubtedly, the stress of command and Arnold's concern about Eighth Air Force casualties had a substantial effect on his health. By May 1945 it had suffered 93,227 combat casualties in Europe, including 24,288 killed, 31,436 prisoners of war, 18,699 missing in action, and 18,804 wounded.

Arnold was promoted to General of the Army in December 1944. He was the only air force officer to hold that rank. He died in Sonoma, California, in 1950.

After his loss of command in January 1945, Possum Hansell knew he would never again have an important air force command. He opted for early retirement at the end of World War II, but returned to active duty in an advisory capacity during the Korean War. After his second retirement, he lectured at air force forums about his experiences in World War II. He continued to defend and advocate the precision bombing of military targets. He wrote his memoir and a second book, *The Air Plan That Defeated Hitler.* He followed LeMay's rapid rise to command of the air force with interest. He retired to Hilton Head, South Carolina, and died in 1988.

Curtis LeMay's postwar career was controversial and turbulent. After a short period as commander of all U.S. Air Force units in Germany, President Truman appointed him to command the Berlin airlift in 1948. Russia had surrounded and besieged Berlin. The president was concerned that Stalin was planning to start World War III and overrun Europe. Although the Western allies had only a small number of troops in western Europe, army commanders attempted to persuade Truman to send ground troops to relieve Berlin.

LeMay told the president such a risky move was unnecessary. He instead proposed airlifting food and other needed supplies to people in Berlin. Truman warned him that the Russians might attempt to provoke an incident that could start World War III. LeMay promised Truman that his aircrews would avoid any controversial incidents.

The Berlin airlift was an amazing success. It was called "General LeMay's Coal and Feed Company." The Russians learned that LeMay was a tough and disciplined adversary. They feared and respected him even more when he was assigned to take over the Strategic Air Command (SAC). For a period of at least ten years, SAC was the only real deterrent to Soviet efforts to expand their hegemony in Europe.

Military experts called SAC the greatest and most powerful military force ever assembled.

LeMay was never comfortable with the news media. He used no props and did not have a dramatic style like Patton or MacArthur. Patton's career was cut short in late 1945 by a tragic automobile accident. In the public's eye, he was highly respected and even a beloved combat leader. Unlike LeMay, his conservative and right wing political views were not known or criticized. He remains a hero in the eyes of the American people.

The most difficult period in LeMay's career was his last four years in Washington as vice chief and chief of staff of the air force. He was first nominated by President Kennedy and reappointed by President Johnson. In 1962 Kennedy was confronted by the greatest U.S. crisis since World War II. LeMay, as a member of the joint chiefs, recommended that Kennedy consider eliminating the Soviet missiles in Cuba with nuclear weapons if necessary.

During the Vietnam War, it was alleged that LeMay advised President Johnson to bomb North Vietnam into the Stone Age with atomic weapons. LeMay has assured me that it was not true; he had been misquoted. He did say he was ready to use nuclear weapons if the United States was attacked by the Soviets. He believed it was folly to tell the Soviets or any other nuclear power that the United States would never initiate the use of nuclear weapons. No president or member of the joint chiefs has ever taken a different position.

Most of LeMay's colleagues felt that he was a failure in the Washington political environment. Major General Delmar Wilson—who first joined LeMay as a member of the 305th Bomb Group in early 1942, flew combat missions with us in 1943, and was on LeMay's staff in the Marianas in 1945—described LeMay as one of the greatest air combat commanders in history, but thought his tenure in Washington was unsuccessful because he refused to recognize the need for diplomacy in his relations with Congress, the president, and his fellow service chiefs. LeMay never learned that he could not deal with the political problems in Washington as if he were a combat commander if the field. LeMay's plain speaking was appropriate and necessary in wartime, but the environment and atmosphere were different in peacetime.

His trouble in Washington started with Secretary of Defense Robert McNamara and the "whiz kids" on McNamara's staff. LeMay did not trust McNamara because he believed the defense secretary engaged in double-dealing with the president, military leaders, and the country. LeMay believed President Johnson extended his tenure as air force chief of staff to support his 1964 election campaign against Barry Goldwater. LeMay was frustrated by the president's personal involvement in planning bombing missions over North Vietnam. He told me that Johnson disregarded his advice that North Vietnam was an agricultural nation that could not be defeated with the bombing methods used on industrial nations. Bombing the jungle trails from North Vietnam was a wasted effort.

He advised Johnson that North Vietnamese war centers could be destroyed in the same way he had destroyed Japanese cities in World War II without atomic weapons. North Vietnam's military weapons were shipped from China and the Soviet Union, and only by destroying Hanoi's docks and harbor facilities could they hope to degrade North Vietnam's ability to wage war. Johnson ignored LeMay's professional advice. He instead played soldier by selecting targets himself and unnecessarily sacrificed the lives of American troops. LeMay was unfairly criticized for the massive bombing of Vietnam that commenced after his retirement in February 1965.

He ended his public career with a disastrous campaign as George Wallace's vice presidential candidate in 1968. Generals Spaatz, Eaker, and other former colleagues were unsuccessful in attempting to persuade him not to participate in what many considered to be a futile and humiliating campaign. I called him on the telephone the day he left to join Wallace and asked him to reconsider. He adamantly resisted all our efforts and explained his decision in typical fashion. He said he knew the campaign would be unsuccessful. Nevertheless, he joined Wallace because it would offer him a platform for disseminating his views about national defense and the conduct of the Vietnam War. He was not a racist. He knew Wallace took extreme positions for political purposes. But Johnson had lied to the American people about the Vietnam War and he believed Hubert Humphrey would do the same if he became president.

LeMay campaigned with Wallace without regard to political realities. He was ridiculed because of his candid discussions on the use of nuclear weapons. These positions and policies about the use of nuclear weapons have been accepted by every president, both Republican and Democratic, since World War II. The liberal press wasn't interested in analyzing his opinions fairly; the media were determined to destroy him.

I was confident that LeMay spoke and acted in good faith. He later conceded that campaigning with Wallace was a mistake. Although he knew that the campaign would be unsuccessful, he was willing to sacrifice his reputation for the future of his beloved country. It was the type of patriotism that few could understand then, and few probably understand today.

Hansell and LeMay attempted to make strategic daylight precision bombing succeed in the bombing campaigns against both Germany and Japan. They believed that civilians should not be direct or indirect targets. After his failed attempt to continue Hansell's precision tactics from 20 January until early March 1945, LeMay felt a change to area bombing was the only possible way to end the war. Area bombing was necessary to destroy all Japanese war production facilities and make the Japanese people feel the hardship of war. In the event of an invasion, the entire Japanese nation would be alive with guerrillas. His decision shortened the war against Japan and saved both Japanese and American lives. The decision to drop two atom bombs on Japan was Harry Truman's. History should judge LeMay by his deeds, not by his lack of political and diplomatic skills.

I was nominated to be a California judge in 1959. In some ultraconservative circles, I was considered to be too liberal to be a judge. LeMay took time from his duties in Washington to telephone and write Gov. Edmund "Pat" Brown on my behalf. As always, he was loyal to the people who had fought with him in World War II. I have never forgotten his admonition to us in 1942: "Avoid a fight if at all possible. If you have to fight, win it." He died in 1990 at the age of eighty-three.

Appendix A: Letter from Colonel LeMay to the Training Command

Office of the Commanding Officer
Station No.105, APO 634

12 January 1943

Dear General Olds:

I haven't forgotten your request for information on how the Group is getting along in the combat zone. The delay has been due to the bad weather we have over here. In order to give you something concrete, I have waited until we have had a sufficient number of missions to at least draw some tentative conclusions.

In general I am proud of my Group. It has given me a great deal of satisfaction to take people right out of schools and after such a short training period, take them into action against the best pursuit and antiaircraft defenses in the world. They have come off without turning a hair and while we have the greatest respect for the German fighting ability, we have no doubt of the final outcome. There are still Americans who can and are willing to fight. I wouldn't trade the 305th for any other Group in any Air Force. However we have had our troubles, weak as well as strong points. Most of these comments, of course, apply only to this Theatre, others are general and you may find something that will be of value to the 2nd Air Force Training Program.

Flying.
  General.

Piloting ability is excellent, we have had no accidents since arriving at our station in England. One of my pilots flew half way across the Atlantic on two engines by jettisoning practically everything but the crew and they were careful to stay out of his line of sight. Three other ships completed the flight on three engines. Incidentally, all failures except one were due to prop governors. Such things as landing with engines shot out, controls and trim tabs shot off, flat tires, etc., are routine matters and are not even mentioned any more, except in battle damage report. Take offs and landings are made at 30 second intervals and my main concern now is to keep more than one ship from using the same runway at the same time. I have long since ceased to worry about whether a 350 hour pilot can fly the airplane or not.

Formation.

All our Groups, as you can tell from your records, were weak in formation flying, especially altitude formation with a full load. In this Theatre good formation flying is absolutely essential, stragglers or anyone leaving the formation for any cause are invariably shot down unless they are lucky enough to get into the clouds and get home on instruments. Due to the extremely bad weather over here all training should be completed in the States. We went into action after arriving in about three weeks, during that three weeks we flew twice.

The type of formation taught is immaterial as long as the pilots are able to place their ships in any desired position and keep them there. Replacement crews will have to adapt themselves to the type of formation used in the Groups to which they are assigned, and Groups have to change their formations from time to time to meet changes in enemy tactics. Right now the 91st, 303rd and 306th are using modifications of the Javlin down and I am using a modification of the stagger. I found that we lacked sufficient practice to fly an effective stagger formation, pilots would get lost on turns, especially when crossing over and in general flew too wide to get effective supporting fire from the rest of the formation. They could fly a normal six ship formation, so I modified that and moved the squadrons into stagger.

The depth of the formation allows the turrets to get on pursuit making head-on attacks. Approximately 80% of all attacks are now being made from 12 o'clock and about the same level as the formation.

Pilots must be taught to fly formation on three engines and with the ship out of trim so they can stay in formation even though damaged by gunfire. Formations usually slow down to protect their cripples, but once a ship is hit and forced to leave the formation, it is practically impossible for it to get back again. The German fighters seem to be concentrating their fire on one ship, cut it out of formation and then shoot it down.

Navigation.

All Navigators seem to have received a good basic training in school. Most of them arrived too late to get much experience in our training period. In the concentration area they were able to get one 2000 mile and one 1000 mile flight in conjunction with fuel consumption tests. They all did a remarkable job on the North Atlantic crossing. Celestial was impossible for the first half of the flight due to the weather. About midway we were able to get some shots through broken clouds. Due to a faulty forecast of winds aloft we had drifted about 200 miles south of our course. When I warned the other ships by radio of this condition, all had either discovered it, or were working out shots which confirmed their positions.

Without exception all Navigators are weak in pilotage, especially over the type of terrain found over here. At home, a railroad, town or river is a checkpoint; here the landscape is one jumbled mass of railroads, roads and towns and once you lose track of your position, it is almost impossible to find yourself again. Pilotage must be used in conjunction with dead reckoning. This condition is further complicated by poor visibility; it is rarely over four miles and averages about three. I would suggest a good course in map reading, using English Aeronautical charts plus some pilotage problems with the windows covered to restrict the Navigator's vision to one mile at normal altitudes. This probably could be given after it was definitely determined that the Group was coming to this Theatre. They should also have some training in Navigating too (*sic*) and in identifying camouflaged targets such as factories, airdromes, etc. This with the shields up to restrict visibility. The visibility is so bad here that most of the time the bombsight must be synchronized on something other than the main target on the runup and then switched to the target when it is positively identified. The problem is further complicated because we are trying to avoid killing Frenchmen. We must drop in the designated target and no other.

Bombing.

The bombing over here has been terrible. 60% of the bombs dropped are not accounted for, less than 1% have hit the aiming point, and about 3% within 500 feet. We have done considerably better than this, but are still not good by any means. The Wing was bombing by three ship elements when I arrived. We started that way, then changed to Squadron bombing and obtained many more hits on the target. I am now advocating bombing by Groups and expect a larger number of hits by that method. At least we will be able to account for all the bombs dropped and when we get a load on a target it will do some damage. Pursuit are also beginning to hit us heavily at the target so we need the protection the Group formation gives.

The poor bombing results, I think, are due to two things: One, there is a lot of difference between bombing an undefended target and running through a barrage of six-inch shell fire while a swarm of pursuit are working on you. Nineteen of twenty-two airplanes we had over the target on the last raid had holes in them. While we lost no ships, the other Groups lost seven and that has its effect on the bombardiers' accuracy. Two, the bombardiers and navigators lack experience in quickly orienting themselves and quickly locating the target under conditions of poor visibility.

The first trouble can only be corrected by actual combat experience; the second corrected by training, but this should be done in the States, not here. It is impossible to get a training mission accomplished here because weather good enough for a training mission is good enough for a raid, so we have to do our practice across the Channel.

Gunnery.

On our arrival here our gunners were very poorly trained, most of them had not received enough shooting, especially at altitude to even familiarize themselves with their equipment. We have over here a tow ship and one range for the Wing, but due to weather and missions, the only practice we have had so far is shooting at FW-190s and ME-109s. However there isn't any better practice for rapidly improving the gunners' accuracy. On some raids, I have had German pursuit try to break up our formation by flying through it from front to rear. We didn't bluff very well and as far as I could see, no one even moved his position an inch. However, they did get through without being shot down by our gunners. On the last two raids every ship coming within 200 yards was shot down. If we can push that out to 500 yards, we will have something.

We have abandoned any type of fire control because there is no place in the airplane where a fire control officer can see enough and even if he could see everywhere, he could not exercise control fast enough. The normal attack now lasts about four seconds, usually they come in pairs, we have never received a mass attack by squadrons or even flights. We have developed a sector method of fire control where waist, radio and nose gunners watch the sector they can cover with their guns and turret- top and ball- over the sectors.

More training should be given gunners, especially at altitude and in formation, in fact all training possible should be done in formation.

Maintenance.

Good maintenance is important here for other than the normal reasons. If you can put more ships over the target than the other

Groups, you seem to get fewer attacks by pursuit. They seem to attack the small formation in preference to the large ones. Maintenance is, of course carried on under handicaps as usual. We have only received about 70% of our O.E.L. equipment to date. Supplies are hard to get even when they are available. Hangar space is limited or non-existent. There is a tremendous amount of sheet metal work in this Theatre. On our last raid, 19 of our 22 ships were hit. Average number of holes, about 15 but varying from 6 to 150. This work by the way is neglected in training: sheet metal workers should be given salvage wings, etc., to work on and patch. Any practice they get will pay dividends over here. Each Group if possible should have one ex-B-17 crew chief as Group Engineering Officer. I know they are scarce but there are enough to equip every Group coming into this Theatre and they are indispensable. I am promoting mine to Major and making him S-4 on paper to do it. He has given the 305th the best maintenance in the Wing and has been a big factor in keeping our losses to the smallest in the Wing. We have lost only two ships so far, one due to prop failure which caught the ship on fire over France, the other ship just disappearing into the clouds coming back from a raid and was never seen again.

Armament maintenance is a problem over here. Guns must be bone dry to function properly at altitude and oiled on the ground to prevent rust. Any slight neglect on the part of the gunners and armament personnel results in rusty guns and failure in the air. Gunners and armament people must be able to disassemble, work in gasoline, wipe dry and reassemble guns in the dark since this is done prior to take off.

Miscellaneous.

Three things stand out in my mind after the first three raids:
1. We were receiving fewer pursuit attacks than the other Groups.
2. We were shooting less airplanes but expending more ammunition per ship shot down.

3. Our losses were far lower than other Groups.

In trying to find the answer to this, my intelligence section is compiling data which they obtain from the combat crews. These figures suggest the following tentative conclusions which grow stronger with every mission.

    1. The 305th has usually more ships in the Group formation than the other Groups.
    2. Apparently are shooting at longer ranges.
    3. Fly a formation stacked more in depth than the other Groups.

The long-range fire is particularly important. Note the following table of pursuit fired on, but not claimed, covering all raids since we started keeping this record:

	Nov 23	Dec 6	Dec 13	Dec 20	Dec 30	Jan 3	TOTAL
Well over 1000 yds	24	23	77	65	8	66	263
1000 yds	6	13	10	5	31	14	79
1000 yds to 200 yds	4	3	0	5	20	12	44
Within 200 yds	5	9	7	4	0	0	25
Come within 100 yds But driven off by Spits	0	2	5	0	0	0	7

There is no doubt some duplication in these figures but they definitely show that we are stopping some attacks by long-range fire. It is also significant that on the last two raids no pursuit came within 200 yards without being claimed. Our gunners are getting better I hope.

I won't bother to give you any details on missions, etc., full reports on those are undoubtedly made available to you from the Chief's Office. At least this letter will let you know that the 305th is still alive and kicking, at least kicking as much as the weather will allow. Please give my regards to Bob Williams and the rest of the boys in the AAF.

Sincerely yours,

/s/ Curtis E. LeMay
Colonel, A.C.

P.S. Some additional information has become available while this letter was being typed. The Wing has adopted our formation and agreed to bomb from a group formation. An attack was made on the Lille Steel Works. The results are rather interesting. The Group flew in the modified stagger one behind the other as close as possible, the interval varying from 500 to 1000 yards. The 305th Group was in the lead at 22,000 feet and the succeeding groups stacked up in elevation. We had 22 ships in our formation.

The customary flak was encountered, moderate in intensity and not particularly accurate, it was not a factor in the mission. We were intercepted by 20 to 25 fighters over the target and they were first sighted just short of the bomb release line and made their first attack just after the bombs were away.

This outfit seemed to be the most experienced and disciplined of any I have encountered so far. They flew a string formation of 5 to 6 airplanes, all attacks were made from dead ahead and on the same level.

During the second attack on the top squadron ships, "A" in the diagram was hit, pieces flew off #2 engine and it was definitely out. One other engine may have failed shortly after. After being hit he fell back about 150 yards, I slowed down to 150 indicated and he was able to regain his place in formation. At about the same time ship "B" got a cannon shell through the windshield killing the Squadron Commander, Major Taylor, who was flying the ship and wounding the Co-Pilot. The ship went into a dive initially then pulled up diagonally across the formation, almost stalled, recovered and managed to get into formation with the top Squadron, who fell in around him to protect him.

The ship received attacks by 4 FW-190s while out of formation. At about this time ship "A" lost another engine and could not stay in formation, he was seen going into the clouds under control, but did not get home. Ship "C" was shot up and had the ball turret gunner wounded. Ship "D" received a few holes. Our Group was the only one receiving any attention by pursuit, two airplanes made one attack on the rest of the Wing. Our score on the pursuit was three destroyed, two probables and five damaged. We lost three, ours shot down and two in the 306th ran together in the air.

We definitely lack firepower in the nose of the B-17. Stacking the formation in depth helps to get our maximum fire out in front, it is mostly long-range fire and not effective enough to definitely stop frontal attacks. The next mission we lead, we will have all turrets, except the flank airplanes pointing forward.

/s/ Curtis E. LeMay

Appendix B: A German Focke-Wulf Pilot Speaks to an American Prisoner of War

Yank, I know you hate this prison
And the way we treat you here.
And I know you miss your family
And the ones you hold so dear.
I know the terror in your soul
When you were sent to fly
'Round Wesermunde and Emden
And were knocked down from the sky.

You don't seem such a demon
As I watch you in your cell.
And you try to act so friendly
Like a Jew that's sent to Hell.
But Buddy, listen—while you think
You've had a gruesome deal,
Just listen to the horror
And the Hell I've had to feel.

You bring your Boeings over,
But we are ready from the start.
For we watch you leaving Dover
On a sound locating chart.
It was fun at first to jump you
And catch you by surprise.
And get your engines smoking
Then knock you from the skies.
To see that bomber twist around
And snap it's burning wing.
And watch it spinning to the ground
Is quite a wondrous thing.

That's one part of the story
But it's quite another tale,
to see my buddies ruined

By your own steel-jacked hail.
That fellow there just made it in,
His leg is shot away.
His neck flows like a fountain;
Now they're bearing him away.
You haven't seen a ruptured spleen
And belly shot away.
On him that's only seventeen
And full of fun and play.

My own best buddy, him and me
Were diving on a plane—
Mein Gott! That feel of living steel!
Oh Lord! That sickening pain;
My leg was shattered, but on I came,
On came my buddy too.
These hooded figures in the waist
Looked God-damned gruesome too.
They caught him heavy on his wing;
They blew his rudder through.
And then bore down with everything
And cut his spine in two.

So, Yankee, lie there 'till you rot!
May more like you go down!
I know now that we're losing
And my buddies aren't around.
I'd rather face the pits of hell
Or swim a molten stream
Than face those turrets when ablaze.
I live a hellish dream,
I realize that threats and lies
Ne'er can allay what's true.
Soon now I'll rise into the skies
In my homeland, too.
And see your bombers, thousands more,
Come roaring through the blue.

I hear their engines beating loud
And see the burning wreck,
Of what I call 'Der Vaterline.'
God-damn your bloody neck.

Appendix C: General Hansell's Letter to General Giles

HEADQUARTERS
38th FLYING TRAINING WING
Williams Field, Chandler, Arizona

27 March 1945

Lt. General Barney M. Giles
Chief of the Air Staff
Army Air Forces
Pentagon Building
Washington, D.C.

Dear Barney:

As you will recall, I had a fairly difficult situation to meet in the Pacific. From command point of view, I had five major obstacles to overcome:

1. I had to redeem the confidence of General Harmon and his staff, since he knew very well that I had opposed his control of Twentieth Air Force operations as Deputy Chief of Staff of the Twentieth Air Force.

2. I had to establish a friendly working relationship with the senior Navy Commanders in the Pacific and overcome their natural hostility to the introduction of another independent command.

3. I had to establish a working relationship with the Air Depot which, as you know, was taken away from my jurisdiction.

4. I had to establish an administrative agreement with the Island Commander and make it clear to him that my chain of com-

mand completely by-passed him and went directly back to General Harmon for administration and to General Arnold for operations, while at the same time I expected from him the logistic support and base defense.

5. I had to lead back into my way of thinking the 73rd Wing which, from its Commander to its lowest Private, was openly hostile to me and everything that I wanted to do.

In view of the fact that most people believed the job couldn't be done anyway, and even such Air Force enthusiasts as George Kenney had stated unequivocally that we could not conduct daylight operations on Japan from the Marianas, I think this was a fairly large order. However, I was well aware of all these difficulties and carefully sought to overcome them all.

As for General Harmon, I reject to say that, in my opinion, I was completely successful there. He wrote me several very nice letters and expressed great confidence in what I was doing. Incidentally, I played ball 100 percent with General Harmon and never sent General Arnold any statement or letter without telling General Harmon what I was doing. His staff was a little more difficult to get around, because they wanted very much to control the XXI Bomber Command. However, I think we finally won them over, too.

As for the second obstacle, the U.S. Navy, I have never received better support from anybody and have never been able to cooperate with anyone any better. When I arrived in the Marianas I had no credentials, other than my own assumption of position and authority. Admiral Hoover was generally considered, by all the Army, and Navy as well, as the hardest-boiled and most intolerant Admiral in the Navy. We hit it off 100 percent again by the simple process of being completely honest and straightforward. Admiral Hoover responded beautifully to that approach. I left the Marianas with a firm friend in Admiral Hoover, and he did everything he could to meet my requests. Incidentally, for air-sea rescue he provided an average of 6 submarines, 2 destroyers, and 10 to 12 flying boats. Although the air-sea rescue was not especially successful, it was not through the lack of effort on the part of Admiral Hoover.

As for the Depot, I had less success in that respect. Up to two weeks before I left Guam, I had received only three percent of my requisitions for supplies and absolutely no maintenance assistance whatever. I didn't complain about this, because I felt the Depot was doing the best it could, but it certainly left me in a spot. Looking back, I am amazed that we were still able to run 938 sorties against Japan in the first 36 days, almost double our estimated capacity for that period. Of course, I might not have done any better if the Depot had been under my control, but at least I would have had a firmer hand in correcting the situation. My biggest maintenance problem was lack of a Deputy Chief of Staff for Maintenance and Supply. At General Harmon's request Steve Thomas was relieved from that job and assigned to General Harmon's staff, leaving me completely without any maintenance expert. I was operating from a field that was less than half complete. My initial operations were from a single runway, 7000 feet long. We had to build our own shops and supply buildings, and they were not finished until long after the assault on Japan had been initiated. Bill Irvine, of course, saved the situation at the last minute, but I had an awfully tough time until he got there. My Headquarters was delayed on route and did not arrive in the Marianas until the middle of December, so I had to run the XXI Bomber Command out of pocket with about 10 staff officers and 15 or 20 enlisted men, operating from an improvised hut—no complaint, but it was not easy.

I did succeed in establishing just exactly the relationship that I wanted with the Island Commander, General Jarmon. We did it by the simple process of pitching in and working to the greatest possible extent of our capacity, proving to him that we meant business, and expected no favors. He, too, responded to this kind of treatment, and toward the latter part of my stay, was occasionally calling me up to see if there wasn't something more they could do for us. I could not hope for a finer relationship there. As for the administrative relationship between General Jarmon and me, I wrote the ticket myself. I wrote a memorandum to him, explaining just how the Twentieth Air Force operated, and outlining precisely what functions I needed from him, and which we would take care of ourselves. He accepted it without ever changing a comma, with the result that the Twentieth Air Force did get firmly established in the way that we wanted it.

I nearly lost my mind about the 73rd Wing. As you know, they had sold themselves on radar bombing at night. They were extremely hostile to my intention to bomb by daylight against precision targets. That was what I believed in, but whether or not I had believed in it I had a directive to that effect. I very seriously considered relieving the Wing Commander and all the group Commanders. However, to have done so would have wrecked the organization for a matter of months. We had told the Chiefs of Staff that we would attack Japan in daylight in the month of November, and I fully intended to see that it was done. I went to Rosie and we had a frank talk, as one man to another. He came through very handsomely and supported my directives very loyally. Little by little, we swung the 73rd Wing around where I wanted it, but at one time I had to call them together and give them the strongest talk I have ever heard a commanding officer deliver to a combat organization. They had to be shaken out of their smugness and made to realize that bombs on the target were the only ones that counted. However, they did come through, and I am very proud of their accomplishment.

There was, unfortunately, one other obstacle which I did not recognize until too late. I had not realized that General Hale felt so strongly about his position in the Marianas. Here is the story of my relationship with General Hale, as I see it:

I arrived on the 11th of October. I at once went to call upon General Hale and he was very cordial. I must confess that I was somewhat dismayed on arrival at Saipan. Instead of two strips each, 8500 feet long, I found only one strip, 7000 feet long, and one strip nearing completion on a field which was not usable. A slight hill rose about 140 feet above the level of the runway at a distance of about 500 feet. I tried a heavily loaded airplane off the other strip and measured its altitude at the end of 6000 feet, and finally had to admit that we couldn't make it. Therefore, I agreed to turn that field over to General Hale and the 7th Air Force, despite the fact that it had been built on priorities established by the Joint Chiefs of Staff for the Twentieth Air Force.

The other thing that dismayed me was this: There were already over 100 airplanes belonging to General Hale's outfit, operating on the single strip of the B-29 field. Willis recognized this difficulty at once and told me that he would have the field cleared by the 1st of November, inasmuch as I had B-29s coming in at the rate of five a day, and they had to get some practice before the initial operation, which was scheduled for the 6th of November. This still left me somewhat dismayed, but I accepted it without comment of any kind. When no airplanes were moved from the B-29 field to the other field, I reminded Willis of the arrangement, and he said that he would have them off by the 6th of November. When my operation was postponed to the 11th of November, and finally the 16th of November, Willis agreed to vacate the field, but made no move to do so.

Finally, I was directed to launch an operation, with maximum force, on the 16th of November, and there were still over 100 airplanes, belonging to Willis' command and to the ATC, on the field. On the 12th of November, when no effort had been made to clear the field and I had over 100 B-29s there, I put my request in writing. I had to address it through Admiral Hoover, and I asked for five things:

1. Submarines for air-sea rescue.
2. Destroyers for air-sea rescue.
3. Flying boats for air-sea rescue.

4. That all fields in the Marianas be cleared as crash landing strips for returned B-29s on the night of the first operation.

5. That Isley Field be cleared of airplanes not belonging to the XXI Bomber Command.

I took this, in person, to Admiral Hoover, who immediately agreed to all of them, and I asked him not to take action on the last item, as that was a matter which I would adjust personally with General Hale. I then went immediately to Willis' office and gave him a copy of the message which I had delivered to Admiral Hoover. I also gave him at that time a detailed plan of my operation against Tokyo, and we discussed it in a very friendly manner. It seemed perfectly clear to all of us that I could not operate 120 B-29s from a single strip, 7000 feet long. And still have 100 miscellaneous airplanes operating from that same strip.

During the course of the conversation, Willis' A-3, a Colonel Eskridge, took me to task and asked me to explain in what way the extra 100 airplanes were interfering with my operations, and why they would have to be moved. This seemed so completely unreasonable to me, that I told him (not Willis Hale, but Colonel Eskridge) that that was a matter which General Hale and I had agreed upon, and I did not consider it necessary to explain to him why 100 miscellaneous airplanes on a single strip was an excessive number, in addition to 120 B-29s.

Willis and I parted on, I thought, good terms, but it seems I had offended his pet assistant and the next I knew of it General Jarmon called me up two days later and Willis was in his office, apparently extremely irate. Willis said that he had made an official complaint against me, through Admiral Hoover, and claimed that I had been arbitrary to him. I must confess that I was completely taken aback and had to have the situation explained to me, because I did not understand that anything had been amiss. I then told Willis that I was very much surprised at his action in sending his message, through the Navy, to another commander, 4000 miles away, when all he had to do was pick up the telephone and I would have been glad to come to his office, which was only five miles away from my own Headquarters. I also felt that it was a very unhappy situation, when a ground commander had to take a part in clarifying a discussion between two Air Corps officers. So I said to Willis, in General Jarmon's presence, that I felt the air field would have to be cleared in order for me to launch my operation, as directed, but that I would rely completely on General Hale's decision, and if he could not clear the field, I would find a way to launch my operation anyway. I repeated my statement to General Jarmon: that I would leave the matter entirely in General Hale's hands, to resolve, as best he could, and that I had every confidence in General Hale's willingness to find a solution which would permit me to carry out my operation.

I must confess it was most distasteful to me to have to adopt this attitude when I felt I was so patently in the right, but I felt very strongly that two Air Corps officers, so far from home, could not afford to have their troubles resolved by someone else. I thought the matter had ended there and made no further comment or report on it. I was busy carrying out operations.

To tell the truth, I think perhaps that General Hale's complaint may have been prompted partly by concern over the failure of his command to provide defense for my bases, as directed by the Joint Chiefs of Staff, and by the expectancy that I would complain about it. As you know, the defense was completely inadequate, and we took a pretty heavy beating. I did not complain about General Hale's failure to meet this obligation, and perhaps I was wrong in not doing so.

There is the story as I see it. I fully realize it is past history, and I have succeeded in readjusting myself to my present circumstances. Incidentally, I have no complaint about my present circumstances. I have an opportunity to do a great deal of flying; I am associated with a fine group of people, and I should like to say that this is the best organized unit I have ever been in—the AAF Western Flying Training Command.

This is not offered as a complaint, nor do I expect anybody to do anything about it, but I will feel better if someone there in Washington knows that there were two sides to the story.

Please drop me a line if you have an opportunity; I know that your duties are, as always, extremely heavy.

Best regards to you and to Hollis.

Sincerely yours,

H. S. HANSELL
Brigadier General, U.S.A.
Commanding

ORGANIZATION CHART

8TH AIR FORCE

AIR SERVICE COMMAND
GROUND-AIR SUPPORT COMMAND
FIGHTER COMMAND
BOMBER COMMAND

AIR DIVISION
COMPRISING 3 TO 5 COMBAT WINGS

BASIC TACTICAL UNIT

COMBAT WING
COMPRISING 3 GROUPS

BASIC OPERATIONAL UNIT

GROUP
COMPRISING 4 SQUADRONS BASED ON 1 AIRDROME

SQUADRON
APPROX. 12 AIRCRAFT

SQUADRONS ARE FURTHER DIVIDED FOR PURPOSES OF FLIGHT CONTROL INTO FLIGHTS (6 AIRCRAFT) AND ELEMENTS (3 AIRCRAFT)